LAW AND THE SACRED

The Amherst Series in Law, Jurisprudence, and Social Thought

EDITED BY

Austin Sarat, Lawrence Douglas, and Martha Merrill Umphrey

Law and the Sacred

Edited by

**AUSTIN SARAT, LAWRENCE DOUGLAS,
AND MARTHA MERRILL UMPHREY**

STANFORD UNIVERSITY PRESS

Stanford, California 2007

Stanford University Press
Stanford, California
© 2007 by the Board of Trustees of the
Leland Stanford Junior University.
All rights reserved.

Printed in the United States of America on acid-free, archival-quality paper

Library of Congress Cataloging-in-Publication Data

Law and the sacred / edited by Austin Sarat, Lawrence Douglas, and Martha
Merrill Umphrey.
    p. cm.—(Amherst series in law, jurisprudence, and social thought)
    Includes bibliographical references and index.
    ISBN- 978-8084755757 (cloth : alk. paper)
    1. Religion and law.   2. Religion and state.   I. Sarat, Austin.
II. Douglas, Lawrence.   III. Umphrey, Martha Merrill.   IV. Series.

K3280.L395   2006
340′.11—dc22   2006012939

Typeset by G&S Production Services in 10/14.5 Minion

For my children, Lauren, Emily, and Benjamin (A.S.)
For Karen, Theo, and Dash (M.U.)

Acknowledgments

The essays in this book were originally prepared for and presented as a lecture series at Amherst College during the 2001–2002 academic year. We are grateful to our Amherst College colleagues David Delaney and Nasser Hussain for their enthusiastic and helpful participation in that series. We thank our students in Amherst College's Department of Law, Jurisprudence & Social Thought for their interest in the issues addressed in this book. Finally, we would like to express our appreciation for generous financial support provided by the College's Charles Hamilton Houston Forum on Law and Social Change and to Amherst's former Dean of the Faculty, Lisa Raskin, for her interest and support.

Contents

ACKNOWLEDGMENTS   *vii*

CONTRIBUTORS   *xi*

The Sacred in Law: An Introduction   *1*
MARTHA MERRILL UMPHREY, AUSTIN SARAT,
LAWRENCE DOUGLAS

The Profanity of Law   *29*
NOMI STOLZENBERG

Pragmatic Rule and Personal Sanctification in Islamic Legal Theory *91*
MARION HOLMES KATZ

Our Papalist Supreme Court: Is Reformation Thinkable (or Possible)? *109*
SANFORD LEVINSON

The Ethos of Sovereignty   *135*
WILLIAM E. CONNOLLY

The Triumph of a Departed World: Law, Modernity, and the Sacred   *155*
PETER FITZPATRICK

INDEX   *185*

Contributors

WILLIAM E. CONNOLLY is Krieger–Eisenhower Professor of Political Science at Johns Hopkins University.

LAWRENCE DOUGLAS is Professor of Law, Jurisprudence & Social Thought at Amherst College.

PETER FITZPATRICK is Anniversary Professor of Law at Birbeck College at University of London.

MARION HOLMES KATZ is Professor of Middle Eastern Studies at New York University.

SANFORD LEVINSON is W. St. John Garwood and W. St. John Garwood Centennial Professor of Law at the University of Texas Law School.

AUSTIN SARAT is the William Nelson Cromwell Professor of Jurisprudence & Political Science and Professor of Law, Jurisprudence & Social Thought at Amherst College and Five College Fortieth Anniversary Professor.

NOMI STOLZENBERG is Nathan and Lilly Shapell Professor of Law at University of Southern California Law School.

MARTHA MERRILL UMPHREY is Associate Professor of Law, Jurisprudence & Social Thought at Amherst College.

LAW AND THE SACRED

The Sacred in Law: An Introduction

MARTHA MERRILL UMPHREY

AUSTIN SARAT

LAWRENCE DOUGLAS

It seems that the specter of the sacred always haunts the law, even in the most resolute of contemporary secular democracies. Indeed, the more one considers the question of the relation between law and the sacred, the more it appears that endless debate over the proper relationship of government to religion is only the most quotidian example of a problematic that lies at the heart of law itself. And in the current historical moment, as some in the United States grapple with the seeming fragility of secular democracy in the face of threatening religious fundamentalisms, the question of the relation between law and the sacred has gained a particular urgency.

Rather than taking up current controversies that address the claims organized religions make on and against contemporary governmental policies, *Law and the Sacred* explores questions about the foundational role of the sacred *as such* in the constitution of law, both historically and theoretically. To focus solely on the First Amendment is to examine doctrinal debates about a thick jurisprudence that depends on the already divided categories of sacred and secular. The chapters in this volume are preoccupied with a prior question: How did that spatial division come to be, in what ways, and with what effects? In addressing these issues, they highlight the ambivalent place of the sacred in the self-image of modern states and jurisprudence. For if it is the case that, particularly in the developed West, contemporary law posits a fundamental conceptual divide between sacred and secular, it nevertheless remains true that the assertion of that divide has its own history, one that defines Western modernity itself. Unearthing that history helps us to see the ways law represses its relation to the sacred to differentiate itself from religion.

Although we intentionally reify "the sacred" in our title to provoke a sense of its comparability with and distinctness from law, the word is more commonly adjectival, attached to or inhering in places or entities that are, by virtue of their sacred character or status, set apart. The Latin root of sacred, *sacer*, has a double meaning: It signifies both something holy or consecrated and something accursed or devoted to destruction.[1] And although current parlance often empties the term of its darker connotations, recognizing the awesome and sublime aspect of that which is sacred can help us to connect sacrality with law in illuminating ways, provoking questions about the kinds of power law accrues when it is imagined as partaking of what Peter Fitzpatrick calls "beyond the existent world."

Even as the concept of the sacred reverberates with religious meaning, it cannot be reduced to a component of religious expression. Rather, sacrality imbues a variety of acts, institutions, and symbolic systems with a quality of mystery and a sensibility of the sublime. As a result, there exists no one definition of the sacred or any agreed-upon understanding of the relation between the sacred and law. As a means of illustrating the most suggestive approaches to the subject, we begin with an exploration of Franz Kafka's *The Trial*.[2] This enigmatic, unfinished novel acts as a screen on which we project various notions of the sacred in relation to law, both because of its overt thematizing of the conjunction and because its power as a work of fiction comes from its own aesthetics of sacrality. We then turn from the realm of literature to that of history and jurisprudence, tracing the association of law and the sacred as it is expressed in theories of nation-founding and in American constitutional interpretation and legal culture.

The Trial

As *The Trial* begins, the protagonist K. finds himself unceremoniously awoken one morning by a couple of slightly bumbling, slightly sinister police hacks who inform him that he has been arrested and then eat his breakfast, attempt to steal his clothes, and leave after minimal interaction. It quickly becomes clear that K. is "on trial" for unspecified crimes; or rather, as the novel tells us, the law seems to have attached itself to his guilt—over what, neither he nor we know. He has not committed any acts prohibited by positive law, and yet as the novel's darkly comical warders, lawyers, and judges inform him and as his readers discern along the way, K. acts like a man with a bad conscience.[3] While he is technically free to roam the city and work at his bank job, once accused, he cannot shake the law.

To what kind of law is K. subject? None that would be recognizable to those who understand law to consist of systems of rules administered by legal actors in a procedurally regular way. Indeed, K. struggles throughout the novel to gain access and insight into the nature and locus of law's authority, only to encounter again and again mere functionaries and adjuncts. Even worse, those encounters regularly represent legal processes as farce—degraded, surreal, violent, and obscene. K. receives notice to go before an examining magistrate, but finds his "court" on the fifth story of a slum building, in a room choked by a contentious mob more interested in watching public sex acts than K.'s long-winded bluster about justice. He opens a closet door in the bank building where he works and confronts a macabre scene in which two of his jailers are about to be whipped because K. has complained about their behavior in his rooms. He wanders the back hallways of a court bureaucracy lined with zombielike petitioners, and the place so saps his energy that he must be helped out the back way and dumped on the threshold, gasping for fresh air. And he seems to find his strongest ally not in his bedridden lawyer, whom he visits only to have sex with the lawyer's servant, but in Titorelli, the court painter, who produces grotesque iconic portraits of lesser judges with whom he curries influence.

How can this kind of law partake in any way of the sacred? The absurdist character of these encounters makes the law, such as it is, appear deeply profane—desecrated and blasphemous.[4] It might be argued that K.'s world is marked by the utter *absence* of law: There are no rules or procedures to follow, and no sovereign authority (monarch, general, legislature, judge) appears to issue edicts, command enforcers, or direct K.'s "trial." How can there be law without these mechanisms of external force?[5] Indeed, this novel does not present the most historically obvious link between law and the sacred: the figure of the divine lawgiver.[6] To the extent that Kafka's novel willfully obscures an identifiable sovereign presence, it can be read as describing a bureaucratic dystopia in which the ruler, or more precisely, the rule of law, is absent, with harrowing results.

And yet the world of *The Trial* is not anarchic. If the central locus of legal power is never overtly visible, it is nevertheless always and everywhere felt by K. Crucially, while K. appears disgusted by its absurd workings, he is nevertheless drawn to a number of perverse manifestations of law and legal spaces. The force he feels is internal and mostly immaterial—if the law is drawn to guilt, perhaps it is guilt that compels K. to seek out the law—and in being "drawn to" law, he is literally compelled by his own desire to find and encounter it in places set outside the ordinary flow of time and space. And where does the law reside? Not in the world of everyday places and procedures but in hallucinatory, otherworldly spaces. The "courtroom," the closet, the stale hallway, the cramped artist studio with hidden doorways—all of these are places set apart from the knowable and comprehensible city in which K. has lived his life. Whatever absurdities or obscenities they may contain, in their feeling of spatial and temporal dislocation, they signal K.'s departure from the common and quotidian and his entry into the realm of sacrality.

Identifying this ethos as "sacred" locates this kind of analysis in longstanding anthropological, sociological, and psychoanalytic literatures that define the sacred as an unstable combination of the venerated and the unclean. As Roger Caillois summarizes the point in *Man and the Sacred*, sanctity and defilement are "two poles of a dreadful domain"[7] set apart from the profane world of the everyday.[8] In this view, religious forces are of two sorts: one benevolent and pure, inspiring love and respect for the gods; the other evil and impure, producing fear and horror.[9] As much akin as opposite, both qualities of the sacred are forbidden, set apart from the profane world, and can in fact exchange values: Sometimes an impure thing can become holy, and vice versa, through a change in external circumstance.[10] This fusion of seeming opposites, and the possibility of their transformation, constitutes what Durkheim calls the ambiguity of the sacred.[11]

Defined by its separation from the profane, the sacred is fundamentally associated with the concept of taboo. First denominated in William Robertson Smith's 1889 *Lectures on the Religion of the Semites*, taboo meant "a system of restrictions on man's arbitrary use of natural things, enforced by the dread of supernatural penalties."[12] That broad definition influenced a wide variety of scholarship, carrying over from anthropology to sociological and psychoanalytic attempts to locate the origins of law. In Freud's influential *Totem and Taboo*, for example, we find an account of taboo that specifically equates it with law. A thing or person that is taboo is set apart; it is dangerous, unapproachable, and contagious, and contact with it makes the thing or person in contact taboo as well. Freud argues that the origin of taboo lies in the original sacrifice of the father by a band of brothers and the subsequent sacrificial feast of both celebration and mourning. In Freud's narrative, these brothers, driven away from the primal hoard by a jealous father, returned, killed, and devoured him. But though they hated their father enough to murder him, they also loved him as a father, and that love produced a deep ambivalence about their act of sacrifice. Out of remorse, the sons prohibited the killing of the totem (their father substitute) and sexual conjugation with the women they had wanted, thus (according to Freud) producing the two most fundamental taboos: those against murder and incest.[13] (As Freud noted, we make taboo those things to which we are most violently drawn.[14]) The rules surrounding taboo are prohibitive, regulative, and hence, order producing,[15] and in them Freud sees not only the origins of law but of conscience as well.[16]

Not only do taboos emerge from an ambivalent relation to the (now sacred) totem; they also signal an internal ambivalence in which the sacred thing is both holy and defiling.[17] Insofar as taboo fuses the transcendent and the bodily, the high and the low, life and death, it indicates something fundamental about the nature of the sacred. "What is sacred," Georges Bataille writes, "not being based on a logical accord with itself, is not only contradictory with respect to things but, in an undefined way, is in contradiction with itself. This contradiction is not negative: inside the sacred domain there is, as in dreams, an endless contradiction that multiplies without destroying anything."[18] The sacred, whether it be made manifest in group ritual or individual encounter, is powerful precisely because it conjoins what we desire and what we fear.[19] To the extent that taboos are contagious—that is, that having come into contact with a taboo person or thing, one becomes taboo oneself—they interpolate, and sometimes entice, those who approach them into their otherworldly, transformational spaces. And to the extent that encounters with taboo are order producing—that is, to the extent that they partake of law—they underscore the potential violence associated with legal power. One does not come into contact with a taboo without repercussion.

We do not know what K. may have done to be "arrested" and put on trial; but as we follow his successive encounters with law, we see him unmoored from the world of everyday life even as he moves nearer and nearer to his inevitable death and the comedic element of his encounters with law disappears. No scene in the novel underscores this feeling of otherworldliness, and overtly signals the mixing of law with the sacred, more than the chapter "In the Cathedral." In it, the protagonist K. finds himself in a dark church to which he has been mysteriously and unknowingly summoned. He wanders aimlessly through the dimly lit and rapidly darkening space until a priest—a prison chaplain—calls him out: "Joseph K.!"[20] Knowing he is free to leave, K. nevertheless turns around, drawn to the priest, who tells him that his case is going badly, that his guilt is "supposed, for the present, at least, to be proved."[21] When K. protests against the abstruse, labyrinthine proceedings brought against him, the priest responds with a parable that Kafka in other places called "Before the Law."[22]

In that well-known parable, a man from the country comes before a doorkeeper to beg admittance to the Law. Although the door to the Law stands open, the doorkeeper tells him that he cannot be admitted at the moment. The country man decides to wait for permission to enter and sits for years in vain. At the very end of his life, he asks the doorkeeper a question. "Every man strives to attain the Law," he says, "how does it come about, then, that in all these years no one has come seeking admittance but me?" And the doorkeeper replies, "No one but you could gain admittance through this door, since this door was intended for you. I am now going to shut it."[23]

The man from the country wishes to be admitted to the law itself—to the emanations of light he sees only as he is dying, not to any mediating embodiment of law.[24] Yet he is forbidden entrance, verbally, and he obeys that proscription. What is it that has kept the man sitting by that door, day after day, neither leaving nor pushing past the doorkeeper? What does the figure of the doorkeeper represent? Is the man from the country free? Is the doorkeeper powerful or inferior to him? Is the doorkeeper a part of the Law or deluded about its nature? It may be that the law resides only in the word of the doorkeeper, or inside the man from the country himself.[25] K. and the priest consider a number of interpretations of the parable, which the priest calls "unalterable scripture," but no particular exegesis seems, finally, to exhaust the possibilities of meaning.[26] But as the priest remarks, "The commentators note in this connection, 'The right perception of any matter and a misunderstanding of the same matter do not wholly exclude each other.'"[27]

Perhaps one meaning of the prison chaplain's parable is that "the law" consists of the rule that one can never reach the law—that it is forbidden.[28] But what does it mean to come "before" such an enigma? To come before (vor) is variously defined as standing outside of something spatially, preceding it temporally, awaiting something, coming under the cognizance of something or someone, or being put on display before something or someone.[29] Each of these definitions posits a relation between two entities but does not tell us the nature of that relation. Is the entity that comes before superior or inferior? Is it utterly outside or does it necessarily define the nature of that which is inside or comes after or is awaited? Could it be prior to the law? The word before marks a threshold that, like the many doors in Kafka's novel, stands open to something or someone not determined or knowable. The door itself, both dreadful and intoxicating, can be understood to signal the operations of taboo without itself indicating what is forbidden. And it is that very undefined quality, which provokes both desire and fear, that from an anthropological perspective gives the sacred its awesome power. Indeed, the hermeneutic debate between K. and the prison chaplain itself suggests that indeterminacy is one central characteristic of sacredness, which this parable places at the heart of the Law's power—an example of the sacred's "inexhaustible morphology." [30]

K. as Sacred Man

Thresholds are places of crossing, spaces between known and unknown, past and future, life and death. The dark, silent cathedral K. visits is just such a space. Its sacrality derives not just from its association with religion but from its liminality: darkened almost beyond toleration during the day, empty but for K. and the prison chaplain, who "belongs to the Court" [31] and who presages the guilty verdict in K.'s case. Here K. stands literally before the law on the threshold of death, already essentially entombed. With no hope of acquittal or expiation, K. has been drawn into the sacred and has become of it. [32] That transformation helps to explain his relation to law and the circumstances of his death.

K.'s "trial" ends in quick, slicing violence. One evening, two gentlemen appear at the door of his apartment as K. sits, dressed in black. At first, they attach themselves to his sides, intertwining their arms with his as they lead him through the city streets; but in the end, K. essentially directs himself to the scene of his own execution, a bleak quarry past the edge of the city. Though his warders seem to desire it, he cannot rise to the occasion to "relieve the officials of all their tasks" and kill himself. He dies, rather, "like a dog," stabbed in the heart under the warders' gaze. [33]

This last grim scene proposes another way of understanding the relation between law and the sacred. Rather than locate the sacred in law, we might rather locate it in K. himself; that is, we might say that in being touched by the law, K. has become a sacred man. But his death is no collective act of ritual sacrifice, no expiation or offering to the gods. [34] Rather, K.'s trial itself can be understood as a legal gesture producing what Giorgio Agamben has called *homo sacer*, or sacred man—he who may be killed but not sacrificed. [35] Originating in early Roman law, *homo sacer* is one who has been abandoned by law and as a result has only "bare life." [36] Rejecting anthropological conceptions of the sacred, Agamben understands sacrality to be in the first instance a political, not a religious, attribution, [37] produced by the sovereign's power to decide the exception—that is, to determine who is placed under the ban, outside the protection of law. [38] Because the relation between sovereign and sacred man is a political relation for Agamben, *homo sacer* is not taboo; he is neither contagious nor, in the final analysis, a particularly religious figure in the ways described by Robertson Smith and others. [39] Indeed, he is not even outside the law; rather, he is utterly enveloped by it to such an extent that he has no life outside of legal power.[40] On Agamben's reading of *The Trial*, for K. law becomes indistinguishable from life, and K. has lived in the state of exception from the novel's beginning.[41]

Agamben understands the prison chaplain's parable as an exemplar of the structure of the sovereign ban. "Kafka's legend," he writes, "presents the pure form in which law affirms itself with the greatest force precisely at the point in which it no longer prescribes anything—which is to say, pure ban. The man from the country is delivered over to the potentiality of law because law demands nothing of him and commands nothing other than its own openness. . . . law applies to him in no longer applying, and holds him in ban by abandoning him outside itself."[42] As Agamben notes, this is precisely the relation the prison chaplain ascribes between himself and K.: "The Court wants nothing from you. It receives you when you come and dismisses you when you go."[43] The structure of the sovereign ban, Agamben argues, is "a law that is *in force but does not signify.*"[44] And that law— sacred in itself—in turn consecrates K. such that he is killed not like a sacrificial lamb but, profanely, like a dog.[45] To stand before such a law, placed in a state of exception, does not provoke any affective ambivalence of the sort imagined in an anthropological account of sacrality; rather, this kind of law renders K. a non-psychologized legal subject by virtue of a totalizing interdiction.

Just before his killing, K. sees a figure lean from the window of a lone house by the quarry, reaching out to him. As he reaches out in return, he wonders,

> Who was it? A friend? A good man? Someone who sympathized? Someone who wanted to help? Was it one person only? Or was it mankind? Was help at hand? Were there arguments in his favor that had been overlooked? Of course there must be. Logic is doubtless unshakable, but it cannot withstand a man who wants to go on living. Where was the judge whom he had never seen? Where was the high Court, to which he had never penetrated?[46]

K. cannot in the end unravel the meaning of this "faint and insubstantial" apparition. Perhaps it signals the existence of a more just social world lying outside the horrifying bounds of the quarry, but at best, it has no more presence than the law K. desires—a just, responsive law—and whose absence he once again decries. If this law marks a missing space in which more arguments might be made on his behalf, the quarry is the place in which arguments do not matter. K. is the man whom the sovereign has excepted from the law,[47] and the quarry is a space of sovereignty, constituted by the fundamental indistinction of law and violence.[48]

The Sacred in Modern Law: Foundings, Sacred Texts, Civil Religion

But perhaps we might question the totalizing effect of Agamben's reading by considering further the question of critique in *The Trial*. Why does K. pull his final warders through the streets toward his own death scene? The horror of that moment in *The Trial* resides in what seems to be K.'s identification with the state and its malign purposes. He is, as Hannah Arendt argues, "capable of entering the world of necessity and injustice and lying, of playing a role according to the rules, of adapting himself to existing conditions."[49] This frightening identification seems to suggest that K. not only has bowed to the inevitable judgment of the state but has acceded to the judgment's legitimacy as well. Indeed, through the whole of the novel, K. has been unable to gain a firm critical purchase on the law: Even as he has condemned it as corrupt and unprincipled, he has been lured toward it to the point of self-obliteration.

And yet K.'s identification with the state is not utterly complete: Bound, ready to die in the quarry, he nevertheless does not take his own life. Kafka casts this moment as one of inaction rather than overt resistance:

> K. now perceived clearly that he was supposed to seize the knife himself, as it traveled from hand to hand above him, and plunge it into his own breast. But he did not do so, he merely turned his head, which was still free to move, and gazed around him. He could not completely rise to the occasion, he could not relieve the officials of all their tasks; the responsibility for this last failure of his lay with him who had not left him the remnant of strength necessary for the deed.[50]

K.'s failure is also ironically the law's failure insofar as K.'s passivity marks the last space of difference between his own self and the state. While such a wan opt-out gesture hardly constitutes a trenchant rejection of a totalitarian regime, we might nevertheless read it as a critique if we place this scene alongside the close of the chaplain's parable. If both K. and the man from the country die abjectly, they nevertheless appear to relate to that abjection, and to the law, differently. Over the course of the parable, the man from the country has grown increasingly "childish" as he waits for the Law, to the point that he begs the very fleas on the doorkeeper's coat to help him gain entrance. As he lies dying, he sees a divine radiance streaming from the door of the Law, as if God were calling out to him. What beckons K. in his death scene is not radiance but "a flicker as of light going up" and the outstretched arms of someone unknown. This flicker of sociality, in contrast to the man from the country's utter isolation, may represent something outside law and its

unreasoning violence; and it is precisely K.'s weakness, his passive refusal to produce his own death, that forces that violence into view. Even as he articulates his
shame in succumbing to the power of the state, K., seeing this elusive figure, knows
he does not want to die. There, in that knowledge and that desire, a critique of the
state's legitimacy resides, however humbly.

The divergences between these two endings propose a refining heuristic useful for an analysis of the relation between modern law and the sacred. On the one
hand, insofar as the man from the country takes a deferential stance toward the
Law, the law is for him an object of single-minded reverence and worship. K.'s ago-
nism and distance from the law, on the other hand, signal the familiar ambivalence
that marks a more nuanced account of the sacred. If law is no less powerful a force
in K.'s life and death than in the country man's, the space opened up by K.'s ambivalence is the space where a critique of law worship, legal violence, and hence, law's
legitimacy can reside.

The tension in *The Trial* between reverence for law's divine emanations and
ambivalence (that is, a conjoining of desire and fear) about law's totalizing power
nicely illustrates the ways in which various positional attitudes toward the sacred
play into both the constitution and critique of law's legitimacy. This tension, which
runs more generally through modern law, concerns less the existence of the sacred in law than the proper relation one ought to exhibit toward the law as it is
expressed in sacred moments, objects, or regimes of meaning. We can see this tension most acutely, particularly in the United States, in three separate but related
domains of legality: theories concerning the moment of founding, interpretations
of the status of constitutional texts as "sacred," and assertions about the status of
law more generally as a kind of "civil religion." In each, a tendency to assume the
existence and directive, determining presence of a revered entity or moral framework resides uneasily alongside, and sometimes clashes with, an ambivalent and
often negating stance toward the direct and determining influence of such an entity or framework.

Foundings

Derrida has written that the founding moment is "the moment in which the
foundation of law remains suspended in the void or over the abyss, suspended by
a pure performative act that would not have to answer to or before anyone."[51] In
emphasizing the act of founding as a "performative," he underscores the problem

articulated by Hannah Arendt in *On Revolution*: the problem of the legitimacy of constituting power. What is it, she asks, that helps us overcome our suspicions that all states are illegitimately founded, caught up in a "vicious circle" such that those who constitute a new government are themselves "unconstitutional" (as Arendt puts it) because they have no authority to do what they set out to achieve?[52] What is it, in other words, that comes "before the law" in a temporal sense to make just the violence of revolution? The confounding "problem of the absolute," as she calls it, at first glance appears to have been solved for the American founders by an assertion of divine warrant: "When in the course of human events it becomes necessary for one people to dissolve the political bands which have connected them with each other, and to assume among the powers of the earth the separate and equal station to which the laws of Nature and Nature's God entitle them . . ." As Derrida writes elsewhere, "They sign in the name of the law of nature and in the name of God. They *pose* or *posit* their institutional laws on the foundation of natural laws and by the same coup (the interpretive coup of force) in the name of God, creator of nature. He comes, in effect, to guarantee rectitude of popular intentions, the unity and goodness of the people."[53] In this view, God functions as an absolute that undergirds the legitimacy of the new order by virtue of its greater harmony with divinely ordained natural law.

Arendt was surely right to note the irony that the founders, harbingers of modernity in politics, invoked religious warrant from God only subsequently to instantiate the divide between sacred and secular that continues in the constitutional system to define modern law.[54] Moreover, this turn to God comes at an extremely inharmonious moment: one of rupture and one that anticipates the impending revolutionary violence that inaugurates a new law, which will in turn legitimate the preceding violence.[55] The reverent invocation of divinity here is not acontextual but part and parcel of the effort revolutionaries must necessarily undertake to sanction their law-making violence, whose justice cannot be guaranteed prior to victory.[56] If in the context of the American Revolution this invocation was not cynical, it nevertheless also illustrated a deeper ambivalence about the relation between law and the sacred at that originary moment. As a necessary guarantee of rectitude and moral legitimacy, these constituting words drew much of their authorizing weight from a reverent relation to the divine; yet the founders themselves kept divinity at a distance both rhetorically and philosophically. Their God did not command; He warranted, and then only indirectly, through the mediating power of Nature. And the new regime He warranted ironically produced the principle of religious toleration and, ultimately, the value of secularism as an organizing principle of the new national government. Thus, if reverence masked the violence that lay at the heart of the Revolution, ambivalence about the imperiousness of religion both inscribed and negated the sacred in the moment of founding.

Sacred Texts

The "cult of the Constitution" in the United States, with its many celebrations and their "fulsome rhetoric of reverence," has a long history, and a significant strain of modern constitutional scholarship argues that the Constitution may be best understood as a sacred text similar to the Bible.[57] For some, the analogy leads to the kind of worship Justice Hugo Black exhibited in the concluding paragraphs of his slim paean, *A Constitutional Faith*: "[The] Constitution is my legal Bible; its plan of government is my plan and its destiny my destiny. I cherish every word of it, from the first to the last and I personally deplore even the slightest deviation from its least important commands."[58] Modern textualist, and to some extent originalist, theories of constitutional interpretation are perhaps the most recent jurisprudential manifestation of this reverent relation to a sacred text. Indeed, Robert Bork, a strong advocate of originalism, provocatively describes nonoriginalist constitutional theories as "heresies."[59]

Vincent Crapanzano paints this strain of contemporary legal scholarship as a reaction to postmodernism, one that "idealizes the past, fetishizes the original, and indulges in nostalgia for that which was never experienced and probably never existed."[60] But in a move that reorients us toward ambivalent conceptions of sacrality, other scholars who analogize the Constitution to a sacred text do so to complicate claims that plain legal meaning can be located in the words of the Constitution, or the intentions or understandings of the founders. Sanford Levinson, one of the contributors to this volume, has written elsewhere that the Constitution lies at the center of a "genuine community of faith" in the United States,[61] acting as a unifying force. Yet, Levinson argues, the analogy between the Constitution and the Bible contains a double message: If the Constitution foments a sense of national integration and identity, it also always has the potential to be a source of fragmentation and disunity precisely because, as a text, it generates competing interpretations.[62] Michael Perry extends Levinson's insight about the Constitution's destabilizing potential, arguing that it is best understood as a sacred, *prophetic* text.

the sacred text constantly *disturbs*—serves a prophetic function in—the life of the community. Indeed, it is in significant part because of its "writtenness" and thus its "permanence" that a sacred text is (in the life of a community that might prefer, from time to time, to ignore it) irrepressible, disturbing, prophetic. And it is in significant part because of its comprehensiveness and indeterminacy and thus its "excess of meaning" that a sacred text (as symbol) achieves its power to disturb from one generation to the next and from one place to another, over the lives of communities separated in time and space and with very different experiences and questions.[63]

Under this view, we might say that the Constitution's sacrality lies not so much in its admirable origins but rather precisely in its capacity to generate an intractable and irresolvable debate about proper methods of legal interpretation (a debate that, like the violence of revolution, has and continues to spill blood, both literally and metaphorically[64]). Along with K. and the prison chaplain, we are drawn to an inexhaustible, unsettling, and unsettleable text.

Civil Religion

Whatever rhetorical and political disturbances the Constitution has produced in the world of legal theorists, in a broader context the document itself has become the central icon of what many have called America's "civil religion."[65] Rousseau originated the concept, writing in *The Social Contract* that "[t]here is thus a purely civil creed whose tenets the sovereign is entitled to determine, not precisely as dogmas of religion, but as sentiments of sociability, without which it is impossible to be a good citizen or a loyal subject." He continued:

> The existence of a powerful, intelligent, benevolent, foreseeing, and provident Divinity, the life to come, the happiness of the righteous, the punishment of the wicked, the sanctity of the social contract and the law—these are the positive tenets. As for negative tenets, I limit them to a single injunction: There shall be no intolerance, which is part of the religions we have excluded.[66]

In drawing upon Rousseau's idea, Robert Bellah has argued that religion, and particularly the idea of God, played a "constitutive role" in the minds of the American founders.[67] They relied on "a collection of beliefs, symbols, and rituals with respect to sacred things and institutionalized in a collectivity" that was nevertheless not specifically Christian in nature and signaled a "genuine apprehension of universal and transcendent religious reality . . . as revealed through the experience of the American people."[68] As Rousseau makes clear and Bellah implicitly argues, civil religion does not replace religion as such; the two complement—even enable—each other by virtue of religion's very disestablishment and free exercise. Indeed, Tocqueville famously argued, "Religion [really, Christianity], which never

intervenes directly in the government of American society, should therefore be
considered as the first of their political institutions, for although it did not give
them the taste for liberty, it singularly facilitates their use thereof" by directing
mores and regulating domestic life properly.[69] In this view, public life is grounded
by and in Christianity as a regime of meaning and morality, and to the extent that
it underwrites the secular, the two are inseparable.

The indirect relation Tocqueville posits between religion and American government is fundamentally at odds with the strong and perhaps more normative than
descriptive claim that the United States is a "secular" democracy.[70] As William
Connolly notes in his book *Why I Am Not a Secularist*, the dominant historical
narrative commonly offered to justify the maintenance of a secular public realm
emphasizes the critical role played by secularization in promoting "private freedom, pluralistic democracy, individual rights, public reason, and the primacy of
the state" over the church as an antidote to the destructive effects of religious
warfare in the early modern period.[71] Under this stark theory of social organization, which we assimilate to the phrase "separation of Church and State," the political world is one evacuated of the sacred and the metaphysical in favor of reason,
tolerance, and the promotion of human well-being and justice in this life rather
than the next. Connolly argues that this thin secularist view represses a richer and
more inclusive range of potential intersubjective relations and obscures the continuing subterranean connections between religion and public life that Tocqueville
noted.

Those connections may be less subterranean now than at any point in the last
fifty years. Yet, however much politics and religion now appear to be intermixing,
it remains the case that constitutional jurisprudence requires the maintenance of
distinctions between Church and State. The difficulty, of course, comes in defining the proper ambit of those distinctions, and in those difficulties, we can see
yet another instance of ambivalence toward the sacred in law. Although the U.S.
Supreme Court has not offered a consistent interpretation of what "nonestablishment" means, as a general matter it can be said that the First Amendment requires
that government be neutral as among religions and (though this is more controversial[72]) avoid preferring religion to nonbelief.[73] But that rule raises the question,
what practices constitute a "religious activity" such that it cannot be supported or
funded by government?[74] And what is a religion, anyway?[75] Thus, for example,
under the Supreme Court's so-called "Lemon test," which while now somewhat
modified is still the leading establishment clause case, to pass constitutional mus-

ter a challenged law must: (1) have a secular purpose; (2) have a primary secular effect; and (3) must not involve the government in an excessive entanglement with religion. The word *excessive* here signals an ambiguity in even this relatively strict conception of the distinction between secular and religious, in a paradoxical gesture of calling into being a line of demarcation while simultaneously undoing it. One can understand this third prong of the Lemon test to say that in spite of the state's strenuous efforts to occupy fully the space of the "secular" to the exclusion of religion, the secular–religious binary can never be fully sustained.[76]

In a country notable for both its religiosity and its religious pluralism, the idea of separating Church and State has had significant symbolic and practical effects. Still, in shifting the conceptual terrain from sacrality to religion, secular democracies appear to wish both to deny the relevance of the sacred to the project of law and to mask the ways in which sacrality remains integral to it. "Religion," a term that denominates a sphere of activities set apart from law, becomes the repository of the sacred, and law is the repository of the profane and a marker of the secular. Yet if we insist upon the distinction between religion and sacrality, we can see more clearly the ways in which, by virtue of masking that very distinction, modern law's relation to the sacred remains deeply ambivalent and that, as such, the sacred lies at the very heart of law.

Overview of the Chapters

In the chapters that follow, our contributors take issue, from both historical and theoretical perspectives, with the conceit that equates law and the profane, religion and sacrality. All of these authors conceive of the "sacred" as a multilayered and shifting realm and attend carefully to its porous relations with law, sovereignty, and jurisprudence. We begin with two chapters that subtly trace the relation between religious and secular law in a premodern era. Nomi Stolzenberg's "The Profanity of Law" forcefully confronts predominant narratives about the secularization of modern law by arguing, counterintuitively, that "secular" law was originally a religious concept, born not of a rejection of divine law in the early modern period but of the all-encompassing religious epistemological framework of the Middle Ages. Stolzenberg reconstructs a tradition of thought that she calls "theological secularism" or "secularist theology"—that is, theological arguments for secular law, enforced by secular political authorities, that can be found in one form or another in all major religions.

Secular theology is both a legal and religious philosophy that developed, under the auspices of religious authority, out of a recognition of human fallibility. In an ideal world, humans ought to be governed by sacred law, but the Christian and Jewish religious authorities on whom Stolzenberg focuses clearly understood that no procedures implemented by humans could guarantee God's perfect justice. Those charged with law enforcement could not be expected to make the kinds of judgments that would infallibly mirror God's own; and legal rules emanating from religious precepts concerned with perfect justice required impossibly high procedural safeguards and so were ineffective in curtailing social disorder. To more effectively produce social order while keeping sacred law unsullied by these kinds of human failings, religious authorities created and authorized a supplement to sacred law in the form of secular legal institutions, accepting that divine law and sacred ideals of justice had in effect to be violated in the temporal world. If secular theology was always necessarily profane insofar as it was contaminated with human fallibility, it was also until relatively recently understood as religiously necessary for the preservation of social comity.

The line between sacred and secular law was not conceptual but jurisdictional, argues Stolzenberg, and produced multiple spaces and types of law for both Christians and Jews in the Middle Ages. The tensions generated by those jurisdictional lines were delicately and effectively negotiated until the rise of secularism in the Enlightenment. It is this theological secularism, rather than the secularism emerging out of the seventeenth and eighteenth centuries, that actually produced the "liberal" legal values of pragmatism, pluralism, and probabilism that we tend to associate with purely "profane" legal systems today. Stolzenberg's chapter complicates our contemporary tendency to bifurcate sacred and profane and provides a corrective genealogy to the simplifications offered by current warring worldviews of modern secularism and religious fundamentalism. If legal systems are conceived as "profane" both in the sense of being outside the realm of the sacred (*pro fanus*, or "before the temple") and, more normatively, in the sense of being unholy and unable to administer divine justice, Stolzenberg reminds us that such profanity is itself a product of religion, not a contrary value to either embrace or disdain.

Marion Holmes Katz's "Pragmatic Rule and Personal Sanctification in Islamic Legal Theory" addresses a similar tension between sacred and secular aims within religious law itself, in this case the shariʿa, as a means of excavating ways of understanding religious law that do not reduce it to a positivistic legal code. If many contemporary interpretations of the shariʿa emphasize the sacred nature of Islamic law and its comprehensive reach over human conduct (and so heighten the perceived contrast between at least Christian and Islamic legal regimes), Katz argues that as a historical matter early medieval Islamic religious thinkers, in ways similar to their Jewish and Christian counterparts, did in fact recognize a realm of temporal power separate from sacred law. Unlike the Jewish and Christian thinkers, however, they did not conceive this arena of prohibition and regulation as autonomous; rather, it was understood to be a discretionary domain of pragmatic and ad hoc action. Over time, Islamic legal scholars, influenced by Sufi thought, began to assimilate this discretionary domain into the overall framework of the shariʿa in sometimes conflicting ways.

Much of Katz's chapter traces the profound but ambiguous influence of Sufi thought in foundational legal theories concerning the goals and purposes of the shariʿa. Sufism takes as its ultimate aim the sanctification of everyday life and the transformation of self through self-renunciation. The shariʿa, like other legal systems, can be conceived more minimally as a set of broad parameters governing human behavior without imposing any particular framework for the cultivation and transformation of self. What, asks Katz, is the role of the "heart" in these varied Sufi interpretations of the shariʿa? Is the shariʿa meant to encourage renunciation and self-denial or to enable worldly benefit and pleasure? Is it central in reaching the highest degree of human virtue, or does it have a relatively modest, secular function, imposing behavioral limits rather than addressing human interiority? Can divine law be understood as something designed to fulfill human needs, or does it necessarily contradict all human passions? For some theorists, the shariʿa, properly understood, constructs a hierarchy of objectives and values that, while allowing for the pleasures of worldly benefit, at their zenith understand pleasure and benefit to come from the contemplation of God. For others, worldly benefit is consonant with virtue only if approached with spiritual detachment or out of strict obedience to divine motive and rationale. These arguments about the ambiguous relation between the shariʿa and the cultivation of self in the history of Islamic legal commentary complicate contemporary assertions about the sacred nature of Islamic law. They also undo what may be perceived in the West as a fundamental incompatibility between the ultimate, interior aims of sacred law and the kinds of regulation that can be accomplished by positive law, which addresses only the exteriorized object of human behavior. If worldly virtue can be cultivated through spiritual practice, then perhaps the conceptual split that so troubles positive law—the split between interior and exterior self—is a false one.[77]

Like Katz's chapter, Sanford Levinson's "Our Papalist Supreme Court: Is Reformation Thinkable (or Possible)?" recognizes the internal fractures that complicate any simple assertions about "religion" and the "sacred." Rather than focusing on hermeneutical conflict about sacred law itself, however, Levinson relates religious arguments about textual interpretation to debates about the role the Supreme Court plays in interpreting the Constitution. Drawing on a heuristic he develops in his book *Constitutional Faith*, Levinson contrasts a "protestant" approach to the Constitution, which takes the text itself as the sole authority for doctrine, with a "catholic" approach, which supplements and in some instances supersedes sacred texts with the traditions and teachings that have developed around those texts over time. Levinson critiques what he sees as an intensification of a protestant "sanctimonious reverence" for the Constitution, a document which in his view contains significant flaws, but he is equally concerned about the tendency of the current Court toward institutional authoritarianism of the sort that has been evident historically in the Catholic Church.

Levinson argues that in case after case, from *Casey v. Planned Parenthood*[78] through *Bush v. Gore*,[79] the Court has shown no interest in engaging in a dialogue about constitutional meaning, acting more like a papacy or monarch than one instrument of governance among several in a democratic society. Liberals, perhaps ironically, have acceded to this "authoritarianism" since the era of *Brown v. Board of Education*,[80] and their continuing support appears guaranteed by their commitment to *Roe v. Wade*.[81] If the general public is inclined to go along with this vision of judicial supremacy, Levinson nevertheless advocates a version of protestantism that decenters and pluralizes our agencies of constitutional interpretation.

William E. Connolly's "The Ethos of Sovereignty" echoes Levinson's political stance as he offers an analysis of the dynamics of sovereign decision making under conditions of democratic pluralism. Pointedly critiquing the decision in *Bush v. Gore*, Connolly asks us to consider the relation between sovereignty and law in moments of constitutional uncertainty in plural societies. The "paradox of sovereignty" first elaborated by Rousseau suggests that societies governed by the rule of law require a kind of sovereign power—an ethos of self-rule—that both precedes and stands above, as well as inside, the law to produce in the first place the conditions that ultimately enable democracy. Although this paradox is most visible at the moment of founding, it recurs as a problem of democratic governance, which requires a particular ethos of self-rule to carry forward. That ethos, argues Connolly, is *part of* sovereignty in a democracy and must be accounted for in any theory of sovereign power; and judicial strategies that resort to the fig leaf of "strict constructionism" mask that necessary component of sovereignty.

In applying the insights of Rousseau's paradox to contemporary conditions, Connolly turns to (among others) Agamben's work on sovereignty and its inter-polation of the sacred. If sovereignty is that which decides the exception, Connolly argues, in the context of modern politics, Agamben's framework must be refined so as to define sovereignty as "a plurality of forces circulating through and around the positional sovereignty of the official arbitrating body." Pluralist democracies reveal Agamben's analysis of sovereign power to be overly formal and incapable of encompassing the messy materiality of culture in such a setting. Thus, alongside the "positional sovereignty" of governmental institutions, "cultural sovereignty," emerging out of that messy materiality, must be accounted for in any adequate theory of sovereign power. Connolly concludes that conceptualizing the ethos of sovereignty in a contemporary context requires an "audacious pluralization of the sacred" and a "corollary relaxation of what it takes to defile the sense of the sa-cred." The sacred is better understood in a more conventional and capacious sense as something to be approached with awe rather than, as Agamben suggests, as that which is both the highest and most susceptible to annihilation.

Connolly's definition loosens the nexus between sovereignty and the sacred and pluralizes the definition of sacrality itself, and his extended critique of Agam-ben's narrow and ambiguous definition of sovereignty in turn enables a skeptical reading of *Bush v. Gore*. In modern American democracy, he argues, the Supreme Court's positional sovereignty operates alongside and in relation to the cultural sovereignty of a democratic populace and "orientations to the sacred" into which much of both the Court and the populace is inducted. In *Bush v. Gore*, the Court exercised its positional sovereignty in opposition to the democratic, cultural ele-ment of sovereignty that prizes voting. To the extent that a discourse of strict con-structionism (which Connolly sees as linked tacitly to the ethos of a narrow, exclu-sionary version of Christianity) masks the partisanship of the Court in that case, it demands contesting—without concomitant accusations of defilement—on the ground that its decision amounts, effectively, to the imposition and enforcement of one faith over others for partisan purposes.

If for Connolly an analysis of modern pluralist societies requires us to loosen the conceptual link between sacrality and sovereignty, Peter Fitzpatrick neverthe-less argues in "The Triumph of a Departed World: Law, Modernity, and the Sa-cred" for the centrality of the sacred to modern law as such. Fitzpatrick, too, takes issue with Agamben's work, in this case his conception of *homo sacer* as unambiguously apart from the law. If under conditions of modernity law claims to be secular, claims to be determinative, and claims to act without regard for otherworldly concerns, Fitzpatrick understands that claim to secularism as a form of negation, "the realization yet denial of the sacred." In Fitzpatrick's view, the sacred is paradoxical: It is both that which is omnipresent and of perfect order and completeness and that which is transgressive of any order, partaking of the miraculous and ineffable. It is, like premodern imaginings of God, both fully determinate and ineffable. The dual nature of sacrality makes perfect closure or resolution of conflict or meaning impossible, and as a result, attempts to determine or enclose are always a denial of what otherwise might have been.

Fitzpatrick understands that denial to be a sacrifice. Sacrifice, he argues, is an act that mediates between sacred and profane, an ambivalent boundary between what is and what otherwise might be. Drawing on Freud's account of the origins of civilization in the killing of the father, Fitzpatrick links premodern sacrifice to the instantiation of law which, performed reiteratively in ritual, asserts continuity while responding to change. Under conditions of modernity, Fitzpatrick argues, we see a kind of unacknowledged sacrifice in the assertion of transcendent universals (the nation-state, sovereignty, and so forth) and attendant, impossible attempts at enclosure. If law has at certain moments been thought to be such a universal—the closed, complete, orderly Benthamite system being only one example—it is by now clear that law so conceived cannot be responsive to change or the chaos of possibility. Thus, if (unlike premodern religion) modern law has no transcendent content of its own, its operations nevertheless bring the indeterminate beyond into the realm of determination: The transgressive and miraculous sacred is precisely what enables modern law's responsiveness to and in the world. In defining law as the neosacral combining of immutable stasis and boundless vacuity in enforceable social relations, Fitzpatrick makes clear his claim that the sacred is both perfected and negated in modernity; and if the sacred has in some sense "departed," it nevertheless conditions and perhaps constitutes the ways we understand modern law.

Taken together, the chapters that follow challenge the meaning and stability of the fundamental divide between sacred and secular that constitutes what we call modernity. Law, thought to be one of the exemplary domains of secularism, instead emerges as a signal location in which the sacred has resided and continues to reside alongside and as a fundamental part of the secular. Although our authors agree neither on the most appropriate definition of "the sacred" nor on the extent to which law and sacrality *ought* to intermix, they suggest both implicitly and explicitly that there is in fact an inescapable relation between the two. As Nomi Stolzenberg concludes, in undermining the either–or logic of modernity, these chapters offer a crucial corrective to the terms upon which contemporary debates about the proper relation among religion, politics, and jurisprudence depend. These debates, in which advocates of religion call for law to return to the field of morality while secularists defend their visions of an unbreachable wall between Church and State, gather heat from the presupposition of a sharp separation between sacred and secular. But in the final analysis, the critical question appears to be not whether religion can recapture law or law can stave off religion but whether we in a modern democratic polity can learn to negotiate the delicate tensions produced by the sacred within law itself.

Notes

1. http://bible-history.com/latin/latin_s.html. Giorgio Agamben explores this second aspect of the term, which lies "before or beyond the religious," in *Homo Sacer: Sovereign Power and Bare Life*, trans. Daniel Heller-Roazen (Stanford, CA: Stanford University Press, 1998).

2. Kafka wrote *The Trial* in 1914–1915 but left it unfinished and in uncertain order. It was published in 1925, the year after his death, by his friend Max Brod. All references in this essay are to Franz Kafka, *The Trial*, trans. Willa and Edwin Muir (New York: Schocken Books, 1992).

3. As Hannah Arendt remarks, "In the case of K., submission is obtained not by force, but simply through increase in the feeling of guilt of which the unbased accusation was the origin in the accused man. This feeling, of course, is based in the last instance on the fact that no man is free of guilt. . . . The feeling of guilt, therefore, which gets hold of K. and starts an interior development of its own, changes and models its victim until he is fit to stand trial." Hannah Arendt, *Essays in Understanding, 1930–1954*, ed. Jerome Kohn (New York: Harcourt Brace, 1994), 70–71.

4. This classic dichotomy between the sacred and profane has been most fully developed by Émile Durkheim and expanded by his followers in the short-lived but provocative College de Sociologe (1937–1939). See Émile Durkheim, *Elementary Forms of Religious Life*, trans. Karen E. Fields (New York: The Free Press, 1995), 34–39.

5. As Jacques Derrida has argued, "there is no such thing as law (*droit*) that doesn't imply *in itself, a priori, in the analytic structure of its concept*, the possibility of being 'enforced,' applied by force. . . . [T]here is no law without enforceability, and no applicability or enforceability of the law without force, whether this force be direct or indirect, physical

or symbolic, exterior or interior, brutal or subtly discursive and hermeneutic, coercive or regulative, and so forth" (emphasis in the original). But Derrida anticipates this paradox of enforceability without physical violence in his refinement of the concept insofar as he understands force as something that can be laid on indirectly, symbolically, via interiority, subtly, discursively, via regulation, etc. Jacques Derrida, "Force of Law: The 'Mystical Foundation of Authority,'" in *Deconstruction and the Possibility of Justice*, eds. Drucilla Cornell, Michel Rosenfeld, and David Gray Carlson (New York: Routledge, 1992), 6–7.

6. Carl Schmitt, *Political Theology*, trans. George Schwab (Cambridge, MA: MIT Press, 1985), 46. Schmitt traces the theoretical and historical interrelations of law and theology from seventeenth-century conceptions of absolute monarchy through theories of natural law to nineteenth-century theories of the organic relation between ruler and ruled. He describes absolutism as giving the state a "decisionist" character of a sort seemingly absent in Kafka's novel. From a historical perspective, under theories of absolute monarchy, the monarch stood just below God in authority and carried out God's will through his own. He was considered no ordinary mortal, having in himself certain qualities of the divine, and was not supposed to be judged on rational principles. See Robert Eccleshall, *Order and Reason in Politics: Theories of Absolute and Limited Monarchy in Early Modern England* (Oxford: Oxford University Press, 1978), 48, 77. See also J. Russell Major, *From Renaissance Monarchy to Absolute Monarchy: French Kings, Nobles, and Estates* (Baltimore: Johns Hopkins University Press, 1994). However outmoded that figure may seem in the world of modern secular states, the connection between theology and sovereignty remains a powerful one. As Schmitt has put it, "All significant concepts of the modern theory of the state are secularized theological concepts not only because of their historical development—in which they were transferred from theology to the theory of the state, whereby, for example, the omnipotent God became the omnipotent lawgiver—but also because of their systematic structure." Schmitt, 36. See also Paul Kahn, who argues that the sacred and the sovereign are deeply intertwined in Western religious and political traditions. Paul W. Kahn, "The Question of Sovereignty," *Stanford Journal of International Law* 40 (Summer 2004), 259–282.

7. Roger Caillois, *Man and the Sacred*, trans. Meyer Barash (Glencoe, IL: The Free Press, 1959), 35.

8. This conception of the term *the sacred* is thicker than the usual contemporary understanding, which tends to stress the exceptional, positive, and transcendent quality of a person, place, or thing. On this point, see Caillois, 132–138.

9. Durkheim, 412. Durkheim offered as examples of the former objects and places held sacred by certain totemic clans; and of the latter, corpses and menstrual blood.

10. On the concept of "ambivalence," see William Robertson Smith, *Lectures on the Religion of the Semites* (Edinburgh: Adam and Charles Black, 1889), 143; Durkheim, 412–417; Caillois, 36; Sigmund Freud, *Totem and Taboo: Some Points of Agreement Between the Mental Lives of Savages and Neurotics* (New York: W. W. Norton, 1950), especially chap. 2.

11. Durkheim, 415. Durkheim attributes this ambiguity (which others term *ambivalence*) to the common origins of both pure and impure (or as he puts it, "lucky" and "unlucky sacred") in the symbolic rites and representations of collective life. For him, religious impulses arise from society itself rather than emanating from an actual metaphysical realm. "What makes a thing sacred," he argues, "is . . . the collective feeling of which it is the object." Durkheim, 416.

12. Robertson Smith, 142. Robertson Smith argued that the vagueness of the boundary between holy and unclean—that is, the ambivalence of the sacred—marked a religion as primitive, though a number of anthropologists have taken issue with Robertson Smith's haughty division between savage and civilized. See Robertson Smith, 143, and in rejoinder, Mary Douglas's *Purity and Danger: An Analysis of the Concepts of Pollution and Taboo* (New York: Penguin, 1970), 21–22.

13. Freud, *Totem and Taboo*, 175–179.

14. Freud, 40.

15. Douglas, 12, 15.

16. Freud, 85. Peter Fitzpatrick offers an extended analysis of Freud's story of origin in his contribution to this volume. Freud explicitly connects taboo with law in *Civilization and Its Discontents*, trans. and ed. James Strachey (New York: W. W. Norton, 1950), 55.

17. Cited in Douglas, 18.

18. Georges Bataille, *The Accursed Share*, vols. 2 and 3, trans. Robert Hurley (New York: Zone Books, 1993), 215.

19. Caillois, 36.

20. Kafka, 209.

21. Kafka, 210.

22. Kafka published "Before the Law" separately in the journal *Selbstwehr* (Prague), 9: 34 (Sept. 7, 1915), later incorporating it into *The Trial*.

23. Kafka, 214–215.

24. Commentators have suggested that this imagery connects Kafka's parable with specifically Judaic renderings of law. See, for example, Jacques Derrida, *Acts of Literature* (New York: Routledge, 1992), 217–220.

25. Helene Cixous explores this last point in a psychoanalytic reading of "Before the Law." See Helene Cixous, *Readings: The Poetics of Blanchot, Joyce, Kafka, Kleist, Lispector, and Tsvetayeva*, ed. and trans. Verena Andermatt Conley (Minneapolis: University of Minnesota Press, 1991), 14–19.

26. On the connection between legal and sacred script, see Andrew D. Weiner and Leonard V. Kaplan, *On Interpretation: Studies in Law, Culture, and the Sacred* (Madison: University of Wisconsin Press, 2002).

27. Kafka, 216.

28. Derrida, *Acts of Literature*, 205.

29. http://dictionary.oed.com/cgi/entry/50019489?query_type=word&queryword=
before&first=1&max_to_show=10&sort_type=alpha&result_place=1&search_id=3hAw-
KLyLWP-13279&hiliteô50019489.

30. Caillois, 13.

31. Kafka, 222.

32. On inexpiable defilement, see Caillois, 48.

33. Kafka, 229.

34. Sacrificial rites, long an object of fascination for anthropologists, classically have
been understood as a ritual of gift exchange between gods and humans that, according to
Durkheim, regenerates a sense of divinity within society. Rituals of sacrifice are collective
acts that reunify and revivify social worlds through actual violence. Here we have only the
barest glimpse of a connection to any social world, at the moment K. sees arms outstretched
toward him and returns the gesture. The scene is defined by the absence of ritual and offers
both K. and the reader no sense of transcendent meaning, as K. clearly understands at the
threshold of death, as he dies "like a dog." On the collective and ritual nature of sacrifice,
see Durkheim, 340–352; Girard, *Violence and the Sacred*, trans. Patrick Gregory (Baltimore:
Johns Hopkins University Press, 1979); Robertson Smith, lectures 6 to 11; Henri Hubert and
Marcel Mauss, *Sacrifice: Its Nature and Function*, trans. W. D. Halls (Chicago: University of
Chicago Press, 1964). See also Alexander Irwin, *Saints of the Impossible: Bataille, Weil, and
the Politics of the Sacred* (Minneapolis: University of Minnesota Press, 2002), 2–7.

35. Agamben, 8. For a helpful and insightful review of Agamben, see Nasser Hussain
and Melissa Ptacek, "Thresholds: Sovereignty and the Sacred," *Law and Society Review* 34:
2 (2000), 495–515.

36. Agamben, 28.

37. Agamben, 75, 9.

38. "The sovereign sphere is the sphere in which it is permitted to kill without committing homicide and without celebrating a sacrifice, and sacred life—that is, life that may be
killed but is not sacrificed—is the life that has been captured in this sphere." Agamben, 83.
Note that being placed under ban is not the same as being placed "outside the law"; rather,
it is a legal relation in itself, one that Agamben sees as in fact the original and central legal
relation. Agamben, 85.

39. Agamben, 73.

40. Agamben's paradigmatic example of such a life is one lived in a concentration
camp.

41. Agamben, 55. As Agamben puts it, "a life under a law that is in force without signi-
fying resembles a life in the state of exception, in which the most innocent gesture or the
smallest forgetfulness can have the most extreme consequences." Agamben, 52.

42. Agamben, 49–50.

43. Kafka, 222.

44. Agamben, 51 (emphasis in the original).

45. Indeed, some commentators who, unlike Agamben, assimilate *homo sacer* to taboo have noted that the preferred method for ridding a community of such a person was not killing, which would put the killer in contact with contagion, but actual abandonment to the elements, in effect making sacred man responsible for his own death. See Caillois 49; Girard, 27, on the Greek figure of *anathema*.

46. Kafka, 228.

47. Agamben's analysis relies on that of Schmitt, who conceived the sovereign as he who decides the exception, a power that lies at the very bottom of state authority. Agamben, 16–17.

48. Agamben, 33–35. See also Walter Benjamin, "Critique of Violence," in *Reflections: Essays, Aphorisms, Autobiographical Writings*, ed. Peter Demetz, trans. Walter Jephcott (New York: Schocken Books, 1978).

49. Arendt, *Essays in Understanding*, 71.

50. Kafka, 228.

51. Derrida, "Force of Law," 36. By "performative," Derrida means the kind of speech act that does something as it is said, that is or appears to be self-instantiating. See generally J. L. Austin, *How to Do Things with Words* (New York: Oxford University Press, 1962).

52. Hannah Arendt, *On Revolution* (New York: Compass Books, 1965), 184.

53. Jacques Derrida, "Declarations of Independence," *New Political Science* 15 (Summer 1986), 11. See also Vincent Crapanzano, *Serving the Word: Literalism in America from the Pulpit to the Bench* (New York: The New Press, 2000), 215–222.

54. Arendt, *On Revolution*, 185–186.

55. Derrida, "Force of Law," 35. As Walter Benjamin writes in "Critique of Violence," "at this very moment of lawmaking, it specifically establishes as law not an end unalloyed by violence, but one necessarily and intimately bound to it, under the title of power. Lawmaking is power making." Benjamin, 295.

56. As Derrida writes, "the inaccessible transcendence of the law before which and prior to which 'man' stands fast only appears infinitely transcendent and thus theological to the extent that, so near him, it depends only on him, on the performative act by which he institutes it: the law is transcendent, violent and non-violent, because it depends only on who is before it—and so prior to it, on who produces it, founds it, authorizes it in an absolute performative, whose presence always escapes him." Derrida, "Force of Law," 36. Agamben notes the sinister dimension of the idea of a founding father, which he links to the Roman father's absolute power of life and death over his sons. This is the meaning of the Latin term *vitae necisque potestas*. Agamben, 89. For her part, Arendt contests the view that a "dictating violence" is necessary for all foundings. She argues that the absolute that authorizes the American founding ultimately is derived not from divinity but from the principle of mutual promise and common deliberation—actions based in reflection and choice, not accident and force. Arendt, *On Revolution*, 214–215. She claims that "[o]nly to the extent that we understand by law a commandment to which men owe obedience regard-

less of their consent and mutual agreements, does the law require a transcendent source of authority for its validity, that is, an origin which must be beyond human power." Arendt, *On Revolution*, 189.

57. Thomas Grey, "The Constitution as Scripture," *Stanford Law Review* 37:1 (Nov. 1984), 1–25; Sanford Levinson, *Constitutional Faith* (Princeton, NJ: Princeton University Press, 1988); Jaroslaw Pelikan, *Interpreting the Bible and the Constitution* (New Haven, CT: Yale University Press, 2004).

58. Hugo Black, *A Constitutional Faith* (New York: Alfred A. Knopf, 1969), 66. Black carried a copy of the Constitution in his coat pocket, often pulling it out to consult its exact language. See Levinson, 31–32.

59. Robert H. Bork, *The Tempting of America: The Political Seduction of the Law* (New York: The Free Press, 1990), 4–11.

60. Crapanzano, 232, and generally 229–235, for an overview of debates about the sacralizing of the Constitution. The reference to fetishism here is suggestive insofar as it signals a bestowing of magical, dreadful powers upon an inanimate object, in this case, the awesome power to restrain judges from the temptation to impose their own politics and value judgments in judicial decision making. As Max Lerner wrote in 1937, "Every tribe needs its totem and its fetish, and the Constitution is ours. Every tribe clings to something which it believes to possess supernatural powers, as an instrument for controlling unknown forces in a hostile universe." Max Lerner, "Constitution and Court as Symbols," *Yale Law Journal* 46: 8 (Jun. 1937), 1294.

61. Levinson, 16.

62. Levinson, 17.

63. Michael J. Perry, "The Authority of Text, Tradition, and Reason: A Theory of Constitutional 'Interpretation,'" *Southern California Law Review* 58 (Jan. 1985), 559 (footnotes omitted). Thomas Grey takes issue with the analogy between sacred text and the Constitution, arguing that the Constitution, unlike the Bible, is not ineffable; its secular premises in principle make it subject to human understanding. See Grey, 16. But as we and some of our contributors argue, simply asserting the presence of secularism cannot guarantee the absence of the sacred in law and may indeed be evidence for it. See Fitzpatrick's contribution in this volume.

64. On Civil War–era conflicts over constitutional interpretation, see Michael Kammen, *A Machine That Would Go of Itself: The Constitution in American Culture* (New York: St. Martin's Press, 1994), especially chap. 4. See also David Ray Papke, "The American Legal Faith: Traditions, Contradictions, and Possibilities," *Indiana Law Review* 30: 3 (1997), 645–657. On the spilling of political blood, see Bork, *The Tempting of America*.

65. See Kammen, 22; Crapanzano, 230. See also Robert N. Bellah, *Beyond Belief: Essays on Religion in a Post-Traditional World* (New York: Harper & Row, 1970).

66. Jean-Jacques Rousseau, *The Social Contract*, bk. 4, chap. 8, in *The Essential Rousseau*, trans. Lowell Bair (New York: New American Library, 1974), 113.

67. Bellah, 173. As Sanford Levinson defines the phrase, it is less inflected with religion: Civil religion is "that web of understandings, myths, symbols, and documents out of which would be woven interpretive narratives both placing within history and normatively justifying the new American community coming into being following the travails of the Revolution." Levinson, 10.

68. Bellah, 179.

69. Alexis de Tocqueville, *Democracy in America*, ed. J. P. Mayer, trans. George Lawrence (New York: Harper & Row, 1966), 292.

70. For a strong critique of secularism, see Richard John Neuhaus, *The Naked Public Square: Religion and Democracy in America* (Grand Rapids, MI: William B. Eerdmans, 1984).

71. Connolly, 20. See also Talal Asad, *Genealogies of Religion: Discipline and Reasons of Power in Christianity and Islam* (Baltimore: Johns Hopkins University Press, 1993), particularly chap. 1, in which Asad argues that only in the nineteenth century did the split between religion and public power really take hold, as evolutionary thought considered religion "an early human condition from which modern law, science, and politics emerged and became detached." Asad, 27. For a judicial articulation of this narrative, see *Everson v. Board of Education*, 330 U.S. 8–9 (1947). For a history of the idea of the separation between Church and State in the United States, see Philip Hamburger, *Separation of Church and State* (Cambridge, MA: Harvard University Press, 2002).

72. See, for example, Justice Rehnquist's dissent in *Wallace v. Jaffree*, 472 U.S. 38 (1985).

73. See Perry, 7. See *Lemon v. Kurtzman*, 403 U.S. 602 (1971).

74. See *McGowan v. Maryland*, 366 U.S. 420 (1961), Sunday closing laws do not constitute a law respecting an establishment of religion; *Engel v. Vitale*, 82 S.Ct. 1261 (1962), prohibiting official prayer in public schools.

75. See *U.S. v. Seeger*, 85 S.Ct. 850 (1965), conscientious objector can gain exemption from combatant training and service if he has a "sincere and meaningful belief . . . parallel to that filled by orthodox belief in God." See also Kent Greenawalt, "Religion as a Concept in Constitutional Law," *California Law Review* 72 (1984), 753–816.

76. See *Lemon v. Kurtzman*, 403 U.S. 602 (1971).

77. On this point, see Asad, chap. 2.

78. 505 U.S. 833 (1992).

79. 51 U.S. 98 (2000).

80. 347 U.S. 483 (1954).

81. 410 U.S. 113 (1973).

The Profanity of Law

NOMI STOLZENBERG

Open thou my heart, Oh Lord, unto thy sacred law,
That thy statutes I may know and all thy truths pursue.

—Jewish Prayer Book[1]

Does not every moment of your practical life give the lie to your religious theory? Do you think it unjust to appeal to the courts if somebody cheats you? But the apostle says it is wrong. Do you offer your right cheek if somebody slaps your left cheek, or would you rather start a lawsuit? But the gospels forbid it. Do you not ask for a rational law in this world, grumble about the slightest increase of taxes and become excited at the smallest violation of personal liberty? But it is said unto you that the sufferings of this *saeculum* do not matter in comparison with the future glory and that long-suffering and hopeful expectation are cardinal virtues. Does the greatest part of your lawsuits and civil laws not deal with property? But it is said unto you that your treasures are not of this world.

—Marx and Engels[2]

It is therefore false to reduce . . . theology to anthropology, thus deifying humanity; for what has to be demonstrated is that humanity is essentially *not* divine and that God, if he exists, is man's enemy. It is the privilege of man to be capable of finite and providential reason and to practice "the prophecy of his future," while perfect saintliness is contradictory to progressive perfection.

—Proudhon, as paraphrased by Karl Löwith[3]

Critics of religion have always pounced on the apparent conflicts and deviations between human and sacred law. For thinkers such as Marx and Proudhon, and others bent on leveling religious faith and the power of religious institutions, gaps between actual legal practices and sacred ideals have supplied endless grist for the mill. But the idea that the law and the sacred conflict did not originate with the critics of religion. On the contrary, conflicts between law and the sacred were a constant preoccupation of religious thinkers and believers in the premodern, presecular world. For them, it was not merely that law *differed* from sacred ideals, or simply failed to live up to them; the concern, rather, was that human legal institutions actually *violated*, and *profaned*, the sacred—and necessarily so. The perception of a link between law and profanity, to be seized upon later by modern critics who would make a mockery of religion, was, in fact, originally a *religious* idea.

Attempting to come to terms with the link between law and profanity was an important theological project that profoundly influenced our legal practices and our basic understanding of law. Yet, despite its importance for the development of modern law, this theological project is long forgotten, lost in the mists of the premodern, presecular past. The idea of an essential link between law and profanity has two facets, both of which are alien to modern, secular thought. On the one hand, we have a notion of law that posits a necessary divergence between law and the sacred and attributes a profane character to law. On the other hand, we have a notion of the profane as the realm of human activity that necessarily includes (we might even say *features*) the business of law. Today, these notions mostly fall on deaf ears, depending as they do on the basic concepts of the profane and the sacred, concepts that have largely lost their meaning in the modern, secular world. In a secular world, the idea that the law is profane is scarcely comprehensible, let alone one we would consider adopting, resting as it does on a framework of concepts, beliefs, and standards of judgment that is altogether foreign to the secular worldview. To characterize a legal system as "profane" (or for that matter, as "holy" or "sacred") presupposes a particular epistemological framework, a basic mindset or framework of meaning, "which defines what sorts of things are accessible to the human mind and human experience,"[4] namely, things pertaining to the divine. It is well understood that different cultures have different epistemological frameworks and that nothing can be humanly known outside one epistemological framework or another. When we draw our commonplace distinctions between "the secular" and "the religious," we generally have in mind not just different domains or practices but different mindsets, or frameworks of meaning, as well. Terms like *profane* and *sacred* derive from a religious framework of meaning, and that meaning is largely lost in the modern, secular world.

But it was not always so. In fact, the very concept of the secular (which bears a close relationship to the concept of the profane) is inherited from conceptual systems that developed in the premodern, presecular world. "The secular" was, in fact, originally a *religious* concept, a product of traditional religious epistemological frameworks. The concept of the secular always served the function of distinguishing religious from nonreligious domains. But nonreligious domains did not, in the premodern view, exist outside the religious epistemological framework. On the contrary, that framework of meaning was all-encompassing, overarching, comprehending within it *every* domain of human (and nonhuman) action and cognition, both the spiritual and the temporal, the holy and the unholy, the ecclesiastical and the secular, the sacred and the profane. In their original usage, oppositions such as the spiritual and the secular, the sacred and the profane, did not denote two different mindsets or conceptual systems or frameworks of meaning (as they do today). Rather, they referred to different institutions, different jurisdictions, different functions, and different domains, all of which were located within a single conceptual universe. That conceptual universe, it bears repeating, was a pervasively religious one. This is not to deny the occurrence in the premodern world of such phenomena as religious skepticism, indifference and cynicism, and all the various forms of transgressive behavior and thought that have been unceremoniously lumped together and dubbed "irreligion."[5] It is, rather, to emphasize the unavailability in premodern times of what we think of today as a secular worldview—that is, one without any God in it—which is to say that the concept of the secular was not originally a secular concept.

To put it otherwise, the concept of the secular has itself, ironically, been secularized and modernized, which makes it hard to grasp the original meaning of the secular and its relationship to profanity and law. The secularization of the concept of the secular has produced the familiar modern conception of the secular as a distinctive, and distinctively nonreligious, *mindset*. By the same token, it has eclipsed the original conception of the secular as a specialized area of God's domain. The resulting gap between the traditional and the modern conceptions of the secular accounts for much of the difficulty we now have in comprehending, or even registering, the claim that the law is profane. Modern secularism simply lacks the epistemological framework to make sense of this claim. And until very recently, it has lacked the incentive even to try to make sense of this claim. But as recent events have perhaps made clear, the question of the character of the law in relation to the sacred is neglected at our peril.

Contrary to the expectations of the likes of Marx and Proudhon, modern life has not been characterized by the "withering away" of religion.[6] Instead, we have witnessed the increasing polarization of religious and secular points of view. This polarization feeds on itself. It is all too easy to dismiss religious critiques of the law and the secular state as the products of fanaticism, religious fundamentalism, and political extremism, with which there is no possibility of constructive engagement.

Conversely, it is all too easy for defenders of religious tradition to demonize the secular world. Both sides demonize the other; both sides talk past each other, without realizing that they share a common root. In fact, religious fundamentalism and modern secularism derive from—and yet are cut off from—a common political and religious heritage, an intellectual tradition borne of the struggle to reconcile the idea of divinity with the practical needs and limitations of the mortal world.

That intellectual tradition exhibited a constant interplay between the ideas of the secular, the profane, and the law. It was a religious tradition, containing the basic conceptual vocabulary that religious fundamentalists invoke today against the modern, secular state, including the concepts of the sacred and the profane. Yet at the same time, it was a political tradition, a tradition of political thought that generated the basic conceptual building blocks of modern—secular—political philosophy. These building blocks include the idea of *secular law* and the concept of *the secular*, more generally, as well as many of the ideas that we now associate with the political philosophy of *liberalism*, such as pragmatism, pluralism, and the need for tolerance.[7] It may come as a surprise to both fundamentalists and secularists to learn that these legal and political ideals originated in traditional religious thought. But in fact, the liberal ideals that fundamentalists spurn and that secularists claim as their own derive from this religious tradition.

Admittedly, there is a certain artificiality to this "tradition" that I am identifying. At no point were its defining elements self-consciously articulated, nor were they ever assembled and singled out as a distinct school of thought or characterized as an intellectual tradition by the historical actors who developed them. There is no name for the tradition I have in mind—although we might refer to it as theological secularism, or secularist theology, for lack of a better term[8]—and it was never the unique property of a single culture or discrete group of people in direct communication with one another. Rather, it is more historically accurate to say that the tradition I am identifying consisted of a loose set of ideas that continually circulated in various theological and political discourses of the past. Theological secularism did not exist as a tradition in the same way that, say, Trinitarianism and millenarianism have formed traditions of Christian thought, or messianism and Hasidism are traditions of Jewish thought, or civic republicanism and liberalism constitute traditions in Western political philosophy. But we have found it useful in other contexts to identify traditions such as "pietism," "mysticism," and "rationalism," even though these terms refer to intellectual trends or bodies of ideas that surface in more than one culture (sometimes as the result of a direct exchange of ideas but sometimes as the result of separate parallel developments) and even though these classifications are the constructs of scholars, external observers, and not terms that adherents of these "isms" would necessarily use to describe themselves. "Isms" and "traditions" are almost always constructed retrospectively—sometimes by followers and sometimes by outsider observers—after a burst of originality has yielded to the ongoing, evolving elaboration and interpretation of the original ideas. Neither the originators nor the elaborators (and of course, there is no clear-cut distinction between the two) need to be aware of the tradition they are in the process of forging (although sometimes they are). It is not their job to construct a tradition or even, directly, to generate ideas. Their job is to solve problems—the elaboration of ideas that constitute an intellectual tradition is a by-product of problem solving that may or may not be recognized and named as such by its participants. The tradition of thought that I am identifying (constructing) here is a tradition in this sense.

Characterizing a particular set of ideas as a theological–secularist "tradition" is, I readily admit, an act of retrodiction on my part, an interpretive act of ordering and giving coherence to a "body of thought" that never really existed as a recognizable body but was in fact amorphous, heterogeneous, and discontinuous (traditions are like that). Furthermore, I "find" this body of ideas circulating in not just one but in numerous legal traditions; in fact, I venture to hypothesize that *every* legal system will reflect similar ideas. Any argument that posits a basic similarity among all legal systems is subject to the charge of resting on false universalizations of local characteristics and overgeneralizations about law. In defense of this unfashionably essentialist style of argument, my position is that the case for finding a common root for liberal and fundamentalist, secular and religious, Western and non-Western conceptions of law in a secularist theology is worth making, or at least stating, if only to provoke the refutations that might help us to see the relationship between these warring conceptions of law more clearly.

But my purpose in this chapter is not to prove the contention that every legal system is rooted in secularist theology. Nor is my aim to demonstrate the presence of theological secularist ideas in every religious tradition. As interesting as it would be, it would also be virtually impossible to examine every legal tradition for evidence of the imprint of theological–secularist ideas, even if one possessed the skills of the best comparativist scholar (which I emphatically do not). My purpose here is twofold: first, to describe the content of the intellectual tradition that I characterize as secularist theology; second, to show that the warring worldviews of modern secularism and religious fundamentalism have a common source in secularist theology and that they both represent developments, and to some extent distortions, of traditional theological–secularist ideas.

In the main body this chapter, I flesh out the content of the ideas that (I) define (as) secularist theology by following their historical development within *our* legal tradition, that is, the so-called Western tradition of legal ideas, beliefs, practices, and institutions upon which modern, secular legal systems are largely based.[9] In particular, I focus on Christian and Jewish conceptions of the relationship between law and the sacred and their respective connections with classical philosophy as well as biblical thought. This part of the chapter reveals that, contrary to the received wisdom (based on centuries of anti-Jewish polemics) that Christianity was based on a rejection of the harsh justice and excessive "legalism" of Mosaic law, Judaism and Christianity each harbor conceptions of law that constitute virtual mirror images of each other, both in their vision of divine justice and sacred law and in their acceptance of the fact that divine law and sacred ideals of justice have to be violated in the temporal world. Most important, for the fateful history of Jewish–Christian relations, Christian and Jewish conceptions of law mirror each other in their respective projections of this profane conception of law onto the legal system of the other, even as they each incorporate the profane system of law that supposedly belongs to the other within their own legal system. The upshot, in both cases, is the elaboration of a particular set of legal arrangements and a particular set of religious and political justifications for those arrangements, which together constitute what I call secularist theology—that is, theological arguments for secular law, enforced by secular political authorities.

Without undertaking the impossible task of establishing the presence of the same set of ideas in all other legal systems, I end by identifying three general intellectual principles or tendencies—pragmatism, pluralism, and probabilism—that are found in Jewish and Christian secularist theologies alike and that, at least at first glance, appear strikingly similar to intellectual tendencies and ideas found in other religious legal cultures. Although passing references to legal cultures as diverse and seemingly remote from Western culture as classical Islamic jurisprudence and the "legal cosmology" of Buddhist Tibet[10] hardly establish the universality of secularist theology, they are at least suggestive of the possibility that secularist theology is expressive of a widely shared human condition and that legal cultures which appear to be deeply alien and hostile to one another in fact share a common stock of ideas.

Central to what I call "secularist theology" are the intertwined concepts of the secular, the profane, and the law. Secularist theology is a legal philosophy, a philosophy about the nature and necessity of law in human society, as well as a religious philosophy about the nature and necessity of a boundary between the sacred and the profane. At the crux of secularist theology is a line of reasoning leading to the conclusion that legal systems fall on the profane side of the boundary line and that the intellectual postures of pragmatism, pluralism, and probabilism are therefore required of law. Although the main body of this chapter is devoted to retrieving this tradition and line of reasoning, the conclusion looks at its evolution (or one might say, devolution) into modern secularist and fundamentalist thought. The opposition that we see today between secularist and fundamentalist thought reflects important points of tension contained in theological–secularist thought. These tensions were always difficult to maintain, but maintaining and containing these tensions is precisely what theological secularism *did* and, in a deep sense, what theological secularism *was*. The collapse of these tensions spelled the demise of secularist theology, leaving in its wake the radically estranged viewpoints of antisecular fundamentalism and antireligious secularism and a broad range of more or less tolerant religious and secular beliefs in between. Even at the extreme poles of modern religious and secularist beliefs, though, secularist–theological ideas never completely disappeared. On the contrary, secularist and fundamentalist legal philosophies each build on different aspects of traditional theological–secularist thought, amplifying one or the other side of the tensions that historically animated secularist theology.

Reconstructing the point of view of secularist theology involves putting the two sides back together, a task that might be likened to trying to repair a pair of chromosomes that, having mutated, no longer fit together, or to tracing the etiology of a modern cultural deformity that finds expression in the frightening levels of mutual incomprehension and antipathy between "the religious" and "the secular" that we see today. It would be hopelessly naive to think that reconstructing the point of view of secularist theology could bring about a solution to the conflicts between religion and secularism that we now face, when the causes of these conflicts are exceedingly complex and hardly reducible to nonmaterial, intellectual causes of the sort explored here. But perhaps it can shed light on the predicament we now are in by helping us to achieve a better understanding of who *we* are and where *we* are coming from, if not also a better understanding of the (religious or secular) other.

Secularist Theology

Classical Origins

The beginning of any account of "Western culture" lies in pagan antiquity. In
the beginning, the holy was separated from the profane. Far from being a godless world, as some critics of paganism would have it, the premonotheistic world
of pagan antiquity was awash with divinity. By definition, the polytheistic world
abounded with gods. "To each community its own local god" was the fundamental
precept of the polytheistic order. This meant in practice that every community
possessed its own god or gods, practiced its own rites, and worshipped at its own
temple. (These facts have led some scholars to propose that the ideas concerning religion embraced by the more radical Enlightenment figures, ideas such as
religious tolerance and freedom of belief, constituted a kind of "modern paganism"—a provocative thesis that, while not universally accepted, at least not without qualification, captures the contemporary resonance between pluralism and
polytheism, on the one hand, and exclusivity and monotheism, on the other.[11])
In the ancient world, the profane referred literally, and without any value judgment, to the area of space directly before ("pro-") the temple ("fanum"): *profanum*.[12] Only in its second definition did the Latin *profanum* acquire the pejorative
connotations of impiousness, wickedness, and ignorance.[13] In its original sense,
profanity was strictly a place designation based on a differentiation between two
sorts of physical and metaphysical space: the sacred—precisely, that which was
consecrated, set apart,[14] as in a *sanctum* (a holy place),[15] or a *sanctuarium* (a shrine
or a private cabinet, a place for keeping sacred things)[16]—and the space outside
the sacred (i.e., the profane), which referred in the narrowest sense to the space
directly in front of the sacred cabinet, temple, or shrine and in a wider sense to any
space (physical or metaphorical) that had not been consecrated. The concept of
the secular in early Christianity came to have much the same meaning: "worldly,
temporal, profane, lay, and secular" became so many synonyms[17] for the comings
and goings and doings of mundane life.[18]

The split between the two different senses of profane, one pejorative and one
not, can be seen clearly in the opposite meanings attached to the verbal form early
on: "to profane" was both to bring an offering to the temple (literally to be before
the temple, *pro fanus*) and to make unholy.[19] Both usages presuppose the existence
of a boundary line dividing the sacred from the profane, but they conceive of very

different relationships between the two sides of the line. In the first instance, the boundary line is respected, and the profane simply occupies the space outside the line that separates the profane from the sacred. In the second instance, the profane oversteps the boundary and crosses over into sacred space (as only the wicked, the impious, the unlearned, or the ignorant would do). In the first, root sense, the profane is not merely compatible with religious piety; it is definitive of it, involving precisely the hallowing of sacred space,[20] the performance of religious obligations,[21] and the reverencing of God (or in the pagan context, of gods or a god).[22] The derivative sense of the profane implies just the opposite—the desecration of sacred space, the violation of religious obligations, and the failure to obey one's god—in a word, sacrilege.[23] But if the latter is an *irreligious* posture, implying impious disrespect and disobedience of divine commands, it is by that same token *not* an *areligious* posture, implying a disbelief in the god (or gods) whose commands are disrespected. On the contrary, it presupposes a religious conception of the world, including a belief in the sacred (otherwise, what is being violated?),[24] no less than the former conception of profanity does.

The tension and the slippage between the two meanings of "profane" are facts to be reckoned with in reconstructing the history of theological secularism. Some viewpoints collapse the difference between the two meanings. For example, as we shall see in the concluding section of this chapter, many forms of religious fundamentalism view anything that is *outside* the jurisdiction of the sacred as, ipso facto, a *violation* of the sacred. From this point of view, there is no distinction to be made between the pejorative and nonpejorative senses of the profane, and there is no distinction to be made between sacred and nonsacred realms. Everything *ought* to be within the sacred jurisdiction according to these reductive views, and whatever escapes it is an affront to religion. Modern secularism can be equally reductive. Instead of equating the two meanings of profanity, modern secularism eliminates the tension between them by simply preserving one and discarding the other. Thus, it adopts the original notion of the profane as a separate sphere of nonreligious activity—the "secular sphere" as it has been known since early Christian times—while relegating the normative notion of the profane to the sphere of private judgment, where, ostensibly, people are free to believe what they like. Religious fundamentalism collapses the distinction between the two meanings of profanity by equating the two, whereas modern secularism empties out the religious meaning of profanity altogether. Neither position recognizes the original conception of a secular realm that is profane in the first sense but not in the second and that, furthermore, provides a defense of the secular realm's profanity, in the first sense, and a refutation of its profanity, in the second sense, *on religious grounds*. Neither position, that is, recognizes the *theology* of secularism.

Unlike fundamentalism and modern secularism, theological secularism preserves the duality of profanity's meaning and, on the basis of that duality, constructs a religious defense of secularism and secular law. It is the essence of theological secularism to recognize *both* senses of the profane and to maintain their separation, thereby creating space for a form of profanity that is neither areligious, nor irreligious but, rather, paradoxically, reflective of religious commitments and beliefs. Contra the various forms of religious fundamentalism that admit no legitimate secular jurisdiction, theological secularism reflects a belief in the necessity of a "nonreligious" sphere of activity that is separated from the sacred realm. Contra modern secularism, theological secularism conceives of that necessity as a *religious* necessity, driven by religious concerns and expressive of religious humility and a sincere belief in god; it likewise conceives of the secular sphere as subject to the will of god and divine law, while being nonetheless "nonreligious" and outside the jurisdiction of religious law in another sense.

Perhaps the best way of understanding secularist theology—both its underlying religious consciousness and the practical arrangements that it prescribes—is to look at it not as an abstraction but, rather, as a practical response to a concrete problem. The basic problem to which secularist theology responds is, not to put too fine a point on it, human imperfection. The imperfection of human knowledge, in particular, is the problem that historically triggered the development of theological–secularist ideas. To put it otherwise, secularist theology reflects an acute awareness of the failures and limits of human cognition, growing out of the perception of a fundamental gap between the human capacity for knowledge and the omniscience of the divine. Of course, it is possible to cultivate an awareness of the frailty of the human conceptual and perceptual apparatus without holding specifically religious metaphysical views. Conversely, it is painfully obvious that holding religious metaphysical views does not ensure being mindful of the limits of human cognition. But historically, the distinctively religious consciousness of an unbridgeable gap between the human and the divine has not infrequently served to sharpen perceptions of the faultiness of human perception and to heighten awareness of the limits of human awareness.

Examples of this distinctively religious consciousness abound. In the Western tradition, the *locus classicus* is, depending on the school of thought, either Plato or

Aristotle. One school derives a religious intellectual tradition that "is both anti-sensible and antirational"[25] from Plato's skeptical philosophy of mind, expressed in passages such as the following:

> Every human soul by reason of its nature has had a view of Reality, otherwise it could not have entered this human form of ours. But to derive a clear memory of those real truths from these earthly perceptions is not easy for every soul—not for such as have only a brief view in their former existence, or for such as suffered the misfortune, when they fell into this world, to form evil connections . . . forgetting the holy vision they once had.[26]

As described by Stanley Fish in his reconstruction of this intellectual tradition, the "cornerstone" of Plato's philosophy of mind "is a profound distrust of the systems of value and modes of perception indigenous to human life."[27] True knowledge, according to this view, can only be obtained through *holy vision*,[28] which is precisely *not* "the [partial and distorting] version of reality yielded by the senses and by a merely rational wisdom."[29]

In this view, the instruments of proof available in the human world—legal proofs are paradigmatic—do not lead to knowledge of the truth but, rather, to its very antithesis: the *illusion* of truth.[30] For this reason, legal proofs and rhetoric, the art of legal persuasion, were roundly condemned by Plato and his followers hand in hand with the condemnation of poetry.[31] Despite its association with poetry, rhetoric is *not* distinguished, in this intellectual tradition, from rational, scientific forms of discourse. To the contrary, rhetoric and science are equated—as ways of producing and communicating knowledge based on merely probabilistic evidence and ordinary sense perceptions—and pronounced to be merely illusory forms of proof (in contrast to dialectic, which alone leads to truth).

The classical tradition of rhetoric is therefore the last place one would expect to find an expression of the religious consciousness of human cognitive limits similar to Plato's. In fact, however, the classical conception of rhetoric, bequeathed by Aristotle in his classic defense of rhetoric against Plato's attack, exhibits more or less the same understanding of the limits and deficiencies of rhetoric as Plato's vision does. Proponents of classical rhetoric were anything but unmindful of the lack of certainty afforded by rhetorical proofs; they understood full well that proofs based on rhetoric rest on inventive interpretations rather than on perfectly objective reconstructions and produce merely probable rather than certain truths.[32] The difference between the followers of Aristotle and Plato on the subject of rhetoric did not lie in a disagreement about what rhetorical knowledge is like (they were rather in agreement about its made-up and less than certain nature), nor did it lie in a difference of opinion about whether other superior forms of knowledge are available in the mortal world (again, they were more or less in agreement that *all* human knowledge practices, including science, medicine, political judgments, and law, have to be based on the imperfect art of rhetoric, save for the philosophical occupation of pure speculation, which is necessarily the province of a few and, by definition, disconnected from the practical world). The difference lay, rather, in their respective evaluations of the practical utility and moral acceptability of rhetoric as a form of knowledge (and in their respective views of the relationship between those two characteristics). Whereas Plato, for the most part, saw little value in rhetoric,[33] Aristotle and his followers accepted the imperfections of human cognition reflected in rhetorical modes of knowledge. The project of classical rhetoric was not to deny the susceptibility of these modes of knowledge to bias and error nor to deny their merely probabilistic and less than certain—hence, illusory—nature. But it was not to deny their practical or ethical value either. Indeed, classical rhetoric made utility the measure of value and recognized the utility of even imperfect, probabilistic modes of knowledge. Rhetoric was thus conceived as a quintessentially pragmatic project of making the best of a bad lot, the lot of living as a mortal in the mortal world, "where we cannot have certain knowledge," so "our knowledge must be probable at best."[34]

Seeking to make human practices of interpretation and judgment as useful and as equitable as possible, classical rhetoric was organized around an awareness of the limits and the pitfalls of the human cognitive capacity. Whether this mindfulness of human cognitive limitations embedded in the classical tradition expressed a distinctively *religious* consciousness of a gap between the human and the divine is a complicated question, the answer to which need not be resolved here.[35] More important, for our purposes, is the emergence of Judaism, Christianity, and Islam as the chief continuators of Aristotle's philosophical ideas.[36] We may never know if religion was at all central to the Aristotelian tradition of rhetoric in the original context—the pagan societies of ancient Greece and Rome—in which it was first developed, institutionalized, and practiced, chiefly by lawyers, a slowly professionalizing class, occupied mainly with practical, human affairs, which placed them outside the sacred realm of rites and oracles, presided over by the priests.[37] What is undisputed is that during the period of time between the twelfth and fifteenth centuries, the proverbial "golden age" of medieval Spain, Aristotelian thought, including the classical tradition of rhetoric, was absorbed into the three major monotheistic religions. Thus, whether or not classical rhetoric contained a religious sensibility at the outset, there is little doubt that the religious sensibilities of Judaism, Christianity, and Islam were grafted onto it (and it onto them) during the Middle Ages (if not, in some instances, before).

The encounters that occurred between the monotheistic faiths and Aristotelian thought (each had its own "Aristotelian moment") did not *create* the religious sense of a gap between the human and divine. That basic notion was a core feature of Judaism, Christianity, and Islam, rooted in biblical (and Koranic) texts, well before any encounter between Greek philosophy and the monotheistic religions occurred. But if the idea that human knowledge falls short of divine omniscience preexisted the encounter between philosophy and monotheism, that encounter could only have sharpened the already present awareness of human cognitive imperfection. In fact, both Platonism and Aristotelianism would have reinforced the sense of human cognitive inadequacy promoted by the monotheistic faiths, and vice versa.

Christian Developments

This is readily seen in the case of Christianity, which early on became fused with both Platonic and Aristotelian ideas and developed a legal tradition directly based on Roman law and its classical *ars rhetorica*. The development of Christian canon law is an inseparable part of the history of the various civil law and common law systems that eventually emerged in Europe. It is therefore of great moment, for purposes of establishing the existence of a tradition of theological secularism and its formative influence on the modern legal culture of the West, to demonstrate the centrality of classical ideas to Christian canon law and traditional Christian legal thought.

The most striking feature of Christian canon law, for our purposes, is its coexistence at all times with other legal systems. From the fourth and fifth centuries, when the first Church Councils were organized and produced the original Church rules, or "canons,"[38] through the establishment of the papacy in Rome, to the present day, the Church never exercised—and never claimed—unrivaled political power. The powers that the Church accrued were undeniably vast. But even at its height, the political authority of the Church did not *displace* other forms of political rule either in theory or in practice. This was not just a matter of Realpolitik (though of course it was also that). It reflected the Church's own understanding of how political power ought to be ordered and distributed.

Church theology, canon law, and the Bible itself always recognized a division between the "spiritual" jurisdiction of the Church and its courts and the "secular" jurisdiction of the State. Indeed, the term *secular* finds its origins in this early Christian usage, meaning, roughly speaking, the worldly, the temporal, the nonreligious, in other words—in its root, nonpejorative, sense—the profane. Building on Mark 12 ("Render unto Caesar what is Caesar's") and Romans 13 ("Obey the government, for God is the one who put it there"),[39] Christian theologians consistently accepted the proposition that secular government is divinely ordained by God. Although this implied a degree of interpenetration between religious and State authority at odds with modern notions of the separation of Church and State, it also implied a theory of a division between Church and State not so dissimilar from modern notions as we might imagine. Augustine's pairing of the "city of God" and "city of the world" and Aquinas's theory of a divinely ordained hierarchy of spiritual and temporal political jurisdictions were perhaps the most influential statements of the fundamental Christian belief in the rightful coexistence of secular and religious realms, but they merely gave expression to a commonplace view.[40]

This theory of dual jurisdictions presupposed the existence of a boundary line separating the sacred from the nonsacred realm, which raises two basic questions: (1) What differentiated the two realms? In other words, what did each realm contain? (2) Why was such a division thought to be necessary? Why couldn't everything be contained in one—sacred—realm? Why couldn't everything be sacred?

The answers to these questions are interrelated. They both turn, in important part, on the basic idea that humans lack the cognitive perfection of the divine. The sacred realm, in the Christian understanding, was occupied by God, of course—by the Father, the Son, and the Holy Spirit; it was also occupied by divine justice and sacred law. But divine justice and sacred law could bear at best only a hortatory relationship to conventional law and human legal institutions for the simple reason that human beings, and human reason, in the Christian conception are flawed. The problem—the practical problem to which Christian theology had to respond—is not just that there are "bad guys" (intentional lawbreakers who violate the sacred order with evil hearts), an inevitability given humanity's penchant for evil in its fallen state. The more intractable problem is that the "good guys," the law *enforcers*, lack the tools to make the correct judgments necessary to doing justice that God alone can make.

The religious consciousness of an unbridgeable gap between divine and human perception is thus intimately connected to the Christian conception of a legitimate secular sphere separated from the sacred realm. Simply put, according to traditional Christian thought, secular law is necessitated by the inadequacy of our grasp on divine justice and sacred law. Which is to say that the secular realm is largely occupied with law—conventional human law, state law, and its attendant institutions, which are designed to apply and enforce the law and serve the needs of society.

This, in a nutshell, is the basic logic of the religious argument for the secular state and secular law, or what I call "secularist theology." The force of this logic is perhaps best appreciated in the context of particular historical episodes in which the allocation of law-enforcement powers to secular political regimes was explicitly discussed. One particularly telling example is the discussion that surrounded the "new criminal law," which emerged in Europe in the late twelfth century. As described by Richard Fraher, who made the topic the subject of a series of articles,[41] the creation of a new criminal law in the high middle ages was propelled by the fact that "procedural guarantees for the defendant were so strongly entrenched in the traditional accusatorial procedure" prescribed by canon law "that prosecution *per accusationem* emerged as a positively inefficient means of curbing criminal behavior."[42] The "conceptual base" for these procedural guarantees, Fraher points out, was "inherited from antiquity."[43] Specifically, "[t]he rabbinic tradition had required two witnesses in order to establish proof and thus supplied a standard for sufficiency of proof in criminal cases. Both the Old Testament and the Roman law required due process before a defendant could be condemned."[44] And "[a] crucial third element appeared in the Roman law's *dictum* that the burden of proof lay upon the accuser and not the accused."[45] The practical result was that convictions were almost impossible to secure under traditional canon law. In other words, sacred law was, literally, too good for this world.

The religious conception of sacred law that made it practically unenforceable reflects the religious consciousness of the limits of human cognition discussed earlier.[46] As Fraher explains, "the fathers of the Latin church had decidedly rejected the preoccupation of fifth-century Roman law with maintaining social control through harsh penal sanctions"; more broadly, they rejected "the conceptual framework from which the [Roman law] vocabulary was drawn" (even as they adapted that legal vocabulary to other ends).[47] Their repudiation of law as an instrument of coercion and social control had many sources. "If the voice of Christian experience in the age of martyrs did not sufficiently discredit the brutal Roman approach to criminal law, the authority of Scripture, cautioning the Christian not to accuse his brother, certainly suggested toleration."[48] It was also consistent with the general spirit of Jesus' rejection of the law and "legalism" of the Pharisees.[49] It is critical to note, however, that this negative attitude toward law and legalism was only aimed at law *in the temporal realm*; it did not extend to the world beyond. As Fraher explains, describing the Church fathers' views, "[i]t was not that any sin would fail to meet its just desert but that [Christian theologians, such as] Augustine and Gregory *were not confident of society's ability to enforce the divine law in this world* and therefore felt safer in leaving vengeance to God and restricting the aims of the church in *this* world to corrective, medicinal ends through penance."[50]

The separation originally made by Christian thinkers between the divine and the temporal thus cut two ways. On the one hand, the Church fathers could afford to dispense with law enforcement in the earthly realm, confident that punishments and rewards would be meted out in the afterlife. On the other hand, their reason for dispensing with temporal law enforcement in the first place was that human beings, charged with enforcing the law, would inevitably fail to make the correct decisions because, as humans, they necessarily lack the perfect omniscience and understanding (the judgment and the mercy) of the divine. The only hedges against these limitations conceived of by the Church fathers were to attach stringent procedural safeguards to the conduct of prosecutions to prevent convictions from being based on inadequate proof or to forego law enforcement altogether. For all practical purposes, these seemed to amount to the same thing.

Not surprisingly, such a purist approach to law enforcement was quickly "supplemented" by a variety of mechanisms aimed at securing what the purist approach could never achieve, namely, convictions.[51] A law that is too good for this world really is too good for this world, a fact that Christians were readier to accept once "the age of martyrs" ended, and they ceased to be the objects of legal persecution and found themselves (after the Roman emperors' conversion to Christianity) in the position of power instead. A system of law that refuses to permit convictions based on less than perfect knowledge is a system in which crimes can be committed with impunity; neither punishment nor deterrence of criminal behavior will be served. By the twelfth century, the perception of soaring crime rates strongly suggested to Christians that the promise of punishment in the afterlife was an ineffective deterrent. Combined with the sense that unrestrained criminality could hardly have been part of the divine plan, the belief emerged in this period that effective mechanisms of law enforcement were a necessary part of the divine plan, even if they conflicted with the requirements of established religious law.

How the need for effective law enforcement was to be reconciled with established Christian law and fundamental Christian tenets, such as "turn the other
cheek,"[52] is a long and twisted tale, which can only be glanced at here.[53] Immediately prior to the emergence of the new criminal law, in the twelfth century, the
favored technique for avoiding the impediments to effective law enforcement had
been the trial by ordeal, conceived as a means to produce the signs or confessions
that would satisfy the stringent requirements of biblical and canon law.[54] The abolition of trial by ordeal in 1215 created a practical void that the new criminal law
was designed to fill.[55] As Fraher says, "the motivation behind the development of
the new criminal procedures . . . was the perceived need for efficient enforcement
of the canon law, for the purpose of deterring deviant behavior" (in particular, the
deviant behavior of clergy members, which, then as now, had become an embar-
rassment to the Church).[56] The legal innovations included "the replacement of
accusatory by inquisitorial procedures, the virtually automatic use of torture as an
investigative and perhaps punitive tool in criminal cases, the employment of lesser
standards of proof when witnesses were lacking, and the creation of summary
procedures to deal with 'enormous crimes.'"[57]

It may seem a great irony that such brutal procedures were adopted as a result
of the Church's moral squeamishness about basing criminal convictions on human
judgments and imperfect proofs. But in fact, it was this very reluctance that generated the need for *alternatives* to the legal procedures understood to be prescribed
by sacred law. Theologians and canon lawyers were perfectly aware that the new
criminal procedures, like the old procedure of trial by ordeal, deviated from the
requirements of sacred law, and they understood full well that in so doing, the new
legal procedures raised the specter of catastrophic mistakes.[58] It was for just this
reason that at least some of these legal procedures were removed from the "spiritual
domain" of the canon law courts and entrusted to the secular government instead.

Indeed, one of the most important and long-lasting of the theological innovations of this period was a principle of deference to secular government to enforce
criminal law. In essence, the Church authorized the secular governments of the
then-prevailing city-states to create and implement an effective system of criminal
law. This was justified on the basis of the newly articulated doctrine, first uttered
by Pope Innocent III in 1203: *publicae utilatis intersit, ne crimina remaneant impunita* ("in the interest of public utility, crimes ought not remain unpunished").[59]
According to Fraher, this doctrine "helped to justify the nontraditional punitive
measures which communal governments enacted to ensure stability and curb

violence in the new city-states."[60] By relegating law enforcement procedures that compromised sacred law's "impossible" standards of proof[61] to the secular realm, upholders of Church principles could simultaneously maintain the purity of religious law (in theory), while in practice overcoming the insuperable obstacles which that law imposed to actually punishing or deterring crime.

It is not insignificant that Fraher links this use of the public utility doctrine to the "enormous popularity of Aristotle" at the time.[62] In fact, the justifications articulated for the new criminal law are a quintessential example of the fusion between religious scruples and Aristotelian pragmatism that characterizes theological–secularist thought. Splitting off secular law and government from the Church's spiritual jurisdiction was not just a concession to power; from the internal standpoint of Church theology, it was a way of "hiving off"[63] functions that, because they had to rely on faulty human judgments, profaned the law. It was a dirty job, but someone had to do it, and to maintain clean hands, that someone had to be a nonreligious (secular) authority. This was the pragmatic solution that secularist theology offered in response to the practical problem of reconciling the standards of the divine (which would not countenance erroneous convictions) with the need for effective crime control and law enforcement (which require that some erroneous convictions be made).

There was, of course, a serious problem with this "solution," reflected and partially concealed in the double meaning of "profane." The legal procedures that deviated from sacred law were not just separated from the realm of sacred law, but they were in direct violation of its impossible standards—standards which were, as a practical matter, impossible to meet. They allowed judgments to be rendered on the basis of merely probable, imperfect knowledge; they allowed erroneous judgments; they permitted innocent people to be tortured, imprisoned, convicted, and put to death. They were thus, in every sense of the word, profane. Yet, they were necessary, and not just on pragmatic but on religious grounds. This was the paradox of secularist theology: Secular law was both *religiously necessary* (or crime would go unpunished and aggression would be unbridled) and *necessarily profane* (for mistakes would have to be made, and innocent heads would roll). Secular law, as conceived by the Christian architects of the new criminal law, was thus both transgressive and normative, both violative of and justified by religious law; indeed, it was religiously mandated. It was authorized by Church doctrines, such as the newly canonized doctrine that no crime should go unpunished. Yet it had to be differentiated and cabined off from the spiritual law. Somehow secular law was both religious and nonreligious; both consistent and inconsistent with religious law. If one thought too hard about it, contracting out the dirty work might not have seemed like an adequate solution to the problem of reconciling the standards of divine justice with the human need for effective law enforcement and human cognitive failings. After all, the dirty work was still being done and still being countenanced by the Church and church law. But for the most part, one didn't have to think too hard about it.[64] It was possible to deny that secular law was profane, in the normative sense, while acknowledging its profanity in the nonpejorative sense in light of its seeming necessity and religious justification—a form of denial made easier by the fact that the favored linguistic convention for referring to the nonsacred domain from early Christian times was to call it "secular," which never carried quite the same sting as calling it "profane." ("To secularize" is not "to profane.")

For all its inadequacies, the theological argument for secular legal authority was eagerly embraced by a Christian public desperate for a solution to the problem of ineffective law enforcement. In a classic Aristotelian moment, both the laity and the clergy welcomed the use of the public utility doctrine to justify secular legal authority on ostensibly religious terms. Indeed, the doctrine was extended to justify changes in the legal procedures of courts in the ecclesiastical realm as well.

For centuries—going back to the original formation of the ecclesiastical realm as a body of religious clerics, formally organized and separated from the Christian laity—the Church had maintained its own "spiritual courts," which followed the legal procedures and substantive rules prescribed by canon law. Indeed, canon law got its start as a collection of rules and bylaws adopted by the Church to "define and determine the organization of the Church and the conduct and duties of its members"—that is, of the clergy.[65] This original focus on the administration of the Church is reflected in the titles and subtitles of the first Church lawbooks, compiled in the fourth and fifth centuries, which announce the subject matters covered by canon law, such as:

1. Ordination, Orders, the life of the Clergy.
2. Monks, nuns, widows, public penitents.
3. Church courts, trials, accusations, etc., councils, church property.
4. Liturgy, Baptism.
5. Marriage, sins of the flesh, murder.
6. Duties and moral conduct of clergy and of laity.

7. The Crown.
8. Theological questions.
9. Heresy.
10. Idolatry.[66]

As these headings reveal, the original collections of Church canons were essentially rulebooks for the clergy, containing the operating instructions for how to qualify, behave, and perform one's duties as a cleric and how to run the day-to-day affairs of the Church. Writing of the character that canon law assumed more than 1,000 years later, during "the long period from the Reformation to the Second Vatican Council," Charles Donahue has described it as "basically an administrative law, parceling out powers and functions, largely among clerics, with papal power increasingly exercised by the Vatican bureaucracy."[67] Minus the Vatican bureaucracy, this is a fairly accurate description of what canon law was like from the beginning: an ecclesiastical law, in the strictest sense, or as Donahue put it, the "administrative law" of the Church, comprising the rules that govern its internal affairs and the conduct of its officers.

Necessarily, this administrative law encompassed matters of both great and little theological import (from heresy to housekeepers)[68] and concerned the conduct of the laity as well as the clergy (since the clergy's regular duties include guiding and ministering to the laity, for example, in the officiation of marriages). As a result, the division of labor between ecclesiastical law and secular law would never be perfectly neat. There would always be overlaps between spiritual and secular law, and the management of conflicts of law and contests over jurisdiction would become a major leitmotif of canon law and Church history.[69]

Given the overlap between ecclesiastical and temporal jurisdictions, it is perhaps not surprising that, at the same time that the Church developed justifications for secular legal procedures to prosecute crime more effectively than traditional canon law allowed, it also enhanced its own prosecutorial powers. The authorization of less stringent standards of proof and procedural protections in the secular courts was only one of the procedural innovations of the new criminal law; most of the others consisted of modifications of the substantive and procedural rules employed by the Church's own legal tribunals. Fraher's work traces how the very same doctrine of *ne crimina remaneant impunita* that justified the circumvention of traditional canon law by the secular city-states also served to justify the circumvention of canon law procedural requirements by the ecclesiastical courts and the

Church hierarchy itself.[70] In the first case, canon law authorized another body of law (the *ius commune*, or common law, of the city-states) to deviate from it; in the second case, canon law in effect authorized itself to deviate from itself. The inquisition, after all (one of the chief elements of the new criminal law) was a religious, not a secular, institution. Like the public utility doctrine that was used to justify it, the inquisition procedure was initially used to deal with "wayward" or "criminous" clerics[71] (as much to avoid outside proceedings against them as to restore discipline to the clerical order).[72]

Just as the use of secular law was rationalized by the Church, the employment of new procedures by the Church's own legal institutions was justified as an "extraordinary measure" required to meet exigent circumstances.[73] And just as the use of the term *secular* helped to finesse the profane character of state law (profane because it violated the requirements of the traditional spiritual law, permitting the conviction of innocent people), the public utility doctrine and similar doctrinal innovations within canon law[74] helped to finesse the profane character of law in the ecclesiastical realm. Although the changes made in canon law and secular law were recognized to deviate from sacred law, they were not explicitly deemed by mainstream Christians to be "profane" (particularly when the stakes were relatively low but even when the stakes were high—as Helmholz observed of a later period, "[f]ew men argued that a judge risked eternal damnation merely by allowing temporal courts to hear disputes between two parsons over which one was entitled to tithes"[75]).

The development of the new criminal law was just one episode in a long history of movements back and forth in Christian thought between a strict adherence to a sacred law that highlights the inadequacy of human judgments and a laxer approach, which stresses the adequacy of human judgments as measured by the pragmatic standards of social utility and necessity. The tension between these two approaches, the purist and the pragmatic, was reflected historically not only in the split between the temporal and spiritual realms but within each realm as well. On the spiritual side, ecclesiastical courts deviated from sacred law every bit as much as the secular courts did, even as these deviations were enshrined in canon law. On the secular side, the recognized temporal power was always viewed (from the point of view of Christian theology) as part of a larger spiritual whole. Throughout centuries of changes in the form and the seat of temporal power, and notwithstanding the multitude of secular political regimes that coexisted with the Church at any one time, the theory that held until well into the modern period was that kingships were divinely ordained and as much a part of Christendom as the pa-pacy.[76] A divinely ordained kingship is by no means a theocracy (neither is the papacy). Yet it is divinely ordained. As the secular branch of government, it repre-sents not the antithesis but rather the counterpart to the spiritual jurisdiction of the Church, both being part of a single integrated political (and religious) system. That being the case, the legal systems of the temporal powers could never be conceived of as wholly lacking in spiritual content or wholly removed from the Church and its ecclesiastical jurisdiction. The law of the king was, in theory, no less beholden to God than the law of the Church; no less expressive of God's will than the law of the Church; and no less a function of God's design than the law of the Church. Secular law was differentiated from religious law not on the grounds of not being part of the divine order but, rather, on the grounds that secular and religious law served different practical (religious *and* political) functions and had different (religious *and* political) jurisdictions presided over by different (religious *and* political) institutions and rulers.

This is not to deny the existence of overlaps in the functions, jurisdictions, and personnel of the two suborders. In fact, the overlaps were significant. As enumer-ated by Richard Helmholz in his discussion of Church law and secular law in Eng-land, there were three different ways in which spiritual and secular law overlapped: (1) "[T]he persons subject to the jurisdiction of the ecclesiastical and the common-law courts were, roughly speaking, the same"—to wit, subjects of the king, virtu-ally all of whom were Christian after the expulsion of the Jews from England in 1290.[77] (2) "[T]here were several areas of human life where the law of the Church and the common law of the realm both claimed exclusive jurisdiction."[78] Finally, (3) "[M]any clerics served as judges in the early common-law courts [and] were in fact mainstays of the system."[79] Scholars have tended to focus on the *conflicts* between Church and State produced by their overlapping jurisdictions (e.g., "If a man punches a parson in the nose, is that a case of assault and battery, or is it the religious offense of impugning the Church's authority?"[80]). But underlying these conflicts is a basic unity between the temporal and spiritual realms. Even when genuine conflicts of law and contests over jurisdiction arose between the two legal systems, the two remained part of a single unified system, specialized parts of a single unitary (religious and political) whole.[81]

This is equally true of the two different secular law systems that evolved in the emerging states of continental Europe and England, civil law and common law (and equally true of the periods both before and after the Reformation.).[82] Civil law and common law, each a species of secular law, were alike not only in their secular but also in their indelibly religious (Christian) character and their relationship to Christian religious law. At once apart from, and a part of, the Church's spiritual law, unquestionably subject to God's law (which at once was and wasn't the same thing as the spiritual law), civil law and common law both expressed the paradoxical quality of secular law in secularist theology. Like the new criminal law enacted by the medieval city-states, civil law and common law each embodied the characteristically secular commitment to effective law enforcement, which, because it required the exercise of human judgment, had to deviate from (and literally "profane") the purity of sacred law. Yet each of these secular legal systems also incorporated norms (e.g., the values of due process)[83] that cut against the need for effective law enforcement and expressed concerns about the fallibility of human judgments that were clearly derived from Christian theology and canon law.

Taken together, as the indivisible though differentiated whole that they were, the various legal regimes of Europe and England gave institutional form to the prevailing secularist theology that recognized, yet sought to justify, the profane character of law *on religious grounds*. Underlying the diversity of temporal and spiritual jurisdictions produced in Western Christendom was a unifying theology, a set of religious arguments supporting the institution of secular political authority and secular forms of law alongside the Church's own courts (which themselves would be licensed to exercise temporal forms of power).

Similar theological arguments have served to justify similar legal arrangements in other religious cultures. One notable example is Jewish law, which produced a version of a secularist theology that replicates (or anticipates) Christian secularist theology in every critical respect. Notwithstanding the different purposes served by secularist theology in Jewish and Christian thought, and notwithstanding the differences between the situation and content of Jewish and Christian systems of law, the similarity in their respective orientations toward secular legal authority is striking. It strongly suggests that secularist theology is not unique to Christianity and the complex system of European canon, common, and civil law but that it rather reflects more widely shared beliefs and concerns.

Jewish Law

Undeniably, there are crucial differences between the legal systems of Western Christendom and Jewish law. One obvious difference stems from the fact that Jews lacked political and legal sovereignty for most of their history, which meant that the power of their legal institutions was greatly circumscribed. Most of the development of Jewish law (which consists of the law of the Torah and the *halakha*, rabbinic interpretations of the law of the Torah, compiled in the Talmud) occurred in the context of political exile, at the sufferance of host states that intermittently accorded Jewish communities a measure of autonomy to operate their own political and legal institutions.[84]

Perhaps the most oft-stated (and often overstated) difference between Christian and Jewish law stems from Christianity's antipathy to Mosaic law and the "legalism" of the Pharisees.[85] According to longstanding (Christian) tradition, the basic break with Judaic law announced by Christ in the Sermon on the Mount served to elevate the moral content and appeal of Christianity over the exclusive particularism of the Jews.[86] According to others, less critical of the Jewish tradition, the break with Jewish law resulted in a diminishment of the legal content of Christian theology as well as the impoverishment of the theological content of Christian canon law.[87] Charles Donahue speaks for this view when he observes that, although "Christianity was an offshoot of Judaism, a religion that has a great penchant for law," and although "Christianity quickly became associated with Roman culture," another culture with "a great penchant for law," Christianity itself exhibits no penchant for law.[88] According to Donahue, the fact that the fathers of Church law used the Greek word *kanon*, suggesting a technical rule, to refer to their statutes, rather than *nomos*, "a word redolent of overarching philosophical ideas,"[89] reflects the fact that canon law, unlike Jewish law, never was and never would be "redolent of overarching philosophical ideas."[90]

Donahue's view is surely exaggerated (canon law is hardly devoid of theological content), but it is certainly true that canon law has historically played a smaller role in Christian theology than religious law plays in the theology of many other religious traditions, for example, Judaism and Islam. (The Hindu religion might be another case in point.[91]) Jewish law indeed is suffused with philosophical ideas, and law is the medium in which the greater part of Judaism's theological, moral, and political ideas have been expressed,[92] which makes it quite different from Christianity in crucial respects.

This difference in the respective contents and functions of canon law and Jewish law reflects another basic difference: Judaism never produced a specialized clerical order comparable to the Christian clergy. Canon law, as we have seen, was in the first instance the law of the clerical order, the administrative law of the Church, ecclesiastical law in the strictest sense. In Judaism, because there is no comparable division between clerical and lay orders, religious law in the Jewish conception could not possibly serve the same functions or have the same character as canon law. Lacking an organized Church, there could be no truly *ecclesiastical* law in Judaism. In the Christian conception, the fundamental division is that between the laity and the clergy, and out of that initial distinction, the differentiation of temporal and spiritual legal jurisdictions emerges. In Judaism, by contrast, the distinction between spiritual and temporal law is not based on a distinction between a law for the clergy and the law for the laity, for there is no comparable social distinction drawn between the two. The crucial distinction in Judaism is not that between a law for the clergy and the law for the laity but, rather, that between a law for Jews and a law for everyone else.

Based on biblical scripture, rabbis developed complex doctrines concerning a law for non-Jews, even though, lacking political sovereignty and power, they had neither the means nor the intention of enforcing that law. The so-called Noahide law, derived from the "Seven Commandments of the Sons of Noah," applies to all humankind (and is sometimes equated with "natural law").[93] Extensive discussions of the legal obligations of non-Jews took place under the rubric of this Jewish law doctrine. And in the same fashion, extensive discussions of the obligations of Jews to follow non-Jewish law took place under the rubric of the Talmudic doctrine of *dina de-malkhuta dina* (literally "the law of the kingdom is the law," often translated as "the law of the state is the law").[94]

Although the interrelationship of these two doctrines is disputed by rabbinic authorities, together they reflect the core ideas of what I have called secularist theology. These include (1) a mindfulness of the unreliability of human judgments, stirred by a religious awareness of the gap between the human and the divine; (2) a sense of the consequent profanity of human justice (and profanation of divine justice) that results from the unreliability of human judgments; (3) a sense of the inefficacy of divine justice in the temporal realm due to the procedural barriers erected by sacred law to prevent miscarriages of justice; (4) an appreciation of the great human need for effective means of law enforcement and the practical value and utility of legal mechanisms for circumventing the stringent sacred law; and (5) a corresponding sanction for the development of distinctively secular forms of justice, designed to circumvent the procedural barriers to effective law enforcement imposed by sacred law. As in Christian theological secularism, these ideas gave rise to a complex, variegated system of multiple legal jurisdictions and types of law, some of which are deemed "secular" or "temporal" and others of which are deemed "sacred," "Jewish," or "religious," although all of them are recognized and authorized by Jewish law.

The first cut in Jewish law is the distinction drawn between a law for the Jews and a law for the gentiles. According to the traditional rabbinic understanding, God prescribed law for all of humanity, but Jews alone were bound by the additional commandments of Sinaitic, or Mosaic, law (the law of the Torah) because only Jews had entered into the special covenant with God to be so bound.[95] Everyone else was subject to the less demanding Noahide Code. The Noahide Code, in the traditional Jewish understanding, contains six basic commandments against idolatry, blasphemy, sexual offenses, bloodshed, theft, and eating the flesh of a living animal. The final, seventh, commandment of the Noahide Code is *dinin*, variously defined as the "obligation to enforce the other provisions of the Noahide Code by appointing judges and other law enforcement officials"[96] or, alternatively, as the obligation to "establish[ ] an ordered system of jurisprudence for the governance of financial, commercial, and interpersonal relationships."[97]

The *halakhah* contains extensive discussions exploring the meaning of Noahide law and the respective obligations of Jews and gentiles to obey one another's law. As Suzanne Stone has remarked, "[t]his large corpus of Jewish legal material defining the obligations of non-Jews who, by and large, are unaware of the existence of the doctrine and who are, in any event, not accountable to Jewish legal authority is to contemporary eyes no doubt strange."[98] That this is so is no doubt a reflection of the modern tendency to equate "real" law with law that is enforceable—a tendency that reveals our own secularist bias. Real law, we tend to think, is law that is enforced by real authorities with real power—that is, states or political institutions like the Vatican, which command the power of a sovereign state, not institutions like the rabbinic courts of the stateless Jews, which clearly lacked the power to subject non-Jews to their law.

But this way of thinking seems clearly to miss the point of the doctrine of Noahide law, in particular, the commandment of *dinin*, which is precisely a call for non-Jews to establish their own system of law, their own rules of contracts, property, and torts, and their own tribunals to apply and enforce these rules of law. According to the rabbis' own understanding, Noahide law is not supposed to be enforced by the Jewish courts. Indeed, the question raised by the interpreters of the *halakha* was not how or whether they could apply the law of the Noahides to the Noahides (i.e., non-Jews) but, rather, how or whether they should, in some circumstances, apply the Noahide law to Jews. Similarly, the doctrine of *dina de-*

malkhuta dina (the law of the kingdom is the law) was elaborated to settle questions concerning whether and when Jews had an obligation to follow the law of the land. Rather like the Christian principle of "rendering unto Caesar what is Caesar's," the doctrine of *dina de-malkhuta dina* served in part to justify Jewish submission to the authority of non-Jewish law—on the grounds of Jewish law—even when that submission entailed the abrogation of certain principles of Jewish law.[99] In this respect, the doctrine was clearly functioning to rationalize pragmatic concessions to superior political power. But this was not the only, or even the primary, function of the doctrine of the law of the king.[100] As scholars like Chaim Povarsky have shown, by marking a boundary line between the jurisdictions of Jewish and non-Jewish law, the doctrine also served to *define* and *protect* a sphere of Jewish legal and political autonomy, safeguarded from incursions by outside law.[101] Most of the applications of the doctrine had the effect of supporting the authority of the rabbinic courts (and other Jewish political institutions) and Jewish law. And even when conflicts of law led rabbinic authorities to apply the doctrine to support the law of the "king," the authority of the rabbinic courts was enhanced inasmuch as they were able to present themselves as the ones granting deference to the secular authorities on the basis of Jewish law.[102]

Clearly, what is going on in the elaboration of these doctrines is the articulation of a complex division of legal authority and jurisdictions, defined and authorized by Talmudic law, much like the theory of multiple legal jurisdictions found in Christian theology and canon law. As in the Christian case, the religious authorities (the rabbis) are conceived of, by Jewish law, as the fundamental legal authorities; and as in the Christian case, these fundamental legal authorities are understood to be the ones to have carved out space where other forms of law are allowed, indeed required, to operate. In theory, then, the deference accorded by Jewish law to other legal systems does not reflect its ineffectiveness; rather, paradoxically, it reflects its fundamental authority.

As in the Christian case, the structure of the system of different legal jurisdictions and bodies of law recognized by *halakha* is complex. A seemingly simple dichotomy between religious and nonreligious law gives way in each case to the elaboration of not just two, but multiple, jurisdictions and systems of law. In the Christian case, as we have seen, the basic bifurcation of temporal and spiritual realms was complicated by the Church's assumption of secular powers for itself. On the grounds of public utility, necessity, and the need for extraordinary measures to be taken to enforce the law, the ecclesiastical courts enacted a new "spiritual" law in the twelfth century alongside their authorization of a new secular law. The new spiritual law, which closely resembled secular law in its relatively lax procedural requirements and standards of proof, was explicitly conceived as a form of emergency law. It was only on the grounds of its emergency powers that the ecclesiastical authorities were thus permitted to deviate from (i.e., violate) the traditional sacred law. The result was that Christian theology sanctioned not just two but three kinds of law: (1) the temporal law of the state (be it civil or common law, a kingdom or a republic); (2) the original spiritual law of the Church, a supposedly pure embodiment of the sacred law combined with a purely administrative law to govern the affairs of the Church; and (3) the emergency "spiritual" law, which was in essence a form of temporal law, designed to serve temporal needs, administered by the Church and the ecclesiastical courts.

Jewish law likewise complicated the basic distinction between Jewish and non-Jewish law, ultimately producing a typology of not just three but four types of law authorized by Jewish law. The fact that Jewish law defined four types of law rather than just the three authorized in the Christian conception reflects the fact that Jewish law, unlike Christian law, subdivides law by peoples or nations in addition to subdividing it according to spiritual as opposed to temporal functions. In the Christian conception, there is no recognition that different peoples or nations might have—or should have—-their own legal systems. Implicitly, the Christian theology of law assumes that everyone is Christian or at least subject to the law of Christian people. Even temporal law, in the Christian conception, is conceived of as a part of the larger Christian body politic: The divinely ordained king is, presumptively, a Christian king subject to the law of God and the Church (even if the Church exercises its authority in part by deferring in some areas to the jurisdiction of the king). By contrast, Jewish law, as we have seen, posits that Jews and non-Jews each have their own separate legal systems. The distinction between Jews and non-Jews is independent of the distinction between religious/spiritual and temporal/secular domains. Thus it is that four, rather than three, different types of law are elaborated in the *halakha*: (1) the sacred law of the Torah, or "pure Jewish law," [103] which is the law supposedly administered by the rabbinic courts for the Jewish people in ordinary nonemergency circumstances; (2) the "law of the king" (or law of the state), sanctioned by the doctrine of *dina de-malkhuta dina*, understood to apply to both Jewish and non-Jewish kings/states; (3) the Noahide law, conceived of as the law of the gentiles, although on some accounts it is construed as a universal law to which Jews also are subject (in addition to being subject to Sinaitic, or "pure religious," law); and finally, (4) a special form of rabbinic law, endowed with the same procedural flexibility as Noahide and state law, authorized to be exercised by the rabbinic courts in cases of emergency, where exigent circumstances demanded the exercise of exigency powers.

Save for the additional wrinkle of the distinction drawn between Jewish and Noahide law, it should be clear that this complex structure of multiple forms of law almost exactly replicates the crucial features of the legal system enshrined in Christian theology. Both systems feature a pure religious, or sacred, law, which on the one hand is supreme over all other forms of law, but on the other hand is limited by its own decree to the jurisdiction of the religious courts, which is separated (again by its own decree) from the jurisdiction of secular rulers and secular law. The systems further parallel each other in their recognition and authorization of a secular law, administered and enforced by a secular state and its secular courts. In both the Jewish and the Christian conceptions, secular legal authority, independent of the jurisdiction of the religious authorities, is not merely tolerated but regarded as necessary and divinely ordained to serve the most basic human needs. Finally, there is an almost exact parallel in the assumption of "emergency powers" by the religious legal authorities sanctioned by the Jewish and Christian traditions. In both cases, religious courts are licensed to deviate from the "pure religious law" on the grounds of exigent circumstances, utility, and necessity (a development that greatly complicates the basic distinction drawn between spiritual and temporal power). Like the ecclesiastical courts, rabbinic courts were authorized to use their "exigency powers" to devise and implement an "extralegal," efficacious system for enforcing the law—when "exigent" circumstances made such a need for effective law enforcement necessary.[104] Thus it was that the basic distinction between two types of law—secular and spiritual—gave way in the Jewish case to *three*, factoring in the two different types of rabbinic law that could now be exercised under the jurisdiction of the rabbinic courts.

All that distinguishes the Jewish structure of multiple legal systems from the Christian structure is the additional distinction that Jewish law draws between a law for the Jews and a law for the rest of the humanity, the gentile "sons of Noah," a body of law that is not just *nonreligious* in character but also (a very different thing) *non-Jewish*. In tandem with the doctrine of *dina de-malkhuta dina*, the doctrine of Noahide law reflected more than a grudging recognition of non-Jewish law. Together, the two doctrines define an essential role for secular law and (either Jewish or non-Jewish) secular rulers.

If the structure of the various legal systems sanctioned by Jewish law resembles the structure of multiple legal systems enshrined in Christian theology and canon law, as it surely does, the question remains whether the rationales provided for this structure in the Talmud resemble the core ideas of the secularist theology found in the Christian tradition. It seems clear that the development of all of these Talmudic doctrines was fueled, at least in part, by the fact that sacred law, the "pure Jewish law" of the Torah, the Sinaitic or Mosaic law, as it is variously called, frustrated the purposes of law enforcement. Not only did biblical and rabbinic law require two witnesses to prove a crime and obtain a conviction, but it also required that criminals be warned of the legal consequences of their actions prior to committing their bad acts. In the case of a murder, for example, the murderer could not be convicted unless someone—a victim or a bystander—had cautioned him against it. It was readily perceived that these biblical rules made it virtually impossible to obtain convictions; indeed, that was their evident function. The criminal law of the Jewish Bible was seen to be a "system of exceptional leniency to the accused." [105] According to traditional understanding, it would allow penalties to be imposed "only in cases of the most serious and egregious violations, when the evidence of guilt approaches certainty as close as is humanly possible." [106] In the case of capital crimes, Sinaitic law created "elaborate procedural barriers to the imposition of capital punishment" that did not exist in Noahide law (as that law was construed in the Talmud).[107] The upshot was that "the Torah's procedural and evidentiary rules make it almost impossible for the death penalty to be imposed" [108]—one of the marks of distinction between it and the morally inferior (but perhaps practically superior) Noahide law.

For pressing practical reasons, then, rabbinic law, like canon law, was compelled to grapple with this system of "exceptional leniency," which essentially precluded the enforcement of its own legal code. The rabbis' practical solution to this problem was the now familiar strategy of "supplementing" the pure religious law with alternative legal systems of law, which are authorized to follow less stringent (and less lenient) procedural rules. Indeed, what Noahide law, the secular law of the state or the king, and the emergency law of the rabbis all have in common is precisely the license to disregard the traditional evidentiary rules of the Bible, such as the two-witnesses and caution requirements. What distinguishes "the Sinaitic judicial system," [109] or "pure Jewish law," [110] from all of these other kinds of law is that it is the one legal system that does not permit judgments to be made absent perfect (or at least near perfect) proof. Conversely, all three of the legal systems

other than the "pure" Jewish religious law of the Torah were depicted by the rabbinic tradition as ones that were ready and able to punish crime "even when the
evidence is less than perfect and when the offender is driven by motives other than
rebellion against God." [111]

The questions, then, are what was the reason for instituting the procedural and
evidentiary barriers in Sinaitic law, and what was the reason for allowing Jews and
non-Jews to follow and enforce less stringent procedural regimes according to Jewish law? And do the rationales provided by Jewish legal authorities resemble the
rationales found in Christian theological secularism? As Suzanne Stone has noted,
the institution of procedural barriers in Sinaitic law "reflects certain assumptions
about . . . the nature of divine justice that Jews are commanded to emulate." [112] She
also notes that "the scriptural authority to dispense with Sinaitic procedure"—by
instituting and following alternative legal regimes—"has proved altogether elusive." [113] According to Enker, the system of procedural stringency and "exceptional"
leniency found in the Sinaitic law expressed the underlying rabbinic attitude that
"[i]f these requirements yield the result that most violators of God's law will not
be punished, so be it. God can and will, it is firmly believed, see to their deserved
punishment." [114] This, of course, is essentially the same as the position taken by
Augustine and other Church fathers. [115] In both cases, it demonstrates an awareness
and an acceptance of the fact that sacred law lacks practical efficacy in the temporal
realm (and a corresponding faith that justice will be meted out in the afterlife).

What, then, justified the adoption of practical alternatives to this sacred legal regime? One theory, favored by Stone, holds that the judicial powers of the
king, the judicial powers of gentile rulers, and the emergency powers of the Jewish courts, sanctioned by Jewish law, all stem from the same source, namely, "the
extension of the provisions of the Noahide Code to Jews." [116] According to this
rabbinic theory, the principle underlying the original establishment of a Jewish
monarchy was that the Jewish people were henceforth to be a "nation like all the
nations." This implied an abandonment of the earlier ideal that the Jews would be
holier than other nations.

If "before Sinai, the Noahide Code governed all humanity," [117] Sinaitic law
reflects the "additional obligations" that "the Jewish people took upon themselves . . . at Mount Sinai—to be a nation of priests and holy people." [118] Had the
Jews lived up to their covenantal obligation to be holy, a temporally enforced law
would have been unnecessary for them. It would be unnecessary because a truly
holy people would obey the law without the threat of penalty; a truly holy people

would voluntarily obey the sacred law. But because the Jews had refused to be holy, coercive enforcement mechanisms in the temporal world were necessary to uphold the law. Thus, the doctrinal innovations authorizing secular, gentile, and emergency law were motivated in part by a perception of a need for law and order in the temporal realm, a need created by the unholiness of Jews and non-Jews alike.

But—and now a familiar series of practical problems begins to form—effective mechanisms of law enforcement necessarily rely on human judgments, which the rabbis were suitably wary of. The problem then (as in the Christian case) was not so much the bad guys (the lawbreakers) as it was the good guys (those who would enforce the law). The solution to the good-guy problem, such as it was, was to impose procedural obstacles to rendering convictions without adequate proof, which, for all practical purposes, came close to preventing convictions from being rendered at all. This, of course, exacerbated the bad-guy problem. The solution to the bad-guy problem clearly called for something else: effective means of law enforcement. This produced the good-guy problem. Thus, the two problems and solutions cycled endlessly throughout Jewish law.

The institution of procedural barriers, the solution proposed in Jewish law to the good-guy problem, reflects the belief that divine omniscience is indispensable to divine justice and the corresponding view that human knowledge is inherently uncertain and unacceptably prone to mistake. Stone provides strong support for the view that this is the rationale behind the exceptional leniency of Sinaitic law, noting that:

> the rabbis were aware that the hardest part of dispensing justice for a human court is the finding of facts. The two-witness rule is designed, according to the internal viewpoint of the Talmud, to assure thorough investigation of the facts so as to arrive at the truth. The procedures thus assure that judges will not find themselves guilty of judicial murder through an error in judgment or through acceptance of false testimony.[119]

This is a powerfully direct statement of what is at risk in the human enforcement of law: the violation of the sanctity of human life and sacred law—*profanity* in the fullest sense. It is, by the same token, a clear statement of the link made in rabbinic thought between the religious consciousness of the gap between divine and human cognition and the perception that human legal institutions are necessarily profane.

The basic justification supplied for adopting the various secular legal regimes, and dispensing with the strict procedural requirements of sacred law, was the need for law and order. Kingships, whether Jewish or non-Jewish, are understood to have been instituted for the worldly purposes of maintaining the peace and protecting the social order—not the higher purpose of achieving holiness that dignifies Sinaitic law (in fact, just the opposite) but a divinely sanctioned purpose nonetheless. The guiding principle of the kingship in both Jewish and Christian traditional conceptions is the social good, which is measured by the standards of public necessity and public utility.[120] (The receptivity of this tradition to Aristotelian ideas should now be clear.) Likewise, the basic purpose of Noahide law and the exercise of emergency power by the rabbinic powers is to preserve the peace and protect the basic social order.[121] Each of these forms of law is a form of secular law, necessitated by the fact that human behavior is *not* perfectly holy (the bad-guy problem) combined with the fact that human beings lack the cognitive perfection necessary for the proper enforcement of divine law (the good-guy problem). Thus it was that, according to Jewish tradition, the Jewish kingship first was instituted when it was conceded that the Jewish people would be "a nation like other nations"—that is, a nation of both bad guys and good guys (both of whom could end up with blood on their hands) rather than the nation of priests and holy people envisaged by the covenant.

There is thus a basic dichotomy in the rabbinic conception between a worldly realm of government and law, which includes both Jewish and gentile states, and another realm that is dedicated to the relationship between man and God. The first realm is a secular one, not in the modern sense but in the traditional sense of a realm that is separated in function, purpose, and institutional form from the "purely religious" realm. Its function is to deal with "the day-to-day concerns of law enforcement and the protection of the social order."[122] Its purpose is to achieve peace, tranquility, and the public good. Its institutional form is the political state. As in the Christian conception, the "nonreligious" or not "purely religious" realm is differentiated from the sacred realm on the basis of its concern with social needs in the temporal world, in particular, the need for social order, which requires effective mechanisms of law enforcement. And again, as in the Christian case, the need for a realm of law apart from the sacred is generated by the necessary inefficacy of sacred law in the temporal realm. As Enker summarizes the rationale underlying the creation of a secular realm in Jewish thought:

> judicial restraint is tolerable, even welcome, with regard to violations of those religious laws that primarily concern man's relation to God. But homicide, and other crimes

between man and man destructive to the social order, require a more aggressive stance. These crimes must be punished even when the evidence is less than perfect and when the offender is driven by motives other than open rebellion against God.[123]

In other words, *publicae utilitas intersit, ne crimina remaneant impunita*—in the interest of public utility, no crime should go unpunished. It is the same pragmatic argument, with the same Aristotelian flavor, offered to justify the exercise of secular legal authority by Christian theology in the twelfth century.

Such rationales reflect concessions to the failings and imperfections of humanity—failings that, Jewish law was compelled to recognize, afflicted Jews as well as non-Jews. The Jews would not, after all, answer to a higher standard, at least not consistently; they would instead be like all the other nations. If there is a principle of universalism here, it is a pessimistic universalism grounded in universal human shortcomings.

The flip side of such pessimism, however, is a sympathetic appreciation for the human condition in the merely mortal world. Such an appreciation is poignantly expressed in the following justification given by the fourteenth-century Jewish jurist, the "Rashba," for the emergency jurisdiction of the rabbinic courts:

> This [the authorization of the courts' emergency powers] is in order to preserve the world. For if you issue decisions based exclusively on the law as given in the Torah, and rule in questions of torts and such only in accordance with this law, why then society would be destroyed, for we would need witnesses and forewarning. As the Talmud says, "Jerusalem was destroyed because they established their decisions only in accordance with biblical law."[124]

This is a truly breathtaking formulation of the principle of practical necessity as a justification for temporal law. Not only is the sacred law too good for this world; its application would actually result the world's destruction! To put it the other way around, if human beings are not good enough for the sacred law, then the sacred law is not good enough *for human beings*. Far better is the law of temporal human institutions, applied by human beings, which, imperfect as it is, is better suited, and more adequate, to the human situation.

It is hard to imagine a more powerful statement of the principles of social utility and necessity that justifies the application of nonideal standards and procedures to a nonideal world. This understanding of human need as being at odds with sacred law is amplified by the rabbinic understanding of the nature of the "emergency" that justifies the rabbis' own use of "extraordinary" powers. In theory, the rabbinic courts' use of their exigency powers in circumvention of the ideal sacred law is strictly an "emergency measure."[125] In practice, the emergency never ends. The implicit theory seems to be that life, the human condition itself, is the emergency. The startling insight here is that sacred law would be destructive of this world and destructive of human life. The corresponding conclusion is that profane law—which entails the commission of "judicial murder"—is necessary and useful because, without it, the world would be destroyed.

Common Themes

It should be clear by now that the conceptions of law in the Jewish and Christian traditions represent mirror images of each other. The two traditions share a religious consciousness of the gap between the human and divine, leading to a mindfulness of the limits of human judgment and cognition. They further share a common conception of sacred law and its unenforceability in the temporal world. To overcome the problem of unenforceability, they both generate justifications for secular law and secular political authority, religious justifications based on human needs and human limitations and on the pragmatic principles of public utility and necessity. Both are thus appropriately characterized as secularist theologies, theological arguments for the necessity and value of secular law.

Of course, neither tradition embraces secular law without ambivalence. Secular law, it must always be remembered, dispenses with the requirements of sacred law and risks "judicial murder." Secular law is at odds with the theological awareness of the inadequacies of human judgment. Secular law is profane. So it is not surprising that each tradition finds a way of defending its ideal of the sacred, while abandoning it in practice, by projecting its image of profane law onto the "other." This, of course, is a well-known psychological strategy. The specific phenomenon of Christians projecting negative images of law onto Judaism is particularly well known. What is perhaps less familiar is the corresponding Jewish tradition of projecting negative images of law onto the legal systems of the non-Jewish other. The representations of Jewish and non-Jewish law within the *halakhik* tradition represent a complete inversion of the familiar stereotypes. The Jewish understanding of the nature of Sinaitic law, reflected in the doctrines of Noahide law and the law of the king, upends the conventional representation of Jewish biblical law as harsh, punitive, and vengeful ("an eye for an eye") in contrast to the merciful dispensation of the New Testament. From the Jewish point of view, it is the Jewish law of the Torah that is more merciful and lenient than the Noahide law of the gentiles, not the other way around.

So here we have yet another similarity between Jewish and Christian conceptions of law. Not only do both endorse a profane, secular law, but they also both engage in acts of collective psychological denial and projection, each attributing to the other the profane form of law that it itself conceived and adopted.

These similarities between Christian and Jewish conceptions of law may seem less startling when we recall that the practical problem which triggered the development of alternatives to traditional canon law was, as Fraher observed, a legacy of Christianity's biblical and rabbinic "inheritance."[126] Notwithstanding the differences between them, Christianity and Judaism share a common corpus of texts, the Hebrew Bible, and the core tenets of monotheistic faith. It is perhaps less than surprising then that these two traditions should have generated such a similar set of ideas about law and its relation to the sacred.

But students of other religious cultures may recognize the features of secularist theology in their subjects as well. Consider, for example, this description of the legal system of Buddhist Tibet, drawn from the work of legal anthropologist Rebecca French. French describes the legal system of Tibet as a single polity, which is subdivided into "religious" and "secular" jurisdictions, even though the entire system is understood to be governed by religious law. The distinction between religious and secular realms tracks a distinction made between two social groups: the "spiritual seekers" or "priests" (in other words, the clerical order) and the spiritual "supporters" or "patrons" (that is, the laity).[127] "Although the Tibetan canon applies to all Tibetan Buddhists, it includes a legal code only for the spiritual seekers."[128] "[T]he dichotomy between the religious community and the law community required a separate and profane legal system."[129] Yet "the sacred realm incorporates the profane even as it defines its included distinctiveness."[130] The "paradox . . . is that even though the legal tradition was presumed to be wholly religious, the dualistic nature of Tibetan religious culture itself actually dictated that 'secular' spiritual supporter laws were of necessity different from 'religious' spiritual seeker laws."[131] The sacred "world of monks [is] governed by the canonical rules of the Vinaya," an ecclesiastical law, while "the world of laypersons [is] governed by the laws of the ancient kings."[132] The law of the kings is classified as a form of secular law in contradistinction to the ecclesiastical law of the Vinaya. But the content of the law of the kings "come[s] directly from the Tibetan Buddhist canon."[133] The law of the kings is "a secular code based on and imbued with the spirit of Buddhism."[134]

"Even though secular actors operated from secular legal codes and viewed themselves as distinct from religious actors, Tibet was a culture perfused with a religious
mentality, and the moral standards of the Buddha and the Vinaya reverberated
through every part of the legal system."[135]

The line drawn in Buddhist Tibet between the law of the priests and the law of
the laity is reminiscent of the distinction between clerical and nonclerical realms
in Christian canon law, while the Tibetan conception of the law of the kingdom
is reminiscent of the Jewish notion of the law of the kingdom embodied in the
doctrine of *dina de-malkhuta dina*, discussed earlier. Traditionally, "there were no
clear divisions between religion and the state" and "Tibetans saw religion, politics,
administration, and law as an interpenetrated whole from which it was difficult to
separate out 'secular law' as a particular category in the Western sense."[136] The Tibetan term for the "law of the kings" or "state law" denotes a conception of secular
law that is more like the medieval Jewish and Christian conception of the divinely
ordained kingship than the modern Western conception of a separation between
Church and secular State.[137]

Perhaps more important than these structural similarities are the philosophical similarities found between the Tibetan Buddhist "legal cosmology" and the
understandings of law displayed in the Christian and Jewish traditions. The most
basic philosophical proposition that unites these different religious legal cultures
is the idea that humans lack the cognitive perfection of the divine (which presupposes the idea that the divinity is all knowing, which in turn presupposes a belief
in the divine). The core idea of Tibetan Buddhism, for example, is that "everything
we apprehend in the world is mere illusion."[138] Without ignoring the profound
differences separating Buddhist from Western thought, it is hard not to perceive
a consonance here with Plato's conception of reality and illusion.[139] Plato, too,
depicted a world of mortal beings in the grip of illusion; his cave parable presents
us with human beings whose faculties of perception are radically cut off from
metaphysical reality, which is understood to occupy a sphere that is transcendent
and inaccessible to human reason. The lesson of the parable of the cave is much
the same (and expressed in much the same terms) as the basic Buddhist belief that
"we suffer from attributing significance to the dreamlike appearances resulting
from the preconceived notions and categories that we carry with us and constantly
use to interpret the world."[140] The fundamental problem, in both Buddhism and
Plato's thought, is that "[t]hese categories of data, acquired through our senses,
keep us ignorant of the true nature of reality."[141]

As Rebecca French has shown, "[t]his notion of illusion is of profound importance in comprehending the Tibetan view of reality, including legal reality."[142] It is of no less importance in comprehending salient traditions of Christian thought, including Christian legal thought. The idea that human perception and reason are illusory has played its most obvious role in the development of the antirationalist traditions of Christian thought, particularly those based on readings of Plato.[143] But the same basic idea underlies the so-called rationalist, Aristotelian traditions of Christian thought as well,[144] albeit less obviously. In particular, it underlies the traditional theological view, which recognizes the fallibility of human judgments and attempts, by way of classical rhetoric or other schemes, to rationalize the modes of human judgment without pretending that mistakes can be completely avoided. If this "rationalist" theology has not usually been framed in the vocabulary of reality and illusion that the mystics characteristically employed, it nonetheless rests on the same basic insight into the fallibility of human perception and the same basic belief in a transcendent reality.

A similar split between "rationalist" and "antirationalist" tendencies occurs in Jewish thought and in Muslim thought, coupled in each case with a similar underlying unity of belief in the fallibility of the human mind. As in Christianity, the most obvious manifestations of the idea that reality is transcendent and that ordinary perception is only a shadow of transcendent truth are found in the respective mystical, Gnostic, Platonist, and neo-Platonist traditions of these two religions.[145] But the same basic idea—that the faculties of human reason and perception are inherently susceptible to illusion and error—plays at least as important a role in the normative traditions of Judaism and Islam, which, like similar Christian traditions, try to reconcile the needs of the mortal world with its inherent limitations in the pragmatic spirit of Aristotelian rhetoric.

What the recurring split between rationalist and antirationalist tendencies suggests is that there is more than one way of responding to the basic problem of human imperfection. One way, which is epitomized by the mystical traditions of Judaism, Christianity, and Islam, along with Buddhism, Platonism, and the various schools of philosophical skepticism that erupted in ancient and early modern thought,[146] is to renounce the faculties of human reason, perception, and judgment, and all the human practices that rely on these faculties and to cultivate a mystical faith and a perpetual suspension of judgment about matters of this world—in short, to withdraw from the temporal world. Another way, the so-called rationalist one, is not to have any less faith in an all-knowing, all-powerful God or any more faith in human perfection[147] but to eschew the mystical flight from the world and to struggle instead to find a way of reconciling the imperfect capacity for judgment of human beings with the requirements of both the temporal and the spiritual worlds.

Theological secularism is a typical product of such a rationalist or, better, anti-antirationalist approach.[148] Conceding that the temporal world imposes certain necessities on human beings (e.g., physical necessities, such as the need for food, and social necessities, such as the need for protection from violence) and further conceding that there are inherent limits to our capacity to respond to these needs, so-called rationalist theologies conceive of temporal power as an adequate substitute for the perfect knowledge that we cannot have and as a positive requirement of life on this earth.

Implicit in theological secularism and rationalism, more generally, are three basic principles or intellectual attitudes, which are worth singling out. One is probabilism, which reflects a readiness to accept mere probabilities as a substitute for certainties. The second is the spirit of pluralism, which also follows from the absence of certain truths. Lacking perfect knowledge, people will inevitably reach different views about the correct way of adjudicating a case or rendering a judgment. If no one has access to divine omniscience and if human cognition is inherently flawed—but all we've got—then interpretive and normative disagreement may have to be accepted, at least to a point. Finally, and perhaps most obviously (though this obviousness is, I think, deceptive), theological secularism reflects the basic intellectual attitude of pragmatism.

These three principles—probabilism, pluralism, and pragmatism—are readily found in the various traditions of theological secularism that we have identified. Probabilism, for example, was a central feature of the modes of proof of the canon law, which in turn served as a model for both civil and common law.[149] Borrowing heavily from the classical rhetorical tradition derived from Aristotle, canon law and Christian theology took probabilistic reasoning to new levels. Probabilistic reasoning and modes of proof are integral to other legal traditions as well, including classical Islamic jurisprudence and Jewish law.[150] But because probabilism departs from the strict requirements of justice—mere probability, after all, and even a great probability are not the same as a certain truth—it is directly implicated in the problem of wrongful convictions and "judicial murder." Hence, it constitutes one of the defining elements of the profanity of law.

The intellectual attitude of pluralism is perhaps most easily discernible in legal traditions like Jewish law and classical Islamic jurisprudence that have historically celebrated interpretive pluralism. Interpretive pluralism is a well-known feature of Jewish law. With no central authority, no pope, no state, and no higher courts claiming infallible judgment or the right to dictate the law, Jewish law tolerated, indeed cultivated, differing legal opinions. Classical Islamic jurisprudence similarly affirmed the necessity and value of interpretive pluralism.

The spirit of pluralism is clearly displayed in the doctrines and traditions that sanction the practice of interpretive pluralism within a single legal jurisdiction (e.g., the jurisdiction of Jewish *halakha* or of Muslim *shari'a* law). That same spirit is also embodied in the diversity of legal jurisdictions carved out by theological–secularist law. Again, the Jewish case is exemplary. By deferring to the law of the gentiles and the law of the state, Jewish law was able to sustain itself. Through the doctrines of the law of the kingdom and Noahide law, it carved out room for different groups and religions to have their own legal systems. That it was able to do so and thereby acquire some measure of legal autonomy for itself from a position of relative powerlessness, often in the face of intense hostility, is a testament not only to the pluralist spirit of Jewish law, but also to the de facto legal and cultural pluralism of the various states that hosted the Jewish minority.

The acceptance by imperial and hegemonic states of substate minority legal systems—often grudging, often accompanied by ulterior motives, and often abruptly revoked, but nonetheless a real and legally sanctioned form of legal and cultural pluralism—typifies the general spirit of pluralism adopted by legal systems committed to theological–secularist views. The spirit of pluralism is perhaps less consistently and less clearly on display in hegemonic legal cultures like those of Christian Europe, Islam, and Buddhist Tibetan than it is in the legal traditions of a stateless minority, like the Jews. But even the most hegemonic cultures have found themselves in the position of a persecuted or exiled minority at one point or another in their respective histories (most recently, in the case of Tibet). Because these communities were not in the position of vulnerable minorities at the time their legal systems were formed, the need for them to stake out space for diverse legal subcultures was not as palpable a matter of group self-interest for them as it was in the Jewish case.[151] Political sovereignty, religious hegemony, and cultural homogeneity were factors that tended to suppress the presence of interpretive and normative disagreements and to diminish the value of (and practical need for) pluralism. Instead, they tended to favor the institution of hierarchical organizations designed to suppress pluralism (like the Catholic Church or, to a lesser degree, the Buddhist monasteries).

But the differences among these different legal traditions on the score of pluralism should not be overstated. Imperial legal systems had mechanisms for suppressing pluralism, but only to a point. Notwithstanding the social and political factors that enabled them to dominate subgroups and dissenters, each and every one of these historically dominant legal cultures historically exhibited a substantial degree of tolerance for pluralism, both with regard to subgroups and with regard to different schools of thought within their own religious legal cultures. One sees this most readily in the Islamic Ottoman Empire, where cultural pluralism was instituted in the form of the millet system.[152] More broadly, as Khaled Abou El Fadl has shown, interpretive pluralism was recognized and affirmed within Islamic jurisprudence as an inevitable consequence of making good-faith legal interpretations. Likewise, the Catholic tradition, arguably the most antipluralist tradition of the lot, found ways to countenance a not insignificant degree of interpretive pluralism, even as it simultaneously sought to suppress adopted doctrinal and institutional innovations such as the doctrine of papal infallibility, clearly aimed at suppressing such pluralism.[153]

Pluralism, like probabilism, at once reflects and conceals the profane nature of law. Pluralism concedes the ideal of perfect justice based on correct knowledge in exchange for multiple views of what justice requires, at least some of which are bound to be wrong. It involves the same practices of judgment as probabilism and entails the same risk of committing "judicial murder." Both pluralism and probabilism are essential ingredients of the secularist theology, which justifies taking this risk (and thus profaning the law) for the sake of avoiding the allegedly greater risk of "destroying the world" through judicial inaction.

Encompassing both the principles of probabilism and pluralism, pragmatism is the overarching intellectual framework of theological secularism. Clearly, it was pragmatic for Jews to find a way to rationalize submitting to the dominant host states that imposed their laws on them, just as it was clearly pragmatic for canon lawyers to find ways of harmonizing the law of the Church and the State rather than continually challenging the State's authority.[154] But we miss the point of the pragmatist philosophy embodied in secularist theology if we reduce it to a matter of making concessions to brute power solely on the basis of group or individual self-interest. As best expressed in the Aristotelian defense of rhetoric, pragmatism is not simply a matter of succumbing to power in the spirit of raw self-interest and Realpolitik. It is rather a matter of recognizing and accepting human needs and limitations, making practical utility (rather than transcendent truth) the measure of value, endorsing the utility of imperfect modes of knowledge (such as probabilism), and generally making the best of things as they are in the "real" world. We seriously misconstrue pragmatism if we imagine that pragmatic judgments are based solely on calculations of self-interest and not on moral values. From the standpoint of pragmatism, pragmatism is itself a moral value. The altruistic goals of pursuing public utility and meeting social needs are as much pragmatic criteria for actions and judgments as self-interest is. Indeed, from the standpoint of pragmatist thought, self-interest and altruism, pragmatism and morality, are false oppositions.

Pragmatism involves turning the mystical insight into the illusory nature of human knowledge about transcendent values on its head. Instead of fleeing from judgment and repudiating the human conceptual and perceptual apparatus for all its blind spots and flaws, the pragmatist valorizes that cognitive apparatus, blind spots and all. Without denying the faultiness of human reason and perception, the pragmatist regards those faculties as useful tools for accomplishing social and scientific goals.

Pragmatism, pluralism, and probabilism are features of every secularist theology, of every theological tradition that supplies a justification for the exercise of secular legal authority and the enforcement of a necessarily profane law. To put it the other way around, the adoption of the principles of pragmatism, pluralism, and probabilism necessitates the acceptance of some version of secular law, which departs from—and runs the risk of violating—sacred legal ideals. That is not to say that these intellectual attitudes or principles show up to exactly the same degree in every theological–secularist tradition. For example, pluralism arguably plays a greater role in Jewish law and classical Islamic jurisprudence than it does in either Catholic or Tibetan Buddhist systems of law. But this is only a matter of degree. Even the latter allow the limited, but hardly trivial, form of pluralism that is embodied in the simple fact of having multiple or at least dual, secular, and religious jurisdictions. Likewise, probabilistic thinking may be most marked in the Christian canon law and the civil law systems; but it is undeniably present in the common law and in classical Islamic jurisprudence and Jewish law as well.

The point, after all, is not the fatuous one that all legal systems are the same. The point, rather, is that there is a basic predicament—the predicament of having to render judgments with limited intellectual equipment at the cost of otherwise allowing crimes to be committed with impunity and thus "destroying the world"— to which all legal systems have to respond. Of course, legal systems do not all experience, or respond to, this predicament in precisely the same way. Indeed, within any single legal system, we see different responses to this predicament, including denial that the predicament exists. What we can say, after surveying the Christian and Jewish legal traditions (and briefly dipping into several others), is that there is one particular way of responding to the predicament that keeps resurfacing. We see not identical, but broadly similar, versions of this response in different legal cultures, including but not limited to our own. This is the response that we have called theological secularism, a set of theological arguments for accepting secular legal authority on pragmatic grounds, as imperfect and profane as secular power is.

Mutations of Secularist Theology: Modern Fundamentalism and Secularism

A tension lies at the heart of secularist theology. On the one hand, secularist theologies are committed to the rendering of judgments, and justice, by secular authorities. On the other hand, secularist theology is mindful of the fallibility of secular courts, unbound by the stringent evidentiary requirements of sacred law. In the spirit of pragmatism, secularist theology endorses making judgments on the basis of probabilistic reasoning, accepting the merely probable in place of certain truths. In the spirit of pluralism, however, secularist theology refrains from endorsing the objective truth of any one interpretation of a legal controversy.

In practice, it is difficult to maintain these attitudes all at once. Psychologically, it is almost impossible to render judgments and maintain the awareness that these judgments are liable to error at the same time. A heightened awareness of the fallibility of human reason is more likely to prevent one from reaching any judgment at all. Conversely, the process of reaching a judgment, in and of itself, seems to have the effect of suppressing our awareness of the fallibility of our own and others' reasoning.[155]

It is customary to describe the intellectual position taken by theological secularists as a "rationalist" one in contradistinction to the "antirationalist" position assumed by skeptics and mystics who eschew making judgments in the temporal "world of illusion." If this label is taken to imply some degree of faith in human reason, enough to warrant exercising human reason, the label is fair enough. But if, as is common, these labels are taken to suggest that the so-called rationalist, the theological secularist, does not share the antirationalist's skepticism about human reason, then they are profoundly misleading. The theological secularist has no less skeptical a view of the illusory nature of human judgments and perceptions than the antirationalist does. But the theological secularist sees no better alternative; indeed, the theological secularist perceives that the only alternative to having human beings, temporal authorities, make judgments that violate sacred law is something even worse: unrestrained aggression leading to the destruction of the world.

It is for this reason that I prefer the term "anti-antirationalist" to "rationalist" to describe the basic attitude toward human reason found in theological secularism. The anti-antirationalism of theological secularism is really just another way of describing the conception of reason embodied in Aristotelian pragmatism—not an "objectivist" conception of reason but, rather, a "subjectivist" one that nonetheless provides a warrant for human action and decision.

There is obviously a very fine line between affirming the validity of subjective legal decisions and validating those decisions as objectively correct. Decision makers will naturally experience a tension between recognizing the subjectivity of legal decisions and making them. Theological secularism may be defined as the systematic attempt, on the part of theologically minded jurists and legally minded theologians, to keep the sense of that tension alive—to sustain the tension between these intellectual postures, to prevent the tension from collapsing and having one intellectual posture (certainty or uncertainty, conviction or doubt) dominate. In practice, this is very hard to do.

The theory of theological secularism always had the tendency to degrade in practice. Awareness of the subjectivity of legal decisions simply cannot be consistently sustained. If practitioners of secular law could not always keep the awareness of their subjectivity and fallibility firmly in mind, the religious sensibility of theological secularism, rooted in an appreciation of the gap between the human and the divine, served as a prod to remember what was constantly in danger of being forgotten. The religious sensibility of theological secularism functioned, albeit intermittently, to heighten awareness of the frailty and limits of the human mind.

With the erosion of religious faith, the ideas of theological secularism, which shaped our legal systems, were deprived of the theological base that had served in the past to heighten our awareness of our cognitive limits. But secularization did not cause the ideas of theological secularism to disappear wholesale. Instead, the result was that secular legal systems continued to reflect all of the basic ideas and principles and intellectual attitudes of theological secularism *except* the religious awareness of the gap between the human and the divine. Pragmatism, pluralism, and probabilism, a belief in the necessity of secular courts and effective law enforcement, the theory of dual (or multiple) jurisdictions for secular and religious law, and most basically, a belief in the necessity of law all continue to play a role in our modern, secular conception of law. All that is missing from the list of theological secularism's core beliefs is the mindfulness of our liability to error, fostered by the religious belief in an omniscient divinity and a gap between the human and the divine. Arguably, mindfulness of the faultiness of human judgments could remain a part of our conception of law without the prod of religious belief. But query what other than religious belief actually serves the function of heightening the awareness of our cognitive limitations that is ordinarily suppressed in the absence of religious belief.

One of the most provocative claims made by Enlightenment scholars is the suggestion that the roots of liberal values, such as pluralism and tolerance, lie in the pagan approach of "to each his own god" and that it was only the advent of the exclusivist monotheistic faiths of Judaism and Christianity that, for a long protracted "dark age," put liberalism into eclipse. In this story, paganism is figured as a sort of protoliberalism, and the monotheistic faiths of Christianity and Judaism becomes the prototype of antiliberalism. From the point of view of the story that we have been telling, however, it is the secularist theologies (of Christianity, Judaism, and other faiths) that look like the source of liberal ideas. Modern-day secularism, and more particularly, secular liberalism, might be seen as the apotheosis of the ideas and ideals of theological secularism. Pragmatism, probabilism, and pluralism, a commitment to separate jurisdictions for Church and State, the basic idea of a secular state, and the value of secular law are all hallmarks of modern, secular, liberal political philosophy. They are also the hallmarks of traditional theological–secularist thought. To put it otherwise, secular liberalism represents the apotheosis of theological secularism — the ultimate secularization of theological secularism, yielding a version of theological secularism in which the concept of the secular itself has been secularized, such that the realm of secular law is no longer seen as a specialized area of God's domain but, rather, as a realm entirely independent of any religious conception.

If liberal secularism embodies the ideas of theological secularism without the theology, then modern-day fundamentalist movements embody the ideas of theological secularism without the secularism. Deprived of the edifice of reasoning that makes the case for a secular law alongside religious law, fundamentalism becomes the placeholder for the perception of the profane nature of secular law. Seizing on the traditional religious insight into the illusory and fallible nature of human judgments, fundamentalism is cut off from the equally traditional religious insight into the destructive nature of sacred law in the temporal realm. In fundamentalism, the traditional religious attitudes of probabilism, pragmatism, and pluralism go by the

wayside, with the ironic result that there is nothing left to temper the fundamentalists' own interpretive and normative judgments, even as they insist on the fallible
nature of human reasoning in the secular realm.

But if the estrangement of fundamentalists from the attitudes of probabilism,
pluralism, and pragmatism cultivates a kind of hubris, the estrangement of secularism from the religious conception of the sacred and the profane does too. Bereft
of a religious sensibility, there is little to temper the confidence of secular liberals
in their own judgments. True, they are explicitly committed to pluralism, probabilism, and pragmatism, values that in and of themselves counsel against hubris. But
as we have seen, in practice, the sense of the subjectivity of one's own judgments is
almost impossible to sustain. Lacking the religious mindset to function as a constant reminder and heightener of the awareness of the limits of the human mind,
liberal secularism all too readily displays a hubris that galls religious believers and
other critics of an overweening liberalism.

Oblivious to the profane nature of the secular, oblivious to the profane nature of law, secular liberalism could not but outrage those religious believers who
themselves do not fail to perceive the profanity of secular law. Of course, not all
religious believers share this hostility to secular law. Many, perhaps most, religious
believers today endorse secular law and liberal values, an endorsement that does
not merely reflect the influence of modern secularism on religion but that is rooted
in their own religious traditions. In the eyes of religious believers who keep faith
with the traditional ideas of theological secularism embedded in their religion, it
is the fundamentalists speaking in their name who are oblivious to the insights
and demands of their religion—and who, in so doing, are corrupting the faith
and profaning the law.

This is a dangerous situation. And it is not a situation that can be alleviated by
simply being more tolerant of religion, including fundamentalism. Liberal tolerance is, in and of itself, for reasons that should now be clear, an offense to those
religious believers who have lost touch with the tradition of theological secularism.
Ironically, the more tolerant and "respectful" of diverse religions secular liberalism
is, the more outrageous to such believers it will be.

The polarization of liberal secularism and religious fundamentalism that we are
witnessing today represents the splintering apart of the ideas and tensions that were
traditionally held together in secularist theology. It is tempting to think that this set
of ideas never could have held together, that it was an impossible project all along.
After all, the lines between antirationalism, anti-antirationalism, and rationalism

are exceedingly fine and often tend to blur. Even before the emergence of modern secularism and fundamentalism, theological secularism was constantly threatening to degenerate into sheer rationalism—an untempered and unwarranted faith in reason—as opposed to sustaining the more nuanced and mindful attitude of anti-antirationalism. In the course of the history of any given legal religious tradition, theological secularism has all too often degraded into its opposite and been eclipsed by contrary theologies. Despite all this, the fact of the matter is that the tensions that define and animate theological secularism were sustained and contained within the theological–secularist traditions of numerous cultures for hundreds, if not thousands, of years. Impossible or not, they did "hold together," and they exercised a lasting influence on the shape of our legal and political institutions and the way we think about religion and law. Theological secularism was always in danger of forgetting itself precisely because the tensions within it are so hard to maintain. It is high time for us to remember.

Notes

1. This passage is contained in the "amidah," said at daily prayers in addition to being included in the high holy day services. It is drawn from Psalm 119, the full text of which reads:

> 119:18 Open Thou mine eyes, that I may behold wondrous things out of Thy law.
>
> 119:19 I am a sojourner in the earth; hide not Thy commandments from me.
>
> 119:20 My soul breaketh for the longing that it hath unto Thine ordinances at all times.
>
> 119:21 Thou hast rebuked the proud that are cursed, that do err from Thy commandments.
>
> 119:22 Take away from me reproach and contempt; for I have kept Thy testimonies.
>
> 119:23 Even though princes sit and talk against me, thy servant doth meditate in Thy statutes.
>
> 119:24 Yea, Thy testimonies are my delight, they are my counselors.

2. Karl Löwith, *Meaning in History* (Chicago: University of Chicago Press, 1949), 46–47. Löwith is quoting Karl Marx and Friedrich Engels, *Marx-Engels Gesamtausgabe*, I., Abt., I/1, 242 ff.

3. Löwith, *Meaning in History*, 64.

4. R. B. Friedman, "On the Concept of Authority in Political Philosophy," *Authority*, Joseph Raz, ed. (New York: New York University Press, 1991), 83, cited in Khaled Abou El Fadl, *Speaking in God's Name: Islamic Law, Authority and Women* (Oxford: One World Publications, 2001), 19.

5. On the difficulty of distinguishing disbelief from misbehavior, see Alan Charles Kors, *Atheism in France 1650–1729: The Orthodox Sources of Disbelief*, vol. 1 (Princeton, NJ: Princeton University Press, 1990), 17–19.

6. The idea of the "withering away" of the state is from Friedrich Engels, *Herr Eugen Dühring's Revolution in Science [Anti-Dühring]* (Chicago: Charles H. Kerr, 1935), 292. Karl Marx does not use the term with regard to religion but does refer to Judaism as having reached a point at which "it must necessarily begin to disintegrate." See "On the Jewish Question," *The Marx-Engels Reader*, Robert Tucker, ed. (New York: W. W. Norton, 1972), 48.

7. On the Christian origins of liberalism, see Jeremy Waldron, *God, Locke, and Equality: Christian Foundations in Locke's Political Thought* (Cambridge: Cambridge University Press, 2000). For liberal ideas within Islam, see Khaled Abou El Fadl, *Islam and the Challenge of Democracy* (Princeton, NJ: Princeton University Press, 2004) and *The Place of Tolerance in Islam* (Boston: Beacon Press, 2002). See also *Liberal Islam: A Sourcebook*, Charles Kurzman, ed. (Oxford: Oxford University Press, 1998) and Lenn E. Goodman, *Islamic Humanism* (Oxford: Oxford University Press, 2005). The identification of a Jewish tradition of political-philosophical thought, including liberal strains of thought, is the project of the multivolume series *The Jewish Political Tradition*, Michael Walzer, Menachem Lorberbaum, Noam J. Zohar, and Yair Lorberbaum, eds. (New Haven, CT: Yale University Press, vol. 1, 2000; vol. 2, 2003). In his introduction to the series, Walzer speaks of "the ways in which" the Jewish tradition of political thought "*follows, parallels*, and *strains against* Greek, Arabic, Christian, and secularist modes of thought"(emphasis added), vol. 1, xxiii–xxiv. He might well have added that the Jewish political tradition *adumbrates* other modes of political thought, especially the Christian and secularist traditions.

8. Throughout this chapter, I use the terms *secularist theology* and *theological secularism* interchangeably.

9. One of the things I hope this chapter will make clear is the extent to which the term *the Western tradition* is a misnomer.

10. Rebecca French, *The Golden Yoke: The Legal Cosmology of Buddhist Tibet* (Ithaca, NY: Cornell University Press, 1995), 57–60. The term *legal cosmology* is French's.

11. See Peter Gay, *The Enlightenment: The Rise of Modern Paganism* (New York and London: W. W. Norton, 1977). The most provocative argument, suggested though not explicitly stated by Gay, endorsed by some scholars and denied by others, is that Enlightenment figures saw in ancient polytheism an adumbration of the pantheistic views ascribed (rightly or wrongly) to radical proponents of religious tolerance such as Spinoza, Bayle, and Hume. Conversely, it is suggested that the radicals of the Enlightenment saw ancient practices of religious tolerance as having been eclipsed by early formulations of monotheism. Whether any particular Enlightenment thinker was monotheistic, pantheistic, or atheistic in his own beliefs and whether any particular thinker equated monotheism with intolerance and pantheism with tolerance—or rather, adhered to quite the opposite view—are much-vexed questions of interpretation in the secondary literature. It may well be that the association

of ancient paganism with liberal tolerance, and monotheism with illiberal faith, is more an artifact of the historiography of the Enlightenment than of any actual Enlightenment figure. Be that as it may, J. G. A. Pocock has noted, "[i]t is clear . . . that the rebirth of modern paganism, as a twentieth-century historian [Gay] has termed 'The Enlightenment,' entailed a fairly drastic rewriting of the history of ancient paganism, which must be made to appear as far as possible deist rather than polytheist, philosophical rather than animist." Pocock, *Barbarism and Religion: Narratives of Civil Government*, vol. 2 (Cambridge: Cambridge University Press, 1999), 107.

12. *Lewis & Short Latin Dictionary*, available at http://www.perseus.tufts.edu/cgi-bin/ptext?doc=Perseus%3Atext%3A1999.04.0059.html; see also *Oxford Latin Dictionary*, 2nd ed. (Oxford: Oxford University Press, 2001), 55, 108, 109.

13. *Lewis & Short.*

14. Ibid. (defining *sacro*).

15. Ibid. (defining *sanctum*).

16. Ibid. (defining *sanctuarium*).

17. Ibid. (defining *saecularis*).

18. Ibid. (defining *mundanus*). In pre-Christian usage, the Latin *saeculum* meant "century," and the adjective *saecularis* referred chiefly to the secular games, which were held regularly at very long intervals. My thanks to Clifford Ando for this point.

19. A similar split and slippage between the two meanings are found in Freud's gloss on the Polynesian word for "taboo." Compare Sigmund Freud, *Totem and Taboo: Some Points of Agreement Between the Mental Lives of Savages and Neurotics*, tr. and ed. James Strachey (London: Routledge & Kegan Paul, 1961), 18–19:

> " 'Taboo' is a Polynesian word. It is difficult for us to find a translation for it, since the concept connoted by it is one which we no longer possess. It was still current among the ancient Romans, whose '*sacer*' was the same as the Polynesian 'taboo.' So, too, the '*ayos*' of the Greeks and the '*kadesh*' of the Hebrews must have had the same meaning as is expressed in 'taboo' by the Polynesians. . . .
>
> "The meaning of 'taboo,' as we see it, diverges in two contrary directions. To us it means, on the one hand, 'sacred,' 'consecrated,' and on the other 'uncanny,' 'dangerous,' 'forbidden,' 'unclean.' The converse of 'taboo' in Polynesian is '*noa*,' which means 'common' or 'generally accessible.' . . .
>
> " 'Properly speaking taboo includes only (a) the sacred (or unclean) character of person or things, (b) the kind of prohibition which results from this character, and (c) the sanctity (or uncleanness) which results from a violation of the prohibition.' " (quoting from the *Encyclopedia Britannica* entry on *taboo* by Northcote W. Thomas).

My thanks to Daniel Stolzenberg for pointing out the double meaning of "profane" and to Martha Umphrey for leading me to the same point in Freud.

20. *Lewis & Short* (defining *consecro* II. B. as "to hallow, recognize as holy" [eccl. Lat.]).

21. Ibid. (defining *"religio"* as "Concerning the etymology of this word, various opinions were prevalent among the ancients. Cicero [. . .] derives it from relegere . . . ; whereas Servius [. . .], Lactantius [. . .], Augustine [. . .], al., assume religare as the primitive . . .). Modern etymologists mostly agree with this latter view, assuming as root lig, to bind, whence also lic-tor, lex, and ligare; hence religio sometimes means the same as obligatio[. . .]" (citations omitted).

22. Ibid. (defining *religiosus*).

23. Ibid. (defining *sacrilegus*, and *sacrilegium* "I. *The robbing of a temple, stealing of sacred things, sacrilege*; II. *violation* or *profanation of sacred things, sacrilege*").

24. As Robert Cover observed, "[t]here is a difference between sleeping late on Sunday and refusing the sacraments, between having a snack and desecrating the fast of Yom Kippur." See Robert M. Cover, Foreword, "*Nomos* and Narrative," *Harvard Law Review* 97: 8 (November 1983).

25. Stanley Fish, *Self-Consuming Artifacts: The Experience of Seventeenth-Century Literature* (Berkeley: University of California Press, 1973), 5.

26. Plato, *Phaedrus*, quoted in Fish, *Self-Consuming Artifacts*, 5–6.

27. Ibid., 5.

28. Ibid., 6, 12.

29. Ibid., 7.

30. Kathy Eden, *Poetic and Legal Fiction in the Aristotelian Tradition* (Princeton, NJ: Princeton University Press, 1986), 8; see also, Fish, *Self-Consuming Artifacts*, 15–21.

31. Eden, 8.

32. Kathy Eden, *Hermeneutics and the Rhetorical Tradition: Chapters in the Ancient Legacy and Its Humanist Reception* (New Haven, CT: Yale University Press, 1997); see also Eden, *Poetic and Legal Fiction*.

33. "Plato . . . finds little to praise in the analogy [between the rhetorical art of the tragic stage and the law court] until his work, the *Laws*, where he compares the best legal constitution, as an accurate *mimesis* of the intentions of the lawgiver, to the finest tragedy." Eden, *Poetic and Legal Fiction*, 8.

34. Robert Newsom, *A Likely Story: Probability and Play in Fiction* (Piscataway, NJ: Rutgers University Press, 1988), 3.

35. The question of whether the intellectual tradition of classical rhetoric was in any sense a *religious* one, containing within it a conception of divinity and a perception of a gap between the mortal and the divine, is an exceedingly complicated one turning on numerous factors, including the religious or nonreligious nature of Aristotle's thought; the religious or nonreligious nature of the *practice* of classical rhetoric, in antiquity and later; and the religious nature of the various intellectual traditions that emerged as the chief continuators the Aristotelian rhetorical tradition.

36. On the impact of Aristotelianism on European philosophy, see Amos Funkenstein, *Theology and the Scientific Imagination from the Middle Ages to the Seventeenth Century*

(Princeton, NJ: Princeton University Press, 1989); Arthur Hyman and James J. Walsh, eds., *Philosophy in the Middle Ages: The Christian, Islamic and Jewish Traditions* (Indianapolis, IN: Hackett, 1983); John F. Wippel, *Medieval Reactions to the Encounter Between Faith and Reason* (Milwaukee: Marquette University Press, 1995). See also Richard M. Fraher, "'Ut nullus describatur reus prius quam convincatur' Presumption of Innocence in Medieval Canon Law?" *Proceedings of the Sixth International Congress of Medieval Canon Law*. Berkeley, CA, July 28–August 2, 1980, Stephan Kuttner and Kenneth Pennington, eds. (Rome: Biblioteca Apostolica Vaticana, 1985). Fraher writes that "social and political conditions led to the widespread adoption—or one might better say adaptation—of the learned law of the Romano-canonical tradition as real-world, workaday law," 498.

For the Christian encounter with Aristotelianism, see Francis Nigel Lee, *A Christian Introduction to the History of Philosophy* (Nutley, NJ: Craig Press, 1969); Richard McKeon, *Aristotelianism in Western Christianity* (Chicago: University of Chicago Press, 1939); John Marenbon, *Aristotelian Logic, Platonism, and the Context of Early Medieval Philosophy of the West* (Aldershot, UK: Variorum, 2000); Gunnar Skirbekk and Nils Gilje, *A History of Western Thought: From Ancient Greece to the Twentieth Century* (London: Routledge, 2001); Fernand van Steenberghen, *Thomas Aquinas and Radical Aristotelianism* (Washington, DC: Catholic University of America Press, 1980). On the Muslim encounter, see Majid Fakhry, *Philosophy, Dogma, and the Impact of Greek Thought in Islam* (Aldershot, UK: Variorum, 1994); Dimitri Gutas, *Avicenna and the Aristotelian Tradition: Introduction to Reading Avicenna's Philosophical Works* (Leiden: E. J. Brill, 1988); Barry S. Kogan, *Averroes and the Metaphysics of Causation* (Albany: State University of New York Press, 1985); Oliver Leaman, *History of Islamic Philosophy* (London: Routledge, 1996); F. E. Peters, *Aristotle and the Arabs: The Aristotelian Tradition in Islam* (New York: New York University Press, 1968). On the Jewish encounter, see Daniel H. Frank and Oliver Leaman, eds., *History of Jewish Philosophy* (London: Routledge, 1997); Lenn E. Goodman, *Jewish and Islamic Philosophy: Crosspollinations in the Classical Age* (Edinburgh: Edinburgh University Press, 1999); Isaac Husik, *A History of Medieval Jewish Philosophy*, trans. D. Silverman (New York: Schocken, 1973); John Inglis, *Medieval Philosophy and the Classical Tradition: In Islam, Judaism and Christianity* (Richmond, UK: Curzon Press, 2001); Husain Kassim, *Aristotle and Aristotelianism in Medieval Muslim, Jewish, and Christian Philosophy* (Lanham, MD: Austin & Winfield, 2000).

37. Richard M. Fraher, "The Theoretical Justification for the New Criminal Law of the High Middle Ages: 'Rei Publicae Interest, Ne Crimina Remaneant Impunita,'" (hereinafter "New Criminal Law"), *University of Illinois Law Review* no.3 (1984): 592. In general, see Jill Harries, *Law and Empire in Late Antiquity* (Cambridge: Cambridge University Press, 2001); Fritz Schulz, *History of Roman Legal Science* (Oxford: Clarendon Press, 1963); Peter Stein, *Roman Law in European History* (Cambridge: Cambridge University Press, 1999).

38. R. C. Mortimer explains that "[t]he word 'canon' meant, originally, a straight rod or line, something by which you measure; and so a definite rule." Mortimer, *Western Canon Law* (Berkeley: University of California Press, 1953), 9. Charles Donahue points to the differ-

ence between *"kanon,* the Greek word for 'rule' or 'guide,'" from which "canon" is derived, and *"nomos,* the Greek word for 'law,'" which he takes "to suggest that canons are not the Judaic law by which, in some sense, the observant Jew believed that he was justified, nor the *nomos* of the Greeks, a word redolent of overarching philosophical ideas," but rather a set of technical rules lacking in theological and philosophical content. See Donahue, "Comment on R. H. Helmholz, Conflicts Between Religious and Secular Law," *Cardozo Law Review* 12: 3–4 (1991): 731–732. As described by Mortimer, the word *canon*

> is applied to creeds, which are the rules of faith, its defined content by reference to which heresy can be measured. It is applied to the books of the Bible; for they fall with the line drawn by the Church and so are those which the rule of the Church recognizes as portions of Holy Scripture. It is applied to the clergy, who fall within the line and so are on the list. For many centuries now it has been applied in this sense only to those clergy who are on the list of a Cathedral; but in Patristic times it was applied to all the clergy on the list of a Bishop. The commonest application of the word, for us, is to the definitions or rules drawn up and agreed upon by a Council. In its strictest sense canon law means laws or canons passed by councils. It came . . . to include a great deal else besides, but in origin and strictly speaking, canon law is the law contained in the canons. And canons define and determine the organisation of the Church and the conduct and duties of its members. They set forth the norm or standard in these matters accepted and expected by the Church. Mortimer, *Western Canon Law,* 9.

39. Mark 12: 17; Matthew 22: 21; Luke 20: 25. The beginning of Romans 13 (New King James Bible) reads:

> 1. Let every soul be subject to the governing authorities. For there is no authority except from God, and the authorities that exist are appointed by God. 2. Therefore whoever resists the authority resists the ordinance of God, and those who resist will bring judgment on themselves. 3. For rulers are not a terror to good works, but to evil. Do you want to be unafraid of the authority? Do what is good, and you will have praise from the same. 4. For he is God's minister to you for good. But if you do evil, be afraid; for he does not bear the sword in vain; for he is God's minister, an avenger to execute wrath on him who practices evil. 5. Therefore you must be subject, not only because of wrath but also for conscience' sake. 6. For because of this you also pay taxes, for they are God's ministers attending continually to this very thing. 7. Render therefore to all their due: taxes to whom taxes are due, customs to whom customs, fear to whom fear, honor to whom honor.

40. See Thomas Aquinas, *A Summa of the Summa: The Essential Philosophical Passages of St. Thomas Aquinas' Summa Theologica Edited and Explained for Beginners,* Peter Kreeft, ed. (Ft. Collins, CO: Ignatius Press, 1990), 522–523, 525, 529–530. Aquinas states that it is necessary for there to be laws framed by people in addition to natural law, as some individuals need law to prevent them from acting in a depraved manner. This law should be framed

to benefit the common good of a community, but it should be flexible enough to allow for individual cases where it would work an injustice to apply it strictly. See also Reinhold Niebuhr, "Augustine's Political Realism," *The City of God: A Collection of Critical Essays*, Dorothy F. Donnelly, ed. (New York: Peter Lang, 1995), 140–141, which notes that while Augustine recognized that members of "the city of god" or those who pursued spiritual endeavors lived within the "city of the world," they were always separate from it as they did not share the same goal as the citizens of the earthly city (*The City of God*, bk. 19, chap. 17).

41. See Fraher, "New Criminal Law"; "Ut nullus"; "Conviction According to Conscience: The Medieval Jurists' Debate Concerning Judicial Discretion and the Law of Proof," *Law and History Review* 7: 1 (Spring 1989), 23–24; and "Preventing Crime in the High Middle Ages: The Medieval Lawyers' Search for Deterrence," in *Popes, Teachers, and Canon Law in the Middle Ages*, James Ross Sweeney and Stanley Chodorow, eds. (Ithaca, NY: Cornell University Press, 1989), 212–233.

42. Fraher, "Ut nullus," 504.

43. Ibid., 494.

44. Ibid.

45. Ibid.

46. Fraher, "Conviction According to Conscience," 27–29. Here Fraher argues strenuously against the view that the critical developments in criminal law procedure that occurred in twelfth-century Europe resulted from a religious skepticism about the human capacity for judgment. But elsewhere, he cites the twelfth-century following of the Roman law of proof as the reason that Pope Innocent III's proclamation, "Rei publicae interest, ne crimina remaneant impunita," met with a mixed response among jurists. See Fraher, "New Criminal Law," 593–594.

47. Fraher, "Preventing Crime," 214.

48. Ibid., 214–215.

49. Donahue, "Comment on R. H. Helmholz," 731; Daniel Boyarin, *A Radical Jew: Paul and the Politics of Identity* (Berkeley: University of California Press, 1994), 134–135, 139–141. See also Alan F. Segal, *Paul the Convert: The Apostolate and Apostasy of Saul the Pharisee* (New Haven, CT: Yale University Press, 1990), 258.

50. Fraher, "Preventing Crime," 215 (first emphasis added, second emphasis in the original) where he cites "the most influential of Augustine's and Gregory's writings on ecclesiastical toleration of wrongdoing . . . collected in Gratian's *Decretum*, C. 23 q.," ibid., n. 10.

51. But see ibid., 219: "By the end of the twelfth century, with the spirit of reform triumphant at Rome, the hierarchy had long since abandoned the policy that earthly misdeeds should be tolerated in this life and left to divine judgment."

52. R. H. Helmholz, "Conflicts Between Religious and Secular Law: Common Themes in the English Experience, 1250–1640," *Cardozo Law Review* 12: 3–4 (1991), 708–710; Fraher, "Preventing Crime," 215, which discusses the principle *de occultis non judicat ecclesia*; Fraher, "New Criminal Law," 593.

53. Barbara Shapiro, *Beyond Reasonable Doubt and Probable Cause: Historical Per-spectives on the Anglo-American Law of Evidence* (Berkeley: University of California Press, 1991), 251.

54. John H. Langbein, *Torture and Law of Proof: Europe and England in the Ancien Re-gime* (Chicago: University of Chicago Press, 1977), 75.

55. Ibid., 5–8.

56. Fraher, "Preventing Crime" 228; see also "Conviction According to Conscience," 46, which contends that not all medieval jurists believed that humans lacked the capacity to judge but that jurists were aware of human fallibility; see also Langbein, *Torture*, 7, which states that human judgment was necessary because the abolition of ordeal by the Fourth Lateran Council effectively destroyed the prior system of God judging the accused via or-deal. The judgment of humans was made palatable by the development of torture, as judges would have no discretion, because the accused would have confessed or two witnesses se-cured; see generally J. H. Baker, *An Introduction to English Legal History*, 4th rev. ed. (Lon-don: Butterworths, 2005), 4–6, which provides an overview of the use of torture and trial by ordeal in England.

57. Fraher, "Preventing Crime," 222; but see "Conviction According to Conscience," 62, where Fraher suggests that the implementation of torture had less to do with the difficul-ties imposed by the two-witness rule and more to do with the Church's campaign against heresy and the secular campaign against treason and sedition, as these crimes often involved little physical evidence. See also Langbein, *Torture*, 6–7, which proposes that the strict re-quirements of proof mandated by Roman canon law resulted in the adoption of torture as a means to extract confessions, thus subverting the two-witness requirement of proof by having the defendant admit guilt.

58. Langbein, *Torture*, 8–10.

59. For a full analysis of the doctrine, its origins and contemporary meaning, and the context of the utterance of Innocent III, see Fraher, "New Criminal Law," 577–581.

60. Ibid., 594.

61. Ibid., 584–586. Here Fraher asserts that the maxim "Rei publicae interest, ne crimina remaneant impunita" issued by Innocent III, was used by judges and lawyers to chip away at defendants' rights under canonical traditions.

62. Ibid., 594.

63. Helmholz, *The Spirit of Classical Canon Law* (Athens: University of Georgia Press, 1996), 116–117. Helmholz describes in general the division between secular and canon law.

64. I do not mean to imply that little thought went into the theological–secularist "so-lution." In fact, some of the ablest minds were recruited to the project of working out this practical dilemma, and many of the discussions exhibit an acute awareness of the issues and difficulties entailed. But that there was a serious problem with the solution—never solved, only finessed—is, I think, undeniable. Needless to say, modern, secular thinkers have not come up with any better solutions to the problem of reconciling the needs of law enforce-

ment with the vagaries of human knowledge and the uncertainties of proof, as recent experiments with emergency law have made painfully clear.

65. Mortimer, *Western Canon Law*, 9.

66. Ibid., 16–17. Subsequent lawbooks from the ancient period added such subjects as (from the Canons of Nicaea) "(1) Of those who castrate themselves. (They are not to be ordained.) (2) Of the newly baptized. (They are not to be ordained immediately.) (3) Of the kind of woman who may be allowed to live in the same house as the clergy (i.e., clerical housekeepers)," or (from the Canons of Neo-Caesarea) "(1) Priests not to marry. (2) No marriage with deceased husband's brother. (3) None to marry often".

67. Donahue, "Comment on R. H. Helmholz," 734.

68. This, to some extent, contradicts Donahue, who maintains there is little of theological import in canon law. See ibid., 730–731, 734.

69. For discussions of the conflicts between Church and secular law, see Helmholz, "Conflicts Between Religious and Secular Law," 707–708, where he discusses the conflict between Thomas Becket and Henry II over the punishment of "criminous clerks"; ibid., 708–709, where he describes the dispute between canon law and common law over which had jurisdiction regarding the inheritance of advowsons, or the right to introduce a cleric as a parson to a parish; ibid., 711, where he states the general conflict of jurisdiction between common and canon law; ibid., 717–718, where he discusses the conflict between canon law prohibiting clerics from shedding blood and their role as judges in common law courts, which enforced the death penalty. Also see note 72 for further references to Henry II's dispute with Becket.

70. Fraher, "Conviction According to Conscience," 24–28; "New Criminal Law," 592–593.

71. Fraher, "Preventing Crime," 223.

72. See Fraher, "New Criminal Law," 577–578, which discusses the conflict concerning "criminal jurisdiction over the English clergy" as the original trigger to the conflict between King Henry II and Thomas Becket in the late twelfth century; see also Donahue, "Comment on R. H. Helmholz," 733, where he proposes that Henry's dispute with and eventual martyring of Thomas Becket led to the realization by both the monarch and the Church that each would have its own sphere of legal control, secular law and canon law, respectively; see also, C. R. Cheney, "The Punishment of Felonous Clerks," *English History Review* 51: 202 (April 1936), 215–236. Cheney proposes that in the century and a half following Becket's murder, the *privilegium fori* was broadened and generally observed in England but that slowly the privilege was eroded until felonous clerks were again subject to punishment by secular courts after being degraded and removed from the ranks of the clergy. (Remnants of the debate regarding the punishment of felonous clerks linger to this day and are visible in the Church's defense of clergy in the 2002 abuse scandal.)

73. Fraher, "Preventing Crime," 223. "Cynus concluded that *inquisitio* had been invented as an extraordinary measure to enhance the efficiency of the criminal process."

74. For example, rules of construction and jurisdiction that legitimized local customary practices that deviated from the traditional formal rules, such as "custom confers jurisdiction" and "the best interpreter of a law is custom." See Helmholz, "Conflicts Between Religious and Secular Law," 716.

75. Ibid., 717.

76. Joseph H. Lynch, *The Medieval Church: A Brief History* (London: Longman, 1995), 118–119. For a more recent consideration of the issue, consider Pope John Paul II Jesus Christ, Messiah Priest General Audience—February 18, 1987. http://www.vatican.va/ holy_father/john_paul_ii/audiences/alpha/data/aud19870218en.html.

77. Helmholz, "Conflicts Between Religious and Secular Law," 708.

78. Ibid.

79. Ibid., 718.

80. Ibid., 719.

81. The point is not just that great ingenuity was exercised by jurists to find ways of harmonizing the systems of secular and ecclesiastical law, as Helmholz has demonstrated, "Conflicts Between Religious and Secular Law," 727. On a more basic level, the need for solutions to the conflicts presented between secular and spiritual law arose from the fact that the two systems of law overlapped and were both contained within a larger political system.

82. Ibid., 721–722.

83. Fraher, "Conviction According to Conscience," 48–50; and "New Criminal Law," 594–595, regarding the relationship between the Church and criminal procedure.

84. See, e.g., "The Charter of the Jews of the Duchy of Austria: July 1, 1244," *The Jew in the Medieval World: A Source Book 315–1791*, Jacob Rader Marcus and Marc Saperstein, eds. (Cincinnati, OH: Hebrew Union College Press, 2000), 31. This is an example of a medieval charter that governed Jews living in the duchy of Austria. Although the document does not specify that Jews could govern themselves, it was taken for granted that they would. The document actually grants the direct jurisdiction to the duke of Austria; see also Kenneth R. Stow, *Alienated Minority: The Jews of Medieval Latin Europe* (Cambridge, MA: Harvard University Press, 1993), 99–100. Stow cites Holy Roman Emperor Henry IV who granted Jews self-governance over themselves in all legal matters to attract Jews to his empire. However, if a Christian was involved, then the normal courts would take jurisdiction, although both Christian and Jewish witnesses could be called. On the general subject of Jewish self-government in the Middle Ages, see also Nomi M. Stolzenberg and David N. Myers, "Community, Constitution and Culture: The Case of the Jewish Kehilah," *University of Michigan Journal of Law Review* 25: 3 & 4 (1992), 633–670; C. Finkelstein, *Jewish Self-Government in the Middle Ages*, 2nd ed. (New York: Feldheim, 1964); Daniel J. Elazar and Stuart A. Cohen, *The Jewish Polity* (Bloomington: Indiana University Press, 1984).

85. James Carroll, *Constantine's Sword: The Church and the Jews—A History* (New York: Mariner Books, 2002), 70; James Parkes, *The Conflict of the Church and the Synagogue: A*

Study in the Origins of Antisemitism (London: Soncino Press, 1934), 37, 50–51; see also Boyarin, *A Radical Jew*, 122–123, 132–143, where he states that although Paul believed that people should not do anything they please, he did believe that it mattered more for Christians to comply with the true law of faith and not the "false law," which focused on physical observance of the law.

86. Boyarin, *A Radical Jew*, 134–140.

87. Donahue, "Comment on R. H. Helmholz," 731–732.

88. Ibid., 731. Donahue identifies three reasons for the lesser role of law in Christianity: (1) "Jesus rejected the legalism of the Pharisees." (2) "The apostolic mission was conceived as a mission to all mankind. . . . For the Church to have insisted on the observance of the whole of its laws would have severely limited, to say the least, its appeal to non-Jews. Thus, the law for the new church was not to be the Mosaic law, at least not the whole of the Mosaic law." (3) "[T]he Church received its first strong non-Jewish intellectual influences from the Greek world, and law was not the Greeks' long suit."

89. Ibid., 732.

90. Ibid., 731–732, 734: "there is relatively little theology in contemporary canon law."

91. Sir William Jones, introduction to "Institutes of Hindu Law or The Ordinances of Manu, According to the Gloss of Culluca; Comprising the Indian System of Duties Religious and Civil: Verbally Translated from the Original Sanscrit," 1794 (University of Southern California Special Collections Department, Los Angeles), iii. This work is a translation of ancient Hindu law written, according to Sir William Jones, around 880 B.C.E. The text exhibits the interconnectedness of religion and the law in such wide-ranging subjects as creation; education ("let the scholar when commanded by his preceptor and even when he has received no command, always exert himself in reading and in all acts useful to his teacher," further let him "always be decently appareled and properly composed"); marriage economics, private morals ("Traffick and moneylending are *satyanrita*; even by them *when he is deeply distressed*, may he support life, but service for hire is named *swavritti* or *dog-living*, and of course he must by all means avoid it.") (emphasis in original); diet, purification, and women ("never let her wish to separate herself from her father, her husband, or her sons; fore, by separation from them, she exposes both families to contempt"); government and military class; private and criminal disputes ("let the king or his judge, having seated himself on the bench, his body properly clothed and his mind attentively fixed, begin with doing reverence to the deities, who guard the world; and then let him enter on the trial of causes. Understanding what is expedient or inexpedient but considering only what is law or not law let him examine all disputes between parties, in the order of their several classes. By external signs let him see through the thoughts of men, by their voice, colour, countenance, limbs, eyes, and action"). The punishments imposed were often similar to those of the Old Testament. For example, "He who raises his hand or staff against another, shall have his hand cut, and he who kicks another in wrath shall have an incision made on his foot." Other subjects covered in the code include commercial and servile classes; the mixed classes and

sections on times of distress; penance and expiation; and transmigration and final beati-tude. See also Patrick Olivelle, ed., *The Law Code of Manu* (Oxford: Oxford University Press, 2004).

92. Suzanne Last Stone, "Sinaitic and Noahide Law: Legal Pluralism in Jewish Law," *Cardozo Law Review* 12 (1991), 1157, 1161: "Jewish legal literature . . . is practical and argu-mentative, rather than speculative or utopian. Legal theory is devoted to explaining the proper governance of Jewish society, as set forth in the written and oral law"; see also, Parkes, *The Conflict of the Church*, 35–37; Carroll, *Constantine's Sword*, 108. Carroll proposes that with the destruction of the Temple and exile from Israel, observances of Torah, law, increased in importance as a way for Jews to maintain a connection to Judaism.

93. J. David Bleich, "Jewish Law and the State's Authority to Punish Crime," *Cardozo Law Review* 12: 3–4 (1991), 831; Stone, "Sinaitic and Noahide Law," 1166.

94. Aaron Kirschenbaum and Jon Trafimow, "The Sovereign Power of the State: A Proposed Theory of Accommodation in Jewish Law," *Cardozo Law Review* 12: 3–4 (1991), 925–927, 936–937; Perry Dane, "The Maps of Sovereignty: A Meditation," *Cardozo Law Review* 12: 3–4 (1991), 1000–1001; Malvina Halberstam, "Interest Analysis and Dina de-Malkhuta Dina, A Comment on Aaron Kirschenbaum, The Sovereign Power of the State: A Proposed Theory of Accommodation in Jewish Law," *Cardozo Law Review* 12: 3–4 (1991), 951–957. See especially Stone, "Sinaitic and Noahide Law," 1211, where she proposes that *dine de-malkhuta dina* was not a concession to foreign law but a method of maintaining legal au-tonomy. See also Gil Graff, *Separation of Church and State: Dina de-Malkhuta Dina in Jewish Law* (Alabama: University of Alabama Press, 1985), 2. Graff contends that the principle not only served as a "means of accommodation" but also as a "legal basis for resistance to the arbitrary demands of the ruling power."

95. Arnold N. Enker, "Aspects of Interaction Between the Torah Law, the King's Law and the Noahide Law in Jewish Criminal Law," *Cardozo Law Review* 12: 3–4 (1991), 1148; Stone, "Sinaitic and Noahide Law," 1159; Carroll, *Constantine's Sword*, 50.

96. Bleich, "Jewish Law," 853, glossing Maimonides.

97. Ibid., glossing Nahmanides.

98. Stone, "Sinaitic and Noahide Law," 1170.

99. Kirschenbaum and Trafimow, "The Sovereign Power of the State," 939. The authors provide as an example the case in which a sovereign forbidding the wearing of hats or *Kippot* to celebrate a national holiday would not be in conflict with Jewish law, as the covering of one's head is not required by the Torah, and therefore the interests of Jewish law are weak and accommodation could be made.

100. Chaim Povarsky, "Jewish Law v. the Law of the State: Theories of Accommoda-tion," *Cardozo Law Review* 12: 3–4 (1991), 950. Povarsky proposes that Jewish law is allowing state law to be used in those instances where either there is no conflict between Jewish law and state law or where "Jewish law by employing its own principles could accept such a [state] law. The integrity of Jewish law is thus being preserved even while state law is be-

ing applied"; see also Kirschenbaum and Trafimow, "The Sovereign Power of the State," 936–940, which states that the principle of *dina de-malkhuta dina* applies in monetary and civil matters but in religious matters only when religious law is not essential or is weak; see also Stone, "Sinaitic and Noahide Law," 1210–1211, which observes that recent scholarship has emphasized the role of *dina de-malkhuta dina* as a means of maintaining Jewish legal autonomy.

101. Stone, "Sinaitic and Noahide Law," 1211; Povarsky, "Jewish Law v. the Law of the State."

102. Stone, "Sinaitic and Noahide Law," 1210–1212.

103. Enker, "Aspects of Interaction," 1155.

104. Stone, "Sinaitic and Noahide Law," 1199: "Although the Talmud did not describe the reported instances of extralegal punishment as an actual, developed system of judicial jurisdiction, later authorities understood this tradition as establishing the legal basis for a systematic exercise of rabbinic 'emergency' powers. With the dissolution of the Sanhedrin, several jurists held that these powers could by exercised by the Exilarch and religious communal leaders."

105. Ibid., 1159.

106. Enker, "Aspects of Interaction," 1144.

107. Stone, "Sinaitic and Noahide Law," 1157.

108. Ibid., 1193.

109. Ibid., 1157, 1193.

110. Enker, "Aspects of Interaction," 1145–1147.

111. Ibid., 1145, which describes the supplementary powers of the religious courts and the king's authority.

112. Stone, "Sinaitic and Noahide Law," 1159.

113. Ibid., 1201.

114. Enker, "Aspects of Interaction," 1144.

115. Fraher, "New Criminal Law," 593; see also note 42.

116. Stone, "Sinaitic and Noahide Law," 1202.

117. Ibid., 1193.

118. Enker, "Aspects of Interaction," 1148.

119. Stone, "Sinaitic and Noahide Law," 1194. At other points in the text, Stone disputes the claim that the doctrines discussed reflect an underlying concern with the gap between human and divine judgment, saying, "It is not at all clear that confessional evidence is excluded from the Sinaitic system because it is an unreliable basis for determining guilt"; ibid., 1180. Her words here seem to support the theory that the *halakha* reflects a concern about the unreliability of human judgment. Fraher similarly resisted the parallel claim about Christian conceptions of human judgment, while also providing support for that claim. Fraher, "Ut nullus," 494, cites the rabbinic tradition of two witnesses as being a contributory element, along with the Roman law requirement of due process in criminal cases, the

Roman law's dictum that the burden of proof is on the accuser and the introduction of an egalitarian view of accuser and defendant being equal, in the creation of a conception of a presumption of innocence in medieval Europe.

120. William C. Placher, *A History of Christian Theology* (London: Westminster John Knox Press, 1983), 156–157; Brian Tierney, *The Crisis of Church and State 1050–1300* (Toronto: University of Toronto Press, 1988); Etienne Gilson, *Reason and Revelation in the Middle Ages* (New York: Scribner, 2000).

121. Enker, "Aspects of Interaction," 1145–1146.

122. Ibid., 1146.

123. Ibid., 1145.

124. Stone, "Sinaitic and Noahide Law," 1201.

125. Ibid., 1198.

126. Fraher, "Ut nullus," 494, where he notes that the rabbinic tradition of requiring two witnesses to establish proof of guilt in a criminal case was an element that added to the creation of a medieval presumption of innocence; see also Fraher, "New Criminal Law," 587. Fraher observed that the Church's continued use of the stringent requirements of proof forced it to ignore all but the most egregious misbehavior of clergy in the medieval period.

127. French, *The Golden Yoke*, 115–117.

128. Ibid., 13.

129. Ibid., 14.

130. Ibid.

131. Ibid.

132. Ibid.

133. Ibid., 14, 42.

134. Ibid., 46.

135. Ibid., 79.

136. Ibid., 100.

137. Ibid.

138. Ibid., 61.

139. On the similarities between Plato's philosophy and Buddhism, see A. N. Marlow, "Hinduism and Buddhism in Greek Philosophy," *Philosophy East and West* 4: 1 (April 1954), 35–45; Thomas McEvilley, *The Shape of Ancient Thought: Comparative Studies in Greek and Indian Philosophies* (New York: Allworth Press, 2002), 165, 168–169.

140. French, *The Golden Yoke*, 62.

141. Ibid.

142. Ibid.

143. Fish, *Self-Consuming*, 5.

144. I am using the terms *rationalism* and *antirationalism* loosely in much the same way as employed by Fish. Various usages of the terms appear in Christian thought with

sometimes more, sometimes less exactitude—with rationalism more commonly being juxtaposed to "irrationalism" (as opposed to "antirationalism").

145. On rationalism and irrationalism within Islam, see Karen Armstrong, *Islam: A Short History* (New York: Modern Library, 2002), 71, 84, 105, 154; John L. Esposito, *Oxford History of Islam* (Oxford: Oxford University Press, 2000); Annemarie Schimmel, *Mystical Dimensions of Islam* (Chapel Hill: University of North Carolina Press, 1975). For Judaism, see Gershom Scholem, *Major Trends in Jewish Mysticism* (New York: Schocken, 1995), 23, 131, 249, 304; and *The Messianic Idea in Judaism and Other Essays on Jewish Spirituality* (New York: Schocken, 1995), 24–30.

146. On the history of the philosophy of skepticism, see Richard H. Popkin, *The History of Scepticism: From Savonarola to Bayle* (Oxford: Oxford University Press, 2003), xvii–xix, where Popkin discusses the origins of the various skeptical positions and their relation to the ability of people to "know" or "not know" something for certain.

147. The so-called rationalists may well exhibit more faith in human cognition than the antirationalists, but that is not the same as having faith that human cognition can attain perfection.

148. The reference is to Clifford Geertz's felicitous phrase, "anti-anti-relativism." See Geertz, "Anti-anti-relativism," *American Anthropologist* 86: 2 (June 1984), 263–278. My preference for the "anti-anti" formulation reflects my sense that theological secularism is anti-antirationalist in that it refuses to give up on the exercise of human reason and the making of human judgments just because human reason and judgment are imperfect. The conventional way of referring to this stance as rationalist is misleading if taken to imply a lack of skepticism about human reason. In fact, the anti-antirationalist shares the skepticism about human reason expressed by antirationalists like Plato. What distinguishes the anti-antirationalist from the antirationalist is that the former puts more faith in human reason than the antirationalist does on the grounds that it does not follow from the fact that human cognition is imperfect that it is therefore inadequate or incapable of being improved.

149. Shapiro, *Beyond Reasonable Doubt*.

150. For the importance of probabilism in Islam, see Abou el Fadl, *Speaking in God's Name*, 39, 45, 85, 149, 160; and Bernard G. Weiss, *The Search for God's Law: Islamic Jurisprudence in the Writings of Sayf al-Din al Amidi* (Salt Lake City: University of Utah Press, 1992).

151. It should be noted, however, that the commitment to diverse legal cultures is present (at least according to *halakhik* views) even before the Jewish community finds itself obliged by the condition of exile to accept the existence of other legal systems.

152. For an overview of the millet system, see Ira M. Lapidus, *A History of Islamic Societies* (Cambridge: Cambridge University Press, 1988), 323–324, 599, 793, 821, 900.

153. On the battle between pluralist and authoritarian approaches to interpretation in Islamic theology and jurisprudence, see Khaled Abou El Fadl, *And God Knows the Soldiers: The Authoritative and the Authoritarian in Islamic Discourse* (Lanham, MD: University Press of America, 2001); and *Speaking in God's Name: Islamic Law, Authority and Women*

(Oxford: Oneworld Publications, 2001). On the Catholic case, see John Courtney Murray and J. Leon Hooper, eds., *Religious Liberty: Catholic Struggles with Pluralism* (Louisville, KY: Westminster/John Knox, 1993).

154. Gil Graff states that "[i]n the transition from corporate community to individual citizen, the principle *dina de-malkhuta dina* was frequently invoked as a measure of harmonizing the requirements of religious law with the demands of the state," although this did not mean it was purely a means of accommodation, as it also "provided a rationale for resistance to the implementation of unjust decrees." See Graff, *Separation of Church and State*, 133–134.

155. See Dan Simon, "A Third View of the Black Box: Coherence in Legal Decision Making," *University of Chicago Law Review* 511 (2004); "A Psychological Model of Judicial Reasoning," *Rutgers Law Journal* 1 (1998).

Pragmatic Rule and Personal Sanctification in Islamic Legal Theory

MARION HOLMES KATZ

The Shariʿa as Law

Popular wisdom on the nature of the shariʿa can be succinctly summarized: It is sacred, and it is law. The shariʿa is sacred both by virtue of the divine revelation in which it is grounded (God's verbal utterance, the Qurʾan, and the nonverbal manifestation of God's will in the normative practice of the Prophet Muhammad) and of the transcendent goals that it ultimately pursues, the achievement of this-worldly harmony with God's will and of otherworldly felicity. It is law in the sense that it encompasses the realm of judicially enforceable rules and the conduct of the state, even while extending to realms of ritual practice and of private ethics exceeding the purview of modern Western "law." Expressing this widespread view, Bernard Lewis writes that "The *shariʿa*, the Holy Law of Islam, embraces the whole range of human activities, and is therefore naturally concerned with the conduct of government in all its aspects."[1] The idea that Islamic law (at least in its ideal form, not necessarily to be identified with classical articulations of the shariʿa) is comprehensive in scope, leaving no purview for human legislation or for secular jurisdictions, is a central tenet of certain modern Islamic ideologies. As the Egyptian radical Sayyid Qutb (executed 1966) declares in his widely read commentary on the Qurʾan, "The Islamic view is that the norms, traditions, systems, and laws people may adopt and accept as a way of life for human society at any particular time in history have no merit or consistency if they are at variance or in contradiction with God's Book."[2]

However, particularly in recent years, a number of scholars have questioned the extent to which the discourses and practices of the shariʿa have in fact historically functioned comprehensively to imbue the articulation and exercise of the law with the sacred. First, there is (even in theory) a sharp discontinuity between *fiqh* (Islamic legal thought) and the actual enactment of enforceable laws. *Fat-was* (the authoritative legal opinions of distinguished religious scholars) have no legal force; although they may be submitted to *qadis* (judges) and may shape their verdicts in given instances, it is essentially irrelevant to the process of *ifta'* whether any legal mechanism exists by which a given opinion might be imposed in practice.

The status of *mufti* (a legal scholar qualified to issue independent legal opinions) is highly prestigious within a shar'i framework, but the tropes of the classical shar'i literature emphasize the undesirability and moral peril of the office of qadi. The qadi's office was compromised both by the stigma of collaboration with the ruling powers and by the necessity to make enforceable decisions, decisions that affected the rights and well-being of the judge's fellow believers and thus potentially implicated him in inadvertent sin, if not in outright corruption. The autonomy of the shar'i scholarly establishment and its aloofness from the taint of governmental power—even power exercised in the conscientious application of the shari'a—is an ideal whose historical grounding has been subject to scholarly debate. Certainly, the trope of the religious scholar who steadfastly refuses the qadi's office—or who assumes it only under severe duress—may reflect scholarly ideology as much as it does the de facto relationship between temporal rulers and scholarly authorities.[3] Nevertheless, it does indicate a widespread reluctance to imbue the actual practice of the law—involving the final selection of legal rules to be applied and enforced in the context of a court of law backed by governmental power—with the aura of the sacred.

Indeed, although the bipolarity of the sacred discussed in the introduction to this volume—the powerful propinquity of the holy and the impure—is generally inapplicable to Islamic ideas of the sacred, it does apply to many Islamic scholars' attitudes toward the holders of temporal power. This is often true even of images of the Umayyad and 'Abbasid caliphates, but applies even more to scholars' attitudes to the military rulers who dominated the Islamic world after their eclipse. In the overwhelmingly influential (if also controversial) work of Abu Hamid al-Ghazali (d. 1111), whose ideas are further discussed later, the motifs of king and court straddle the symbolically potent borderline between the sacred and the impure. King and court are both central metaphors for the divine and loci of a contagious moral and religious taint. Of course, on one level, this ambivalence reflects a simple dichotomy between the divine King and the earthly usurpers of his power[4]; at a deeper level, however, the motif of kingly might functions as a powerfully ambiguous symbol.

Like the Jewish and Christian thinkers discussed by Nomi Stolzenberg, Islamic legal scholars acknowledged the pragmatic need for laws, jurisdictions, and mechanisms of enforcement that fell outside the purview of the shariʿa. This recognition was expressed in the concept of *siyasa*, defined as the discretionary power exercised by temporal rulers in the interests of public order and general welfare. The domain of siyasa was complementary to that of shariʿa; in the area of penal law, the word *siyasa* came to refer to penalties imposed by the authorities outside the framework of the *hudud* (a limited set of offenses whose punishments are mandated by the shariʿa). Thus, premodern Islamic scholars recognized the existence, necessity, and (consequent) legitimacy of a non-sharʿi governmental domain. Patricia Crone has argued that by the time of al-Ghazali, when the role of the caliphate had declined to the point that theorists were compelled to acknowledge the centrality of governmental authorities bereft of religious qualifications, "the Muslim world had developed something similar to the division between state and church in medieval Europe."[5]

However, the domain of siyasa was (at least in the eyes of religious theorists) one of ad hoc pragmatic action rather than of law. Crone notes that the rivalry between caliph and sultan was played out in political terms and did not lead to the demarcation of separate jurisdictions: "the scholars and kings of the Islamic world ruled the believers/subjects on the basis of the same law, the Shariʿa, not, as in the Latin West, on the basis of two different legal systems . . . devised by different sets of authorities."[6] The nonexistence of alternative rules, procedures, and jurisdictions may have been more a matter of theory than of fact; for instance, in discussing the sphere of competence of the police (*shurta*), the great North African historian Ibn Khaldun (d. 1406) defines it in terms of siyasa functions that could not be performed within the framework of the sacred law. He notes that the shariʿa plays no role in the proactive detection and investigation of crime; this function is performed by the police, who can also extract confessions under duress should the public interest so require. These are things from which qadis may remain piously aloof (*tanazzaha ʿanhu al-qadi*).[7]

However, the realm of sultanic decrees and dynastic justice was not, in general, conceptualized as an autonomous form of law. The term *qanun* (a Greek loan word) did, over time, emerge as a term for "law" that served as a secular complement for the religious term shariʿa. At least by the later fourteenth century, the term *qanun* was used to refer to concrete bodies of dynastic law; the Aq-qoyunlu ruler Uzun Hasan (ruled 1466–1478) was known to have issued a set of qanun regulations that continued to be applied after the rise of the subsequent dynasty. (Substantively, this qanun is thought to have represented "a practical register of local customary law."[8]) In the Mamluk period, dynastic law appeared sufficiently autonomous so that the Egyptian historian Maqrizi (d. 1442) "explicitly defines the distinction between Shariʿa and *siyasa* jurisdictions" and defines the latter term according to a prevalent (folk) etymology relating it to the Yasa, the code of laws attributed to Genghis Khan.[9]

In response to the overwhelming reality of Turkish power holders devoid of any religious qualifications, efforts were made to assimilate the domain of siyasa into the overall framework of shariʿa law. The independent and controversial Hanbali thinker Ibn Taymiyya (d. 1328) pioneered efforts to integrate these areas into the religious law through the concept of *siyasa sharʿiyya*. While the religious might shun power in the belief that "positions of command are incompatible with true faith" and wielders of power might eschew religious guidance because they considered it impractical, Ibn Taymiyya argued that a comprehensive and yet flexible understanding of the shariʿa could meld the two. By striving to "unite the Qurʾan and iron" (i.e., power), in this view, "the world will serve religion."[10] This vision was largely fulfilled under the Ottoman Empire (fourteenth to twentieth centuries); while qanun played a central and overt role in the Ottoman legal system, it was combined with shariʿa in a unified court system staffed by religious scholars.[11] Although the shariʿa was not the sole source of legal norms in historical societies (and profane legal rules and practices were extensively acknowledged even by religious scholars), its relationship to secular law was thus not one of clearly demarcated separation, and secular law was not comparably elaborated as a discourse, a career path, or a set of institutions.

The history of Islamic legal thought and practice thus suggests that the shariʿa is something less (as well as more) than law in the modern Western sense. On the one hand, it was conceptualized in ways largely unconcerned with issues of governmental enactment or judicial enforcement; on the other, its partial disengagement from issues of pragmatic public order left an acknowledged sphere of governmental discretion, if one that was not theorized as a separate domain of legal thought and practice. It is certainly not the case that, as was argued by earlier generations of Western scholars, the shariʿa was an ideal construct whose simultaneously ethereal and rigid nature left it detached from social practice; studies like those of Wael Hallaq and David Powers have illustrated the intimate connection between legal discourses and social realities.[12] However, shari'a was not always (in the modern sense) law, nor was the law always shari'a.

The Shari'a as Sacred

The characterization of the shari'a as "sacred" may in some ways seem less problematic than its characterization as "law." However, the shari'a was not unchallenged among medieval Muslims as a framework for the pursuit of sanctity, and in contrast with some of the available alternatives, it appeared positively profane. The most famous articulation of the position that the shari'a is, in fact, profane appears in the great synthesis of the jurist and Sufi mystic Abu Hamid al-Ghazali. Al-Ghazali argues that *fiqh* (jurisprudence) applies exclusively to externals, while Sufism addresses the conditions of the heart. Early in his magnum opus *Ihya' ulum al-din*, he defends this position to a hypothetical challenger:

> [God] created this world as a provision for the Resurrection, so that [human beings] could take from it that which was good to prepare themselves for the journey. If they were to make use of it justly, conflicts would come to an end and the *fuqaha'* (legal scholars, i.e., scholars of the shari'a) would be out of work. However, they have [always] made use of it following their desires, from which conflicts arose. Thus there was need of a sultan to govern them, and the sultan required a law (*qanun*) by which to govern them; the *faqih* is the one who is knowledgeable about the law of governance (*qanun al-siyasa*) and the means of mediation among the people when they come into conflict as a result of their desires. The *faqih* is the sultan's teacher and his guide to the means of governing the people and keeping control of them, so that by virtue of their good behavior (*istiqama*) their worldly affairs would be in order. Indeed, [*fiqh*] is related to religion, not directly but through the intermediation of the world.[13]

It is striking that al-Ghazali uses the Arabic words *qanun* and *siyasa* in this passage, although it quite clearly refers to scholars of the shari'a—who would ordinarily be considered the religious scholars par excellence.

Al-Ghazali's imaginary disputant replies with an objection: "This may be true of the rules relating to personal injury, criminal punishments, fines, and the resolution of disputes, but it does not apply to those things categorized as acts of worship, such as fasting and prayer." Al-Ghazali counters this response by turning to the requirement of the shari'a most intimately connected to interior be-

lief, the pronunciation of the confession of faith ("There is no god but God, and
Muhammad is the Messenger of God"):

> As for *islam* [i.e., conversion through utterance of the confession of faith], legal dis-
> course (*fiqh*) discusses what is valid and what is invalid with regard to it and its con-
> ditions; the only thing it considers in this regard is the tongue [i.e., what the person
> confesses openly]. As for the heart, it is outside the realm of *fiqh*.

Here al-Ghazali cites the example of the Prophet Muhammad, who rejected the
execution of a man who had clearly made the verbal confession of faith out of fear
of the sword; suggesting that his state of faith was inaccessible to human scrutiny,
he asked rhetorically, "Didn't you split open his heart?" According to the shari'a,
that is, mere lip service renders a person's life and property sacrosanct. However,
al-Ghazali notes,

> As for the world to come, there wealth is of no use; the only thing that matters there is
> the light, secrets, and sincerity of hearts. These are not matters of *fiqh*. If a *faqih* were to
> delve into them it would be as if he were delving into theology or medicine; he would be
> going outside of his discipline.

Al-Ghazali's arguments suggest, surprisingly, that the shari'a is sacred only in
terms of the ultimate source of its provisions, the commandments of God. Its
function in human life is a secular one, the imposition of behavioral limits protecting Muslim polities from the social havoc wrought by selfish passions and safe-
guarding the lives and properties of their subjects. Such protections are relevant to
the religious life only as necessary preconditions; al-Ghazali likens the shari'a to
the measures taken by the ruler to ensure the physical safety of pilgrims to Mecca,
which are necessary to the effective performance of the Hajj but do not themselves
partake of its spiritual significance.[14]

To a certain extent, al-Ghazali's argument is directed not at the inherent potentialities of the shari'a as a means to self-improvement but to the study of the shari'a
as a social and intellectual pursuit. He is keenly aware both of the intellectual pride
that can result from successful study of the law and of the worldly gains that accrue to its practitioners. The discipline of legal study can degenerate into a form of
intellectual play that is pursued for its own sake, with little regard for the ultimate
aims of the religious life.

However, there is a more profound disconnection between the shari'a and al-
Ghazali's ideals of self-refinement. Significantly, his low estimation of the shari'a
is based not only on a dichotomy between the inner and the outer but on a gradu-
ated scale of renunciation. Immediately following his exposition of the external

and political nature of the fiqh, al-Ghazali further explains the qualitative difference between mere adherence to the strictures of the shariʿa and the cultivation
of hearts. He does this by establishing a typology of *waraʿ*, or pious self-restraint.
The first stage is the *waraʿ* required to be considered a qualified witness, judge, or
public official under the shariʿa; it requires that one refrain from open transgression (*al-haram al-zahir*). The second is the *waraʿ* exercised by those who refrain
from anything whose status is open to ambiguity or doubt. The third is the *waraʿ*
of those who eschew even licit things if they may lead to what is forbidden. The
fourth, and highest, level of *waraʿ* is to eschew anything that might distract one,
even briefly, from consciousness of God.[15] Al-Ghazali is here essentially arguing
that the law fails to refine the heart, to use one of his favorite locutions throughout
this lengthy work, because it demands from the believer only a minimum of renunciation. One can satisfy the moderate demands of the shariʿa while continuing
to indulge in a plethora of desires that distract one thoroughly from the awareness
of the divine, leaving one's heart thoroughly burdened with the impurities whose
elimination is the main goal of al-Ghazali's Sufi ethics.

The problem of the continued gratification of the lower self, or *nafs*, within
the bounds of the shariʿa is most clearly apparent in al-Ghazali's discussion of the
concept of *zuhd*, or renunciation. One who "sells" this world in exchange for the
next is a renunciant (*zahid*) with respect to this world; yet this is not the highest
level of renunciation.

> Someone who rejects (*yarghab ʿan*) all but God Most High, even the gardens of para-
> dise, and loves none but God Most High is an absolute renunciant (*al-zahid al-mutlaq*).
> Someone who rejects every share (*hazz*) that he might gain of this world, yet does not
> renounce similar shares (*huzuz*) of the next, but covets houris, palaces, rivers and fruits
> [in paradise], is also a renunciant, but at a lower level than the first. Someone who
> abandons some shares (*huzuz*) of this world but not others, for instance, someone who
> abandons wealth but not status or gluttony but not self-adornment, does not merit the
> name of "renunciant" absolutely; his rank among renunciants is like that of someone
> who repents of only some sins among the repentant. It is a valid form of renunciation,
> just as repentance of some sins is valid repentance. Repentance consists of abandoning
> things that are forbidden (*al-mahzurat*); renunciation consists of abandoning things that
> are allowed, which are the share of the lower self (*al-lati hiya hazz al-nafs*).[16]

Here the key concept is the *hazz*, or "share"; one's efforts are defective to the extent
that one seeks any benefit, even the most licit—and even if it is deferred to the
afterlife. To seek gratification or reward is to vitiate the spiritual benefit of one's
action.

The shari'a is not purely profane, however, because it is rooted in the all-important life of the spirit. Al-Ghazali affirms that the discipline of Islamic law is akin to the discipline of the Sufi path "because it examines the works of the limbs, and the source and origin of the works of the limbs are the qualities of the heart."[17] However, the discipline of the shari'a as currently practiced neglects this dimension. Having enumerated a long list of positive and negative moral characteristics, al-Ghazali laments:

> If a legal scholar were asked about one of these concepts, even (for instance) about sincerity, or reliance on God, or the way to avoid hypocrisy, he would refrain from expressing an opinion. This is despite the fact that [knowledge of these qualities] is his individual obligation, whose neglect can cause his perdition in the afterlife. If [on the other hand] you were to ask him about mutual cursing [a form of divorce when a husband makes an unsupported accusation of adultery against his wife], zihar [a form of divorce where a husband declares his wife to be "like his mother's back"], racing, and shooting [two legally problematic pastimes], he would present to you volumes of subtle ramifications that ages might pass without any need arising for them.[18]

In al-Ghazali's view, this estrangement between the disciplines of law and of spiritual self-refinement is not a primordial one. With particular attention to the figure of al-Shafi'i (d. 820 C.E.), the eponymous founder of one of the four classical schools of Sunni law and the subject of a great deal of hagiography, al-Ghazali endeavors to demonstrate that the most august early jurists were also accomplished ascetics whose sentiments anticipated those of later Sufis. In the remainder of his magnum opus, al-Ghazali offers a comprehensive overview of the shari'a that invests it with a depth dimension drawn from Sufi ethics and continues with a resumé of the Sufi path.

The influence of Sufi thought, as I argue later, has generated many of the ambiguities in the relationship between observance of the shari'a and cultivation of the self as understood by leading legal theorists. Historically, almost all Sufis have accepted the validity of the obligations of the shari'a, so there is no fundamental opposition between the two forms of discipline; indeed, in terms of personnel, the overlap has been considerable. Prominent Sufis have frequently been jurists, and prominent jurists have frequently been Sufis. For this very reason, however, the two discourses are scarcely separable; ever since the flowering of classical Sufi thought in the tenth and eleventh centuries, legal discourse has been penetrated by Sufi terminology, and vice versa. Thus, since that era, most jurists have been aware of the distinctively Sufi disciplines that claim to take the refinement of the self as their ultimate aim. Because these disciplines far exceed the strictures imposed by an exoteric understanding of the shari'a, they implicitly challenge the idea that the shari'a alone suffices to tame the unruly passions of the lower self.

The wide appeal of Sufi ideals of self-cultivation has suggested to many Muslims that adherence to the shari'a is not a comprehensive or self-sufficient mode of actualizing the sacred in the life of the individual believer. Specifically, the Sufi ideals of *wara'* (pious self-restraint, even in matters allowed by the shari'a) and *zuhd* (renunciation, whether in terms of material self-denial or of psychological self-abnegation) were far more exacting than the relatively accommodating limits established by the law. It is perfectly possible to be wealthy, comfortable, well fed, and sexually fulfilled while remaining in strict adherence to the shari'a; the same is not true of Sufi ideals, which (while only occasionally reaching the extremes of celibacy and mendicancy) advocate not merely ethical enjoyment but radical detachment—if not from the physical enjoyment of wealth, sex, and honor, then from emotional investment in them.

The contrast between the demands for renunciation presented by the Sufi path and the more limited forbearance dictated by the shari'a becomes even more pronounced when we turn to jurists who emphasize the shari'a's nature as a beneficent law designed by God to fill human wants and needs. The key term around which such discussions revolve is *maslaha*, meaning "interest" or "benefit." Scholars who analyze the shari'a in light of the concept of maslaha hold that it beneficently provides for human wants and needs, rendering believers' lives optimally harmonious and happy. Because of its emphasis on concrete benefits to human beings, this approach potentially conflicts with the Sufi axiom that spiritual improvement can be achieved only through self-denial. The shari'a is seen to function as a mechanism for the realization of (legitimate) human needs and goals rather than a pedagogy of their frustration. As Wael Hallaq has written, the idea that the shari'a is intended to provide for human maslaha implicitly "amounts to arguing that the Shari'a is designed to respect the needs and even personal pleasures of God's subjects."[19]

One possible resolution of these potentially conflicting ideals lay in the construction of a hierarchy of human objectives culminating in the transcendent. One such synthesis can be seen in the work of the jurist and Sufi 'Izz al-Din 'Abd al-'Aziz ibn 'Abd al-Salam al-Sulami (d. 1262). In his work of legal theory, *Qawa'id al-ahkam fi masalih al-anam*, al-Sulami's opening premises at first seem strikingly secular to the point that they evoke Jeremy Bentham's concept of utilitarianism.

Thus, al-Sulami quite simply defines the benefits (*masalih*) pursued by the shari'a as "pleasures (*ladhdhat*) and those things that lead to them, and joys (*afrah*) and those things that lead to them"; the harms (*mafasid*) it seeks to avert are "pains (*alam*) and those things that lead to them, and sorrows (*ghumum*) and those things that lead to them."[20] It is a function of human nature that we be attracted to pleasure and joy and averse to pain and sorrow. Furthermore, it is implanted as an instinct in human beings (*al-tiba' majbula 'ala dhalika*) that greater benefits must be given precedence over lesser ones.[21] Al-Sulami also parallels Bentham in equating considerations of pleasure and pain with moral judgments; in the vocabulary of the Qur'an, al-Sulami argues, "The terms 'benefits' and 'harms' are synonymous with 'good' and 'evil' actions (*al-hasanat wa'l-sayyi'at*), because good actions are always beneficial and vice versa."[22]

Because of the firm grounding of the principle of maximization of benefits in human nature, al-Sulami believes that most benefits and harms (and thus most provisions of the divine law, *al-shara'i'*) can be known intellectually. The difficulty arises when people fail to correctly recognize the relative value of different benefits. More subtle difficulties arise because benefits and harms are rarely unmixed. There are very few benefits in human life, for instance, that are obtained without burdensome effort. The desire for them (*al-shahwa*) can also be disagreeable, which entails an innate conflict between pleasure and pain.

The fundamental distinction between al-Sulami's system and Bentham's is, of course, al-Sulami's belief in a life after death. Not only does the eternal duration of the life to come give it precedence over the exigencies of this life, but it is the domain in which the inextricable mixing of pain and pleasure that we experience here below will ultimately be resolved; in Paradise, pleasure will be unalloyed.[23]

Through the introduction of otherworldly considerations, al-Sulami's system comes to resemble that of al-Ghazali. Since the intuitive sense of the hierarchy of benefits and harms shared by all humans applies only to the pleasures and pains of this world, its judgments can be completely overturned by considerations of otherworldly benefit; the pleasures of the next life are so utterly incommensurate with those of this world as to outbalance them completely. Unlike worldly benefits, which can be known intellectually, otherworldly benefits can be known only through the techniques of fiqh. All people strive for pleasures and joys and attempt to avoid pains and sorrows, but they differ in the rank of the pleasures they pursue. The highest rank is that of those spiritual adepts who seek the pleasure of mystical states in this world and of the beatific vision in the next. Below them are those who seek the conventional pleasures of Paradise in the world to come, and at the bottom are those who seek exclusively the pleasures of this world.[24] Ultimately, the hierarchical ranking of pleasures demands that even in a system based, like al-Sulami's, on the pleasure principle, worldly pleasures must often be forgone. In the end, the juristic principle of maslaha and the Sufi ideal of taming the appetites of the lower soul are brought into harmony.

A similar synthesis of worldly benefit and spiritual self-refinement is suggested by the famously independent Hanbali jurist Ibn Taymiyya in a fatwa on the permissibility of playing chess. Ibn Taymiyya's relationship to Sufism is, at first glance, very different from those of al-Ghazali and al-Sulami. While al-Ghazali is famous for his affirmation of a moderate Sufi path as an integral component of normative Sunni practice and al-Sulami is known to have practiced mysticism under the direction of more than one of the most prominent Sufi masters of his day,[25] Ibn Taymiyya is known as a stern opponent of what he perceived as the deviations and exaggerations of many contemporary Sufis. However, Ibn Taymiyya also affirmed central Sufi terminology and ideals and sought to integrate them into his construction of the law.[26] In this legal opinion, Ibn Taymiyya bases himself on the theory of the "objectives of the shari'a" (*maqasid al-shari'a*), which holds that the rationales for the individual provisions of the law are grounded in the preservation of believers' religion, life, intellect, offspring, and wealth. For Ibn Taymiyya,[27] the fundamental values preserved by the shari'a are ranked in a strict hierarchy. The preservation of life, wealth, and progeny are not independent and equivalent values but subordinate means to the single absolute end served by the shari'a, the cultivation of a right attitude toward one's Creator. Ibn Taymiyya writes,

> The interests of physical well-being take precedence over the interests of financial well-being; the interests of spiritual well-being (lit., "the well-being of the heart," *maslahat al-qalb*) take precedence over the interests of physical well-being. Wealth is sacrosanct only because it is the source of physical subsistence.[28]

The culmination of the hierarchy of values protected by the shari'a is the worship of God; as God states in the Qur'an, "I have created humans and jinn only to worship Me" (verse 51:56). "The worship of God," Ibn Taymiyya argues, "comprises the knowledge and love of God and obedience to Him; what is more, it comprises everything that He loves and approves"—presumably, then, all of the shari'a.[29] The locus of all of these values, according to Ibn Taymiyya, is the heart. It is in the heart that knowledge, love, and fear of God are found; it is with the heart that one repents, places one's trust in God, and sincerely consents to His decrees. Thus, it is the well-being of the heart that takes precedence over all other considerations in a true understanding of the objectives of God's law. All of the virtues associated with the heart are comprised within the concept of the "remembrance of God" (*dhikr allah*).

Ibn Taymiyya's ranking of the objectives of the divine law has concrete implications for his legal reasoning. The points just discussed are drawn from a legal opinion (fatwa) on the permissibility or prohibition of the game of chess, and they play a decisive role in the jurist's conclusions about the shar'i status of the game. In keeping with his observation that most jurists focus overwhelmingly on the believer's physical and financial welfare, Ibn Taymiyya notes that many scholars assume the prohibition of chess to be contingent on its use as an occasion of gambling. He himself, however, sees a deeper and more compelling rationale for its proscription. Chess is forbidden because of its uniquely absorbing character, which engrosses the player in strategy to the exclusion of all other awareness—including the awareness of God.[30] As in the case of al-Sulami, we here see a synthesis of technical legal reasoning with an emphasis on spiritual consciousness, *dhikr*, more commonly associated with Sufi discourse.

Although interesting, Ibn Taymiyya's synthesis seems to function primarily in the limited context of evaluating the shar'i status of a pastime absorbing enough to detract from the believer's consciousness of God. It is significant that he is willing to use the objective of dhikr as a generative principle underlying a concrete legal ruling (the prohibition of chess), but he does not seem to use it as a foundational axiom consistently informing his understanding of the shari'a as a whole. For a comprehensive synthesis of the juristic concept of maslaha with the Sufi ideal of renunciation, we must turn to one of the most original legal thinkers of the Islamic Andalus, Abu Ishaq al-Shatibi (d. 1388). Al-Shatibi's legal writing seems to have been motivated in part by his disapproval of Sufi influences on the interpretation of the shari'a. Wael Hallaq has compellingly argued that in al-Shatibi's works of legal theory, "the main thrust of his theoretical exposition is directed at the mystics of his time, who . . . were a powerful force advocating, *inter alia*, what he thought to be a rigid and unduly demanding application of the law."[31] Indeed, one charge against him was of active enmity toward the Sufis.[32] Nevertheless, al-Shatibi's understanding of the objectives of the shari'a is ingeniously contrived to contend that the shari'a disciplines and denies human desires, even while affirming that it functions to serve human welfare.

Al-Shatibi, in fact, begins his discussion with a bold affirmation that the ultimate goal of the shari'a is to free the individual from the dominion of his own desires. "The objective (*maqsad*) of the establishment of the shari'a," he writes in his great work of legal theory, the *Muwafaqat*, "is to free the responsible actor from the bidding of his passions (*ikhraj al-mukallaf min da'iyat hawahu*), so that he may be a servant of God by choice as he is by compulsion."[33] According to al-Shatibi, "There are many pieces of evidence demonstrating this, one of which is the explicit [Qur'anic] text indicating that God's servants were created to serve God and to subject themselves to His commands and prohibitions"—the same verse adduced by Ibn Taymiyya. Negatively, the passions are directly contrasted with obedience to the divine will in many Qur'anic passages. Al-Shatibi concludes that God has established "revelation, that is, the shari'a" and the passions as the two exclusive and opposite options, than which there is no third (*fa-qad hasara'l-amr fi shay'ayn . . . , fa-la thalitha lahuma*). Thus, every time God mentions the passions (*al-hawa*), He condemns them. Al-Shatibi's third argument is that it is evident from experience that following the passions is rarely conducive to human welfare; thus, even peoples without a divine law, such as those living in the periods between the extinction of one religious dispensation and the advent of the next prophet, have agreed in condemning those who are ruled by their passions and restraining them for prudential reasons. Here he is presumably referring to the principles of the various schools of Greek philosophy.[34]

Al-Shatibi proceeds to attempt to demonstrate that divine law is always and inevitably in contradiction to the passions. This is not immediately evident, in that divine law leaves many areas open to the free choice of the individual (the category of *mubah*, permissible or neutral) and frequently commands that which is in any case desirable. In al-Shatibi's view, however, the opposition between divine law and human whim is an essential one, omnipresent even in cases of apparent congruence between the two. First, the juristic categories of "mandatory" and "forbidden" (i.e., absolute command and prohibition) are fundamentally in opposition to choice. Any chance correspondence between the command or prohibition and the fleeting desires of the individual is purely contingent and does not impair the basic fact of submission. It might seem that the intermediate three juristic categories of desirable, undesirable, and neutral leave great play to the preferences and desires of the individual. However, al-Shatibi argues, these categories in fact constrain individual choice as much as absolute command and prohibition; nothing is neutral at the bidding of the individual. "How many a slave of the passions (*sahib hawa*)," he reflects, "wishes that a given neutral action were prohibited, so that if legislation on the point were left up to him he would forbid it . . . !" Someone might even wish that a given action were mandatory today, only to wish it prohibited tomorrow. "Thus," concludes al-Shatibi, "the fact that a neutral action is deemed neutral does not place it unconditionally at the will of the responsible actor (al-mukallaf)."[35]

The theory of the objectives of the law (maqasid), however, raised possible objections to al-Shatibi's argument that the shari'a was inherently inimical to human desires. As a hypothetical opponent argues, the Qur'an explicitly denies that the world was created frivolously or in vain; thus, divine law must be established with some objective. If the shari'a is established with some objective or benefit in view, the benefit must accrue either to God or to His creatures. It is impossible, however, that the shari'a be established in pursuit of God's interests; as a supremely self-sufficient (ghani) being, God cannot possibly have any needs to fulfill. The objectives underlying the shari'a must, thus, pertain to human beings. This being accepted, there must be an underlying correspondence between divine law and the desires of individuals "because every rational being seeks his own interests and that which conforms to his desires (hawahu) in this life and the next, and the shari'a has ensured this objective for them through its obligations; so how can it be denied that the shari'a is established on the basis of humans' desires and the promptings of their passions (aghrad al-'ibad wa-dawa'i ahwa'ihim)?"[36] In other words, how can the shari'a be said systematically to oppose the gratification of human desires if in fact it consistently serves human needs?

"The answer," writes al-Shatibi, "is that even if it is accepted that the shari'a is established for the interests (masalih) of human beings, it is incumbent upon them on the basis of the command of the Divine Legislator, and according to the limits He has imposed, not on the basis of their passions and desires. For this reason, the obligations of divine law are burdensome to people (thaqila 'ala 'l-nufus); perception (al-hiss), custom and experience all attest to this." Any action that is performed merely in conformity with one's passions, without reference to its being commanded, prohibited, or left to the discretion of the individual, is inherently void (batil bi-itlaq); because every act must have a motivation and a rationale, and if obedience to the Divine Legislator has no part in it, it is nothing but conformity to passion and desire. Any such action is completely void because it is completely in contradiction to the Right (al-haqq). As for actions of worship, it is obvious that they are void. As for profane actions (al-'adat), they are null with respect to the lack of any merit or divine reward (thawab) accruing on the basis of the command or prohibition; in this respect, their performance or nonperformance is equal.[37] Only if one performs a given action with a view to its being commanded, prohibited, or left to one's discretion in the shariʿa, according to al-Shatibi, has one performed it in the requisite manner. If the two motives (of personal desire and submission to the divine law) are commingled, the act is rewarded or nullified according to the motive that predominates.[38]

The objectives (*maqasid*) of the shariʿa are divided into two categories: fundamental (*asliya*) and secondary/subordinate (*tabiʿa*). The fundamental objectives are those in which the acting individual has no share (*la hazz fiha li'l-mukallaf*)— that is, there is no room for personal choice with respect to them; they are universal and unchanging. In all times and all societies, they comprise the preservation of religion, life, intellect, offspring, and wealth. As becomes clear from the later parts of al-Shatibi's discussion, individuals also lack a "share" in the fundamental objectives in the sense that they derive no immediate personal benefit from their performance. Religious obligations such as prayer and almsgiving fall into this category; they are intrinsic elements of the fundamental objective of preservation of religion and yield no immediate gain to those who perform them.[39] Some of the fundamental objectives of divine law are individual duties (*ʿayniya*), and others are incumbent on the community as a whole and can be performed by any individual on behalf of the group (*kifaʾiya*). Al-Shatibi seeks to demonstrate that the individuals who perform such communal duties have no "share" (hazz) in them by pointing to the fact that it is universally considered improper for public servants to seek personal gain from the performance of their functions; judges may not demand money for their rulings, nor may jurists for their legal opinions.[40]

In contrast to these fundamental duties, the secondary duties do yield immediate benefits to those who perform them; in al-Shatibi's terminology, the individual has a "share" in them. These subordinate duties are the means to the ultimate ends of preserving religion, life, intellect, offspring, and wealth. God in His wisdom has created human nature such that the intermediate actions leading to the ultimate objectives of the law are inherently gratifying. Eating, drinking, sexual congress, and other such actions yield immediate benefits of comfort and pleasure that serve as powerful incentives to their performance.[41]

In cases where the human constitution naturally inclines toward the satisfaction of a given urge, the divinely implanted drives ordinarily guarantee that the necessary actions will be performed. For instance, human beings naturally crave the satisfaction of their sexual and nutritional needs. Thus, there is no need for stringent

divine commandments enjoining procreation or eating. These and other actions
are merely recommended, rather than commanded, by the divine law.[42] The less
direct the personal gratification derived from a given action, the more need there is
for strong commands dictating its performance. When a desirable action or omis-
sion actually conflicts with humans' inborn desires, the relevant commandments
and prohibitions are particularly rigorous. The same is true of those actions, like
prayer and other acts of worship, in which the actor has no personal "share." (Al-
Shatibi acknowledges that people may derive various kinds of personal gratification
from performing their religious duties, but none of them are inherent or desirable objectives of the divine commands.[43]) Hence, command and prohibition are
always present in inverse proportion to the gratification of the individual's desires.
Where no immediate personal benefit is to be hoped, commandments are stringent and rewards abundant; actions yielding direct gratification, in contrast, are in
general neither rigidly commanded nor richly rewarded.

However, even actions yielding immediate benefit can be raised to the level of
disinterested obedience to command. It is possible, al-Shatibi argues, to perform
such actions *as if* one had no personal interest in their performance. Even if an
act is both personally gratifying and neutral in the eyes of divine law, it can be
performed purely for the sake of God. One can achieve this, al-Shatibi states, by
"receiving permission [to perform a given act] on the basis that that which is permitted is a gift from God to His servant." Then "it is divested of personal interest"
and becomes "just as if he obeys a demand without considering anything else."[44]
An example of this is would be an action, like engaging in trade, that benefits the
actor financially. If he is sufficiently detached from the benefit deriving from his
action, he will treat it as if he is no more entitled to its fruits than any other human
being. He will be like the overseer of the public treasury, administering wealth on
behalf of the community. Thus, many pious people have pursued crafts and trades
with great material success, only to distribute their wealth to all needy persons
without privileging themselves.[45]

At this point, al-Shatibi comes full circle to his original argument: The ultimate
objective of divine law is to release the individual from the promptings of his passions so that he can be a true servant ('abd) of God. Although one does, in fact,
benefit from the performance of many of the requirements of the shari'a, it is thus
necessary to perform them as if one had no share (hazz) in their fruits. By disci-
plining one's motivations so that each action, no matter how personally beneficial,
is performed purely because it is commanded or allowed by God, each action will
in effect be equivalent to an act of worship ('ibada).

Conclusion

The shari'a is widely understood as sacred law, a characterization that would be accepted by many Muslims. Nevertheless, as we have seen, both halves of this characterization are subject to qualification and debate. Although the shari'a is certainly law in the sense that it offers authoritative norms for the behavior of individuals and society, it is not always coextensive with law in the modern sense. Its relationship with the state is variable and complex, and it often coexists with alternative (essentially secular) jurisdictions. Perhaps more surprisingly, it holds a complex and negotiable place in evolving Islamic constructions of the sacred. The cases examined here, where the role of the shari'a is critiqued or reframed in terms of Sufi ideals, indicate that alternative constructions of the sacred deeply influenced even serious and renowned legal thinkers.

Notes

1. Bernard Lewis, *The Political Language of Islam* (Chicago: University of Chicago Press, 1988), 28.

2. Sayyid Qutb, *In the Shade of the Qur'an*, trans. and ed. M. A. Salahi and A. A. Shamis (Leicester: Islamic Foundation, 1999), vol. 1, 249.

3. In his study *Religion and Politics under the 'Abbasids* (Leiden: Brill, 1997), Muhammad Qasim Zaman argues that the relationship between the dynasty and the 'ulama' was characterized more by patronage and collaboration than by conflict.

4. As Patricia Crone has noted, although al-Ghazali assigned a pivotal role to the de facto holders of military and political power, "the power they exercised had no positive moral meaning in itself." See Crone, *God's Rule* (New York: Columbia University Press, 1994), 247.

5. Ibid., 248.

6. Ibid., 249.

7. Ibn Khaldun, *Muqaddimat Ibn Khaldun*, ed. E. M. Quatremere (Beirut: Maktabat Lubnan, 1970), vol. 2, 30–31.

8. V. Minorsky, "The Aq-Qoyunlu and Land Reforms," *Bulletin of the School of Oriental and African Studies* 17 (1955), 450.

9. Bernard Lewis, "Siyasa," in *In Quest of an Islamic Humanism: Arabic and Islamic Studies in Memory of Mohamad al-Nowaihi*, ed. A. H. Green (Cairo: American University in Cairo Press, 1984), 9.

10. Frank Vogel, *Islamic Law and Legal System* (Leiden: Brill, 2000), 202.

11. Ibid., 205–206.

12. See, for instance, Wael Hallaq, *Authority, Continuity, and Change in Islamic Law* (Cambridge: Cambridge University Press, 2001), chap. 6; David S. Powers, *Law, Society, and Culture in the Maghrib, 1300–1500* (Cambridge: Cambridge University Press, 2002).

13. Al-Ghazali, *Ihya' 'ulum al-din* (Beirut: Dar al-Fikr, 1414 A.H. / 1994 C.E.), vol. 1, 28–29.

14. Ibid., vol. 1, 29.

15. Ibid., vol. 1, 30.

16. Ibid., vol. 4, 230–231.

17. Ibid., vol. 1, 31.

18. Ibid., vol. 1, 32.

19. Wael B. Hallaq, *A History of Islamic Legal Theories* (Cambridge: Cambridge University Press, 1997), 182.

20. 'Izz al-Din ibn 'Abd al-Salam, *Qawa'id al-ahkam fi masalih al-anam* (Cairo: Maktabat al-Kulliyyat al-Azhariya, 1388 A.H. / 1968 C.E.), vol. 1, 11–12.

21. Ibid., 7.

22. Ibid., 5.

23. Ibid., 8.

24. Ibid., 11–12.

25. See *Encyclopaedia of Islam*, new ed. (Leiden: Brill, 1960-), s.v. "Sulami, 'Izz al-Din."

26. For a collection of selections from the work of Ibn Taymiyya relating to matters of Sufism and law, see Ibn Taymiyya, *Fiqh al-tasawwuf*, ed. Zuhayr al-Kubra (Beirut: Dar al-Fikr al-'Arabi, 1993).

27. Taqi al-Din Ahmad ibn 'Abd al-Halim Ibn Taymiyya, *al-Fatawa al-kubra*, ed. As'ad Sayyid Ahmad (Cairo: Maktabat Dar al-'Uruba, n.d.), vol. 2, 17–18.

28. Ibid., vol. 2, 17.

29. Ibid., vol. 2, 18.

30. Ibid., vol. 2, 10, 14–15.

31. Hallaq, *History*, 163.

32. Ibid., 163.

33. Ibrahim ibn Musa al-Lakhmi al-Shatibi, *al-Muwafaqat*, ed. Abu 'Ubayda Mashhur ibn Hasan Al Sulayman (al-Khubar: Dar Ibn 'Affan, 1417 A.H. / 1997 C.E.), vol. 2, 289.

34. Ibid., vol. 2, 290–292.

35. Ibid., vol. 2, 292–293.

36. Ibid., vol. 2, 293–294.

37. Ibid., vol. 2, 294–296.

38. Ibid., vol. 2, 296–297.

39. Ibid., vol. 2, 300, 305.

40. Ibid., vol. 2, 300–302.

41. Ibid., vol. 2, 302–303.

42. Ibid., vol. 2, 305–306.

43. Ibid., vol. 2, 309.

44. Ibid., vol. 2, 314.

45. Ibid., vol. 2, 315–316.

Our Papalist Supreme Court: Is Reformation Thinkable (or Possible)?

SANFORD LEVINSON

On the Phenomenon of Constitution Worship and Institutional Authority

This chapter is part of a series of reflections delivered at Amherst College on the common theme "law and the sacred." This conjunction obviously generates multiple meanings. One of them is to counterpoise a basically secular legal system against a quite different realm of social life that we call "the sacred." There is good reason to be interested in how the American legal system has dealt with claims made by its religiously observant members on behalf of what they regard as such "sacred" dimensions of life. Doctrinally, this issue has often been posed by way of interpreting the Free Exercise Clause of the First Amendment in the context of religious practices that deviate from ordinary morality, standard examples being bigamy or drug use.[1] However, this question, whatever its obvious interest, is not the topic of this chapter.

Instead, I return to an earlier work of mine, *Constitutional Faith*,[2] in which I view the law itself as possessing some elements that we often identify with "the sacred." Thus, I suggested that American culture, particularly in its political dimensions, could be understood in significant part as being constituted by a "civil religion" whose components itself took on sacralized dimensions. This is, I believe, especially true of the U.S. Constitution, which is (too) often treated as a holy text. Moreover, I argued that one could gain illumination into enduring controversies about the U.S. Constitution by placing them within the context of traditional issues that arise in the study (and practice) of conventional sectarian religions.

Consider, for example, the implications of James Madison's desire that Americans would grow to "venerate" the Constitution rather than spend much, if any, time rationally reflecting on its strengths and weaknesses, the latter of which might be sufficiently serious to require radical amendment.[3] "Some men look at constitutions," wrote Thomas Jefferson in 1816, "with sanctimonious reverence and deem them, like the ark of the covenant, too sacred to be touched."[4] I believe that Madison's hope (or Jefferson's implicit fear) is being ever more realized, for Americans seem remarkably uninterested in confronting potential problems with our constitutional system. This excess of veneration sometimes takes on overtones of idolatry, especially when some treat the framers of the Constitutions as godlike figures, in effect immune from ordinary proclivities toward human error. Thus, one of the pernicious consequences of what might be termed Madison's victory is that it has become next to impossible to generate any serious discussion of what I have elsewhere called "constitutional stupidities."[5] Indeed, that very term is taken by some to be almost unpatriotic or, in terminology more relevant to this book's topic, "sacrilegious." I confess that I strongly share Jefferson's distaste for the "sanctimonious reverence" that is directed at what may be a significantly flawed document. One might even be tempted to adopt a Marxist description of the U.S. Constitution as too often joining more conventional religions in serving as "opiate[s] of the people," dulling our intellectual senses and discouraging much-needed confrontations with the actual circumstances of our lives.

I believe, for example, that a partial explanation for Americans' quite remarkable esteem for their presidents is the fact that the Constitution makes the president the head of state—the semiotic equivalent of monarchs in other political systems and not only what Ross Perot might label the "chief employee" of the people, subject to the criticism any employee might receive from a disgruntled employer. "For all their genius," British writer Geoffrey Wheatcroft has written, "the American founding fathers made a grave error in combining the office of head of government and head of state. Visiting Washington over many years, I have always been taken aback by the sheer reverence shown to the president—head of state of a great country but still a mere politician."[6] Moreover, the allocation by the Constitution to presidents of fixed terms of office serves to make literally unthinkable the prospect of replacing a manifestly deficient president in midterm through ordinary political processes (rather than the Sturm und Drang of impeachment). Thus, the Constitution itself doubly encourages a psychology of viewing presidents as wise father—or in the future, wise mother—figures, especially when times are genuinely threatening and all of us need reassurance that we will in fact be protected from monsters. Far from serving as a genuine mechanism for vigorous self-government, the Constitution in some ways serves to generate mass infantilization.

However, the major focus of *Constitutional Faith* is altogether predictable fault lines that are present even—or perhaps *especially*—among those who profess to venerate the Constitution and proclaim our good fortune in having it as the foundation stone of our political lives. One of these fault lines involves the very question of what counts as "the Constitution." Is it a particular *text*, found at the National Archives and in any textbook on constitutional law? I describe those who assert this as "protestants" insofar as the foundational claim of some key Protestant reformers was the claim "sola scriptura"; the truths of the Christian religion, that is, are found *only* in Scripture.[7] They were opposing the "catholic" position that Scripture, however important it might be, is significantly supplemented—and some would say supplanted—by the traditions and teachings of those who define themselves as the community of Christians. Similarly, there are constitutional catholics who would insist that the Constitution's text provides, at best, only a starting point for analysis, with the "real" Constitution found as well (and as a matter of fact, more importantly) in our political traditions, including, of course, the practices of our political institutions, including courts, legislatures, and executives, and the deepest values of the general culture as well. This means, among other things, that it is never sufficient to read a single purportedly authoritative text; instead, one has to become learned about a variety of complements to this text that constitute America's own "unwritten Constitution."

There is also an institutional fault line: Protestants were moved to proclaim the primacy of Scripture in part because they were in open revolt against the institutional claims of the Catholic Church to be the authoritative custodian of tradition. One manifestation of this revolt was the proclamation of scriptural primacy; just as important, though, was the institutional claim, especially by the more radical dissenting sects, of "the priesthood of all believers" that assaults the most fundamental of claims to institutional authority made by the Church. Although many Protestant churches, as they organized themselves into new denominations, attempted to stifle the anarchic implications of viewing each believer as equal in authority to interpret Scripture, others to this day remain radically decentralized with regard to the authoritative enunciation of Christian doctrine. Indeed, in what is now sometimes called the "Third Great Awakening" of American society in the past quarter-century, it is the distinctly nonhierarchical evangelical churches that have gained millions of new members, even as the more traditionally organized, formerly "mainstream" churches have become increasingly marginalized.

For what it is worth, the U.S. Supreme Court has seemingly adopted the view that any particular individual must be given a status as authorized interpreter of his or her religious tradition, even if such views as are enunciated might appear highly idiosyncratic to other members of a given group whose tenets are ostensibly being applied.[8] "Intrafaith differences," Chief Justice Burger once reminded us, "are not uncommon among followers of a particular creed, and the judicial process is singularly ill equipped to resolve such differences in relation to the Religion Clauses." It is no part of the Court's function to inquire who among contending participants within a given religious community "more correctly perceived the commands of their common faith. Courts are not arbiters of scriptural interpretation."[9] To put it mildly, this is a profoundly "protestant" notion of religious possibility, giving significant protection to individual idiosyncrasy. We will say later in this chapter that the Court is distinctly less generous to constitutional protestants, where its position turns distinctly catholic.

The Roman Catholic Church, of course, claims to be "the rock" upon which Jesus called for the building of his church and for which he gave Saint Peter the keys. The leaders of the Church are viewed as being in apostolic succession to Jesus and his disciples. The ultimate implication of this is that the propositional content of the Christian religion—assertions as to what it "means"—is constituted by what the Vatican proclaims. This is most dramatically illustrated on those rare occasions when the pope speaks ex cathedra and claims the mantle of infallibility. For a member of the Catholic community, at least from the perspective of the Vatican itself, it becomes logically impossible to say that "the pope has made a mistake" because the very baseline constituting religious truth is just what the pope proclaims. But the Vatican makes almost as powerful claims in behalf of the teaching magisterium of the institutional Church. As an empirical reality, it is obvious that millions of Catholics, particularly in Western Europe and the United States, reject a variety of the Vatican's teachings, especially regarding sexual and reproductive behavior. Of course, the Vatican has never in the slightest recognized the legitimacy of treating the teachings of the magisterium as only "suggestive," rather than "authoritative," as to the meaning of Christianity. There is little embrace by the institutional Church of the legitimacy of what the Court termed "intrafaith differences" on such issues as the ordination of women or the legitimacy of the exercise of reproductive choice that includes contraception or abortion.

By now, the constitutional analogy should be obvious: Does one view the U.S. Supreme Court as the institutional fount of constitutional meaning, or can members of a "constitutional faith" community legitimately possess their own views of what the Constitution "really" means? Justice Jackson once wrote of the Court that

"We are not final because we are infallible, but we are infallible only because we are final."[10] Still, whatever may have been Jackson's doubts about judicial infallibility, he expressed none about finality. If, as Charles Evans Hughes once declared, the Constitution is simply what the Supreme Court declares it is,[11] then this makes it analytically difficult even to recognize the notion of judicial error (or fallibility) because the Court is itself "final" when declaring what the Constitution means and, therefore, what counts as legal "truth." To say that the Court made a mistake, however, requires an outside leverage point that enables one to recognize the error in the first place. "Finality," then, might apply only to a given case, definitively indicating who won or lost it, however unjustly, or it might refer far more broadly to establishing a definitive legal norm.

As against an infallible (or even final) institution, one might instead view the Court as simply one body, among many, engaged in dialogue. The judicial conversation is not only intrainstitutional, as exemplified, for example, in the existence of concurring and dissenting opinions to those of the majority, but also extrainstitutional. The Court speaks not only to (or with) other institutional actors in state or national legislatures or executive or judicial offices, but also, and perhaps most important, with a citizenry that itself remains free to reject proffered judicial interpretations in favor of what their own intelligence tells them the Constitution means. This would obviously constitute a far more "protestant" alternative to what is often (correctly) termed "judicial supremacy." In my book, I presented the case for a mixture of doctrinal catholicism—I think it is utterly foolish to define the Constitution only by reference to the canonical text—and institutional protestantism.

With regard to the latter, especially, I tried to link the argument with an American tradition going back at least to such luminaries as Thomas Jefferson and, indeed, James Madison himself, at least as represented in the Kentucky and Virginia Resolutions of 1798 that they authored. Madison is the best evidence for the proposition that "veneration" of the Constitution does not entail that one venerate as well the Supreme Court. Jefferson and Madison, of course, were not alone in their critiques of judicial supremacy. Andrew Jackson, Abraham Lincoln, and Franklin Roosevelt are only the most prominent successor presidents who issued sharp challenges to what might be termed "judicial supremacy" even as they warmly supported the ideal of "constitutional supremacy." It is, of course, the very ability to distinguish these two supremacies that identifies one as an institutional protestant because the catholic position is that "constitutional supremacy" does indeed entail "judicial supremacy."

Even in 1988, when *Constitutional Faith* was published, I readily realized that
my position was a minority one. One reason, I believe, was the fact that opposition
to judicial supremacy had been, at least since the 1950s, identified with the right
wing, not with progressive figures like Jackson, Lincoln, or Roosevelt, and indeed, a
plethora of less known figures who had issued manifestoes against an overweening
Court throughout the first half of the century. The reason for this transformation
is fairly easy to explain: The Warren Court was viewed by most liberals as a vital
agent of needed change, whether with regard to segregated schools, malappor-
tioned legislatures, or making the public schools more hospitable to students who
were not mainstream Christian in their religious identity. It was, indeed, *Brown v.
Board of Education*[12] that generated, three years later, in *Cooper v. Aaron*,[13] the first
self-description by the Court of itself as "ultimate interpreter" of the Constitution.
Cooper asserted, for example, that *Marbury v. Madison*[14] had established the "basic
principle that the federal judiciary is supreme in the exposition of the law, [a]
principle [that] has ever since been respected by this Court and the Country as a
permanent and indispensable feature of our constitutional system."[15]

This reading of *Marbury* is certainly debatable; I believe that scholarly weight is
in favor of a significantly more modest interpretation of *Marbury*.[16] If one is looking
for a Marshallian citation for judicial supremacy, a far better one, I believe, is his 1819
opinion in *McCulloch v. Maryland*,[17] which concerned the constitutionality of the
Second Bank of the United States. There Marshall concludes the first paragraph in
the opinion with the astonishing claim that "by this tribunal alone can the decision
be made. On the Supreme Court of the United States has the constitution of our
country devolved this important duty." Interestingly enough, Marshall cites not a
single case for this proposition, though one might well have thought that *Marbury*
would deserve mention if he in fact believed it stood for the extravagant proposition
he is enunciating (and would later be enunciated in *Cooper*).

But this is a relatively minor cavil. What is truly astonishing about the *Cooper*
opinion is the second assertion about judicial supremacy as "[a] principle [that]
has ever since been respected by . . . the Country as a permanent and indispensable
feature of our constitutional system." To believe this requires that one willfully
ignore the repeated attacks on judicial supremacy mentioned earlier. I have written that "[i]f a student wrote such a statement in a final exam, it would receive a D
at best."[18] Still, one of the things we know about the U.S. Supreme Court is that,
through the power of performative utterance, it can apparently create "historical
truth" out of the same whole cloth that for most Americans it uses to create "legal

truth." It is very hard, for example, for students—and even for some of their professors—to realize that there is no good reason to accept as authoritative the Supreme Court's versions of American history as found in any given opinion. It is not only that they are not trained in the specific skills of the historian; more to the point, judges writing opinions are, first and foremost, skilled lawyer-advocates trying to persuade an audience. Few opinions ever confess to recognizing the stunning uncertainties and ambiguities of the evidentiary record that would make any professional historian cautious indeed before offering the confident and unnuanced assertions regularly found in the pages of the *United States Reports*.

Still, almost no political liberals protested the Court's egregiously misleading statement in *Cooper*, lest they give aid and comfort to even more egregious racist governors like Arkansas's Orville Faubus, who had precipitated the *Cooper* case by attempting to forestall even the most halting of moves toward desegregated schooling in Little Rock. Nor did many liberals challenge similar assertions of "ultimate authority" when they were repeated in 1969 and 1974 in *Powell v. McCormack*[19] and *U.S. v. Nixon*.[20] The Court was seen as "progressive" in its repudiations, respectively, of an attempt, led by conservatives in the House of Representatives, to exclude Harlem Representative Adam Clayton Powell from serving the term of office for which he had been elected and then of Richard Nixon's attempt to forestall discovery by the special prosecutor of crucial Watergate-related tapes by claiming executive privilege. But it is not only these rather exotic decisions, or even necessarily the banner decisions of the Warren Court, that account for the continued wedding of political liberals with the institutional Supreme Court.

U.S. v. Nixon was preceded, the year before, in 1973, by *Roe v. Wade*,[21] in which the Court invalidated laws in almost all of the states that had prohibited or otherwise strictly regulated abortion. If *Brown* was the key judicial decision for the midcentury generation of constitutional thinkers, then, most certainly, *Roe* served to organize much of the debate for the closing quarter-century (and of course, into the new millennium). The Court could rely on liberals to support its assertions of strong judicial supremacy as long as it was viewed as heroically resisting pressure from political conservatives to overrule *Roe*.

This might help to explain why the most important attack on judicial supremacy during the last forty years was delivered in 1986 by Edwin Meese, the attorney general of the United States during the Reagan administration.[22] "It is still the Constitution which is the law," Meese told an audience at Tulane University, "not the decisions of the Court."[23] This recognition of a gap between law and institution constitutes institutional protestantism; for institutional catholics, there can be no gap. Meese's statement elicited from the then-director of the American Civil Liberties Union the accusation that Meese had issued "an invitation to lawlessness," a view reflected in a *New York Times* column by Anthony Lewis describing Meese as "invit[ing] anarchy." Harvard Law School Professor Laurence Tribe said that Meese's position "represents a grave threat to the rule of law because it proposes a regime in which every lawmaker and every government agency becomes a law unto itself, and the civilizing hand of a uniform interpretation of the Constitution crumbles."[24]

Ironically enough—and I shall have more to say about this presently—all of these ringing defenses of judicial supremacy occurred even as the Court was becoming perceptibly more conservative in a variety of areas as a result of the appointments to the Supreme Court by President Reagan of Justices O'Connor and Scalia. (And of course, Anthony Kennedy would replace Lewis Powell the next year, in 1987.) Indeed, from one perspective, it was more than a bit surprising that Meese would choose to attempt to undermine the legitimacy of the Supreme Court just when it was on the verge of being captured by a conservative majority, as indeed occurred during the George H. W. Bush administration with the appointment of Clarence Thomas to replace Thurgood Marshall. (Bush had also replaced William J. Brennan with David Souter, though Souter has turned out far less conservative than he was predicted to be.) As already suggested, I strongly suspect that the easiest explanation for this otherwise odd behavior lies in the politics of abortion.

Liberal support for (and conservative skepticism about) judicial supremacy was seemingly vindicated in this regard when the Court in 1992 issued its decision in *Planned Parenthood v. Casey.*[25] A bitterly divided Court upheld the principle of reproductive liberty enunciated in *Roe*, though there was no genuine agreement by the five-justice majority why this should be so. The most important opinion was thought to be a concurrence issued by Justices O'Connor, Kennedy, and Souter, all, of course, Reagan and Bush appointees. What was truly remarkable about that concurrence is that there was no concession that *Roe* had been rightly decided in the first place. Instead, its central feature was its discussion of the importance of following precedent, which, by definition, means the importance of adhering to what the Supreme Court had earlier said. It was quite literally an authoritarian opinion.

"Precedent" as the Substitution of Court for Constitution

The emphasis on precedent, particularly with regard to constitutional inter-pretation, is perhaps the best example of the triumph of institutional catholicism over its protestant analogue. Precedential decision making can be summarized as the notion that case Y should be decided in accordance with a case X that had resolved similar issues. I could certainly speak at length about the theoretical dif-ficulties of deciding when cases are sufficiently alike to justify the claim that fidelity to precedent requires a particular decision. For now, I am assuming that we can identify the relevant cases and determine that Y is indeed sufficiently like an earlier decided X so that it should be decided similarly *if* we feel bound by precedent at all. But the obvious question is *why* we should feel so bound. The central paradox of the maxim "follow precedent" is that it has its greatest impact when we can all agree that the initial decision was wrong. In such cases, it is *only* the existence of the prior decision that counsels the given result in question. If we look at prior de-cisions and find them intellectually compelling, to adhere to them is *not*, I would argue, the same phenomenological experience of "being bound" by precedent. In the former instance, one has in fact been persuaded by an argument, made at an earlier time, that one believes continues to make great sense at the present time. So if one says that *Roe* is a fine decision that should continue to be followed, that is not really a precedent-based argument inasmuch as one would presumably make the identical argument as to present constitutional meaning even if there were no *Roe* on the books. One does not ordinarily complain of being "fettered" when one in fact has no objection to what one is doing. Instead, as Bentham argued long ago, "The deference that is [ostensibly] due to the determination of former judgments is due not to their wisdom, but [only] to their authority."[26] As Gerald Postema notes, this argument on behalf of precedent echoes the legal positivism of Thomas Hobbes, who had earlier resisted the claim that law is founded in "Rea-son" and instead emphasized that "It is not Wisdom, but Authority that makes a Law."[27] And the particular authority that one is privileging is obviously the judiciary itself.

As if instantiating the position taken by Hobbes, the *Casey* plurality devotes many pages to defending the proposition that "a decision to overrule a prior case should rest on some special reason over and above the belief that a prior case was wrongly decided." Not surprisingly, many readers concluded that at least one of the justices in the plurality *did* believe, like the four dissenting justices in the minority, that *Roe* had been "wrongly decided." According to the plurality, it is better, both most of the time generally and in this case in particular, to maintain adherence to what is recognized as a "wrong" conception of the Constitution than to overrule it in the name of a presumptively "correct" reading. What we see is the negative vindication of Meese's argument inasmuch as it is indeed "the decisions of the Court," rather than "the Constitution," that serve as the template of "law." It is as if the justices had taken their oath to "uphold the decisions of the Supreme Court, except in extreme circumstances," rather than the oath they *do* take, which is to support, protect, and defend the Constitution of the United States.

The plurality self-servingly describes the people of the United States as accepting "the Judiciary as fit to determine what the Nation's law means and to declare what it demands." Such acceptance, generated by a mixture of "substance and perception," constitutes the "legitimacy" of the Supreme Court, the maintenance of which should be one of the central missions of the justices. According to the plurality, the possible perception by the public that the Court was reversing course because of changed political circumstances, such as new justices arriving on the Court representing different political sensibilities from those dominant two decades earlier, would be fatal to the Court's legitimacy. And this in turn would "seriously weaken the Court's capacity to exercise the judicial power and to function as the Supreme Court of a Nation dedicated to the rule of law."[28] But recall that "the judicial power" seems to include the power to offer definitive resolution of highly contentious political issues.

One way of understanding this argument is that the very admission by the Court that it is capable of making mistakes in its interpretations of what the Constitution means would weaken its authority with the mass public. Or to be a bit more charitable to the plurality view, they may be arguing that the public might believe that the basis for a change of the Court's position in the specific instance of abortion was the result not of abstract legal reasoning but, rather, an injudicious capitulation to public pressure brought by critics of *Roe*, who regularly march in Washington and picket the Supreme Court on the anniversary of the decision. The public must be assured, according to the plurality, that the Court is impervious to public pressure of any sort. One of the things this means, of course, is that the very exercise of one's First Amendment right to engage in public demonstrations against the Court serves to entrench the Court in the position it has taken, lest one think that the Court is in any way responsive to public opinion!

It should be obvious that I have all sorts of problems with the approach adopted by the plurality. Far better, I believe, were the two opinions by Justices Blackmun and Stevens that did in fact embrace *Roe*. Or for that matter, also far better, at least in terms of intellectual coherence, were the dissenting opinions by Justice Scalia and Chief Justice Rehnquist that convincingly refuted the argument about the importance of rallying around a Court even if one finds an earlier decision disastrous, as opponents of *Roe* and its successors most certainly do.

None of this stopped a number of liberals from publicly applauding the concurring opinion. In an article originally printed in *The New York Review of Books* as "The Center Holds" and then tellingly reprinted in his book *Freedom's Law: The Moral Reading of the American Constitution* as "*Roe* Was Saved," Ronald Dworkin describes the opinion of O'Connor, Kennedy, and Souter as exemplifying "the traditional constraints lawyers in our tradition have always observed: integrity of principle and respect for precedent."[29] But of course, once one believes that the result was generated by "integrity of principle," respect for precedent seems almost literally beyond the point. But why one should respect precedent, if one views the earlier cases as *violating* principles of constitutional integrity, was left undiscussed.

Ever-Expanding Claims of Judicial Authority

It should, then, occasion little surprise that it would be groups of politically conservative intellectuals who organized symposia with such dramatic—some would say apocalyptic—titles as "Treason in the Courts"[30] and "The End of Democracy? The Judicial Usurpation of Politics."[31] This latter symposium appeared in a leading journal of religious conservatives, and the introduction declared that "[a]gain and again, questions that are properly political are legalized, and even speciously constitutionalized." Indeed, the editors perceived "an entrenched pattern of government by judges that is nothing less than the usurpation of politics," and they even questioned whether "conscientious citizens can [any] longer give moral assent to the existing regime," given such decisions as *Roe* and other decisions that were described as under the sway of a "culture of death." Obviously, most political liberals were appalled by the symposium; more to the point, even many of the authors' conservative allies were put off by the radicalism of the arguments and the potential stripping from the Constitution, at least as interpreted by the Supreme Court, *any* degree of veneration.

It is fair to say that the Supreme Court has remained wholly unrepentant with regard to its claims of interpretive authority. Indeed, *Casey* was succeeded by a spate of opinions reaffirming the Court's supremacy with regard to defining constitutional meaning. Consider, for example, the fate of the Religious Freedom Restoration Act (RFRA), passed in 1993 by an almost unanimous Congress and gladly signed by President Clinton, who, like President Bush before him, had supported the act. Why is it called a "Restoration" Act? The answer is simple: A 1990 case, *Oregon v. Smith*,[32] had held that the Free Exercise Clause of the First Amendment did not protect Native Americans against criminal punishment if they ingested peyote even as part of centuries-old ceremonies that were undoubtedly part of their traditional religious practices. According to the majority opinion, written by Justice Scalia, "neutral" laws of "general application" could be enforced without exception, whatever its burden on religious practices. Only if there was good reason to believe that the law in question was nonneutral in the sense of being passed *to stifle* the practices of a religious group would it be unconstitutional. There was no such evidence here. In a concurring opinion, Justice O'Connor protested the demise of the so-called "compelling interest" test, by which burdens on religious practices required that the state present especially strong justifications for enforcing its policies in such circumstances; astonishingly enough, however, she seemed casually to assume that just such a "compelling interest" was present. She therefore provided no more protection to the particular Native American practice than did her intellectual nemesis Justice Scalia.[33] Other justices did dissent; they would have protected the practice.

The decision was greeted by a storm of criticism, and the result, three years later, was RFRA, which required the presentation of a "compelling interest" whenever the "free exercise of religion is substantially burdened." Congressional power was predicated on its right, under Section 5 of the Fourteenth Amendment, to pass legislation implementing the rights guaranteed by the amendment, which, at least since 1940, have included the state's duty to recognize the right to free exercise of religion.

So the situation was that the Court had held that protection of "free exercise of religion" did not include exemption from otherwise neutral laws of general application. Congress, after conducting copious hearings—and being lobbied by many different groups, ranging from religious organizations to the American Civil Liberties Union—said in effect that the Court was wrong. Passage of RFRA was necessary as a prophylactic measure to safeguard against the possibility of religious oppression. It was, in effect, better to "overprotect" religious liberty, even by stifling what might otherwise be legitimate state activity, than to "underprotect" it by putting heavy burdens on the religious to litigate and to meet difficult burdens of proof whenever threatened by state legislation.

The Supreme Court considered RFRA's constitutionality in 1997 in a case arising in Texas.[34] The city of Boerne, near San Antonio, which is increasingly tourism oriented, refused to allow a Roman Catholic Church to remodel and enlarge its facilities. The city argued that the Church's facility was covered by a local historic-preservation zoning ordinance whose purpose was to maintain the charm of the town and draw ever more visitors. The remodeling, it was thought, would be contrary to these commitments of the overall community. The Church claimed that enforcement of the ordinance burdened its ability to carry out its religious mission and that RFRA required Boerne to allow the remodeling in question. The Court, through Justice Kennedy, almost contemptuously invalidated the congressional statute and, therefore, dismissed the Church's claim to legal protection.

The animating principle behind *Boerne* was that Congress had no independent authority to interpret the Constitution. Whatever the Court had determined to be the reach of the First Amendment was dispositive. Needless to say, *Marbury* was invoked, as were a number of other judicial decisions. It should be obvious, though, that judicial decisions can be authoritative about the extent of judicial power (and the limits of congressional power) *only* if one has already accepted the premises of judicial sovereignty. Someone who is skeptical about this proposition should never find persuasive a declaration by the Court that it is indeed authoritative, regardless of how many decisions it can point to. It would be as if religious Protestants should be expected to accept claims to papal authority within the entire Christian world simply because the pope, backed by the Vatican, reiterates such claims. Rejection of this claim is precisely what constituted the Reformation.

Similar dismissals of any interpretive role for Congress were expressed in later decisions involving both the Americans with Disabilities Act[35] and the Violence Against Women Act.[36] As Professors Robert Post and Reva Siegel have demonstrated,[37] the Court applied a doctrine that was originally developed to restrain its own role in upsetting state practices (i.e., that state practices would generally be tolerated if they passed tests of "minimal rationality," save for special instances) and turned this into a limitation on congressional power as well. That is, only if the Supreme Court would agree that a particular state practice, such as discrimination against the disabled, was unconstitutional would Congress be able to invoke its own authority under the Fourteenth Amendment to bar such discrimination. But, the majority blithely assured its readers, such discrimination was thoroughly "rational" and not otherwise barred by the Constitution; Congress was constitutionally barred from coming to a different conclusion. The Supreme Court treated Congress precisely as then-Cardinal Ratzinger, in his role as head of the Congregation for the Doctrine of the Faith within the Vatican, treated such dissenting Catholic theologians as "Hans Kung, Leonardo Boff, Charles Curran, Matthew Fox and Tissa Balasuriya, all of whose lives and work," according to one reviewer, "he has damaged."[38] Excommunication was not necessary; silencing—and the concomitant ignoring of such views—was sufficient.

Alexander Bickel once wrote that "[v]irtually all important decisions of the Supreme Court are the beginnings of conversations between the Court and the people and their representatives."[39] It should be absolutely clear that the current Court has almost no interest in any such conversations, at least if that implies a genuine dialogue among its participants. Instead, the Court's self-conception is that of the hectoring lecturer thundering out propositions that admiring and attentive students copy down and then regurgitate on exams. Indeed, as New York University professor of law Richard Pildes has shown, the contemporary majority tends to identify a vigorous democratic dialogue and attendant challenges to established institutional practices, such as the two-party "duopoly," with "disorder."[40] The majority of the current Court seems to be suffused with a deep contempt for Congress and, concomitantly, for the political majorities that Congress ostensibly represents, which it appears at times to regard as a barely legitimate part of the American political system.[41]

Bush v. Gore, surely the most significant decision by the Supreme Court in recent years, can be relatively easily understood once one recognizes the justices' mixture of contempt for Congress and their capacious understanding of the extent to which the country relies on the Court to offer definitive resolution of contentious issues rather than leave them to the vagaries of the political process. Perhaps members of the Court were aware of articles published while *Bush v. Gore* was under consideration suggesting that "the closest thing to unanimity is that the American people trust the U.S. Supreme Court more than any other institution to make the final call about how to proceed."[42] To reject this call from the people would itself have threatened the Court's high stature, or so a justice might have thought.

Research conducted prior to the presidential election and then after the Court's decision in *Bush v. Gore* is extremely interesting with regard to the role of the

Court.[43] Gallup poll numbers show that around Labor Day of 2000, 62% of the public approved of the "way the Supreme Court is handling its job" and only 25% disapproved. Interestingly, independent voters were least enthusiastic about the way the Supreme Court was handling its job, with 57% approval.[44] Democrats were in fact most enthusiastic, with a 70% approval rating, as compared to support from only 60% of Republicans. This may lend credence to my colleague Lino Graglia's view[45] that the Court remains, in at least some respects, considerably more liberal than is suggested by legal academics, including myself, who describe the current Court as tending toward "revolution" in its commitment to ideological conservatism.[46] Or it may simply corroborate the suggestion by Stanford Law School Dean Larry Kramer that "for most people approval or not of the Court turns on their perception of *Roe v. Wade*. I think it is difficult to overstate the popular obsession for associating this issue with the Court, as if it were the only thing of moment the Court really does."[47]

Many commentators predicted that the Court's decision handing George W. Bush an office that many of us continue to believe he did not legitimately win would have grave consequences for the Court's legitimacy. From the perspective of five years later, one must concede that such predictions were almost grotesquely incorrect. Even in the month following the decision, the Court's approval ratings dropped only three percentage points (to 59%) after its decision in *Bush v. Gore*, though disapproval ratings jumped from 25% to 34%. Not surprisingly, Republican approval had jumped by a full one-third, from 60% to 80%; presumably only 15% remained sufficiently angry about the Court's commitment to reproductive choice to declare that they "disapproved" of the Court. Democratic support had plunged by a similar rate; now only 42% of Democrats approved of the Court, and 50% disapproved. Independents basically remained stable, going down from 57% approval in September to 54% in January.[48]

By June 2001, the overall approval–disapproval figures were identical to what they had been almost the year before, 62% to 25%. Democrats were clearly learning to live with, if not to love, even the *Bush v. Gore* Court, as 54% then approved; the 50% who had registered disapproval in January were reduced to a mere 32%. Republican enthusiasm had diminished a bit, though it was still a robust 74%. Independents' regard for the Court was at a peak of 59% approval.

Wisconsin Professor Herbert Kritzer, analyzing a similar question involving "confidence" levels in various American institutions, including the Supreme Court,[49] found that the public's "confidence" actually seemed to increase from

2000 to 2001: Whereas only 47% of the public indicated in June 2000 that they had a "great deal" or "quite a lot" of confidence in the Court (as against 49% who had only "some" or "very little"), 50% of the sample polled indicated such levels of confidence in June 2001. (Indeed, even in mid-December of 2000, 49% manifested the highest levels of confidence.) Not surprisingly, Democrats and Republicans responded differently to the Court's decision in *Bush v. Gore*. If, however, the Court was gambling that it could maintain broad public support even while throwing the election to George W. Bush and establishing ever better relations with the congressional Republicans, it was a winning decision. A group of distinguished political scientists, examining the effect of *Bush v. Gore* on the legitimacy of the Supreme Court, found that "support for the Court" was undiminished between 1987–2001 among both whites and African Americans[50] (though the latter throughout the period were less supportive of the Court than were whites). Indeed, they offer as "the conclusions in which we have the greatest confidence" the following:

> (1) the ruling in *Bush v. Gore* did not greatly undermine the legitimacy of the Court, (2) probably because the effect of pre-existing legitimacy on evaluations of the decision was stronger than the effect of evaluations on institutional loyalty, and (3) institutional loyalty predisposed most Americans to view the decision as based on law and therefore legitimate.[51]

Interestingly enough, the Court more recently has lost some of this support, largely, it appears, because of the unhappiness of Republicans with such decisions as *Lawrence v. Texas*, invalidating Texas's antisodomy law; the *Grutter* decision, upholding affirmative action at the University of Michigan Law School; and *Roper v. Simmons*, invalidating the death penalty for persons who committed their crimes while still under eighteen in a decision that cited foreign legal materials.[52] Gallup polls conducted in May and July 2005 indicated significant drops in both approval of and confidence in the Supreme Court across political parties. Thus, while "[i]n September 2004, 57% of Republicans said they approved of the way the Supreme Court was handling its job," that number had dropped to only 44% less than a year later. Approval among independents dropped from 52% to 42%, while Democratic support "showed only a modest decrease among Democrats (44% to 40%)," though, of course, Democrats had begun with a lower level of support. With regard to "confidence" in the Court, a May poll found that only "41% of Americans say they have 'a great deal' or 'quite a lot' of confidence in the Supreme

Court. This result is one of the lowest that Gallup has recorded since the question was first asked in 1973, and it is also lower than last year's rating, when 46% of Americans expressed this level of confidence in the court."[53] A January 2005 Gallup poll found that only "42% of respondents report that they have a great deal or quite a lot of confidence in the U.S. Supreme Court."[54]

None of these polls explicitly asks the public whether it accepts the proposition that the Court indeed possesses a papal-like authority to offer definitive pronouncements about constitutional meaning. It is considerably more radical to reject judicial supremacy than to express a degree of unhappiness with the current Court. No doubt the appointment of John Roberts as Chief Justice contributed to at least a slight redistribution in the degree to which persons are happy with the Court, though one doubts that he will be significantly more conservative than William Rehnquist. One might expect greater redistribution with the confirmation of the very conservative Justice Samuel Alito to replace the more moderately conservative Justice Sandra Day O'Connor. But "unhappiness" does not easily turn into outright rejection, at least for most people. The United States remains, jurisprudentially, a distinctly "catholic" country with regard to the institutional authority of the Court. Though there are certainly liberals who attack the inflated claims of judicial authority, many liberals are wary of appearing to join forces with former House Majority Leader Tom DeLay, who railed against liberal federal judges and suggested that the Congress do whatever it could to clip their power, including threatening impeachment of judges whose decisions it disapproved of.[55] And as the Bush administration appears to wish to minimize any role for the judiciary in checking its conduct of "the global war on terror," most liberals, whatever their relative unhappiness with the Court, are justifiably unwilling to collaborate with the administration in undercutting judicial authority.

Is It Possible to Envision an Institutional "Reformation"?

Given that I have spent the bulk of my scholarly career not only describing the possibility of a "protestant" alternative but also attempting to advocate its merits, I realize far better than before exactly the extent to which I am swimming upstream, risking sounding like a crank if not, indeed, a heretic. Let me then conclude by returning to my title: I presume that I have adequately demonstrated the papalism of the current Supreme Court. But I also asked if "reformation" was either thinkable or possible. One might say that the answer to this first question is obviously yes because you see in front of you someone who continues thinking about a more protestant form of constitutional institutions. And I am not alone. Mark V. Tushnet, for example, in 1999 wrote a book with the vivid title *Taking the Constitution Away from the Courts.*[56] But it appears clear that there is no popular base for a genuine "reformation" with regard to our conception of the Court. Even if it is, as a formal matter, "thinkable," it certainly does not seem possible, given the current shape of American politics. Liberals continue to love the Court because of abortion and its halfhearted willingness to confront some of the more exaggerated claims of the Bush administration to unfettered power in the conduct of the "global war against terrorism." Nonreligious conservatives are presumably thrilled with decisions like *Bush v. Gore* and the Court's willingness to invalidate a variety of nationally imposed regulations on state and local government. Both presumably believe they have more to lose than to gain by engaging in any genuine attack on the Court and its papalist or monarchical pretensions.

And of course, even if conditions were such that a "protestant" movement became genuinely possible, led, perhaps, by Republican populists like DeLay, there remains the awesome question of whether the Constitution itself puts impassable barriers in the way of reform possibilities. Consider, for example, the issue of lifetime tenure on the Court. Two eminent constitutional lawyers picked this as the "stupidest" feature of the Constitution.[57] I have my own candidate for "stupidest," but I certainly agree that life tenure has become indefensible. One can protect "judicial independence" without granting federal judges the possibility of inhabiting their offices for three decades. I would prefer that the United States emulate the practice of many countries around the world in limiting members of their highest constitutional courts to terms of ten or twelve years. Or given the contingent fact that the Supreme Court is composed of nine justices, I would advocate single eighteen-year terms, thus guaranteeing a retirement (and new blood on the Court) every two years.

Almost everyone believes, however, that any such reformation would take a constitutional amendment.[58] Yet Article V makes it next to impossible to amend the Constitution in any important respects, especially with regard to the basic organization of American institutions. What are sometimes termed the "majestic generalities" of the Constitution—including the Bill of Rights and the Fourteenth Amendment—are sufficiently indeterminate to allow changed meaning simply through the appointment of new, ideologically sympathetic judges. The very existence of what I increasingly term the "iron cage" of our constitutional system serves not only to dampen interest in what appear, practically speaking, to be impossible alternatives but also to reinforce a psychology of happy acquiescence to what seems unchangeable.

Are things really as bleak as I suggest? Yale Law School Professor Jack Balkin protests that "[t]he claim that catholicism has won the day is the sort of argument that only a lawyer would make." He claims that "[n]o political scientist worth his or her salt would blithely assume the accuracy of this claim." He points to the mass of evidence presented by political scientists and historians of constitutional development that the Supreme Court has almost never actually been treated as offering definitive interpretations of the Constitution, at least if significant social groups objected to them. It is certainly true that if one looks at the behavior of decision makers in the field, one often finds great differences between "the law" as described in the *United States Reports* and what sociologists of law call "law in action." Standard examples involve such issues as school prayer and police practices involving the rights of those suspected (or even more so, those convicted) of criminal conduct, though one can also obviously point to the continuing resistance to recognizing the rights to reproductive choice ostensibly guaranteed by *Roe* and reaffirmed in *Casey*.

Moreover, as Robert Dahl pointed out many years ago,[59] the Supreme Court is unable to stand in the way of a determined national majority for very long. It will, after all, sooner or later capture control of the presidency and Senate and be able to effectuate "transforming" appointments that modify, if not outright overturn, prior decisions. Indeed, in the *Casey* apostrophe to precedent issued by O'Connor, Kennedy, and Souter, there were significant departures from the actual holding in *Roe v. Wade*, even if they chose not to emphasize that point. So perhaps the lesson should be to watch what the overall political system, including the Supreme Court, actually *does*, not simply what is *said* about its operation.

Indeed, Balkin suggests, "the best analogy to constitutional catholicism is, not surprisingly, the actual history of the Catholic Church itself." The defining characteristic of the reign of Pope Benedict XVI appears to be an almost desperate attempt to recapture control over a Church whose membership behaves in accordance with the values of the surrounding culture, not those articulated by the institutional leadership in Rome. American Catholics are much more likely to be so-called "cafeteria" Catholics, picking and choosing which parts of the Church's teachings to obey and, concomitantly, which parts to ignore. Orthodox Jewish critics of Conservative or Reform Jews often use the same invidious metaphor. (There is no reason to believe that a culinary approach to religion is restricted to the United States.)

The current struggles wracking (and perhaps wrecking) the Catholic Church with regard to sexual abuse can be understood in part as the result of a "protestant" revolt against the current institutional leaders. And it appears increasingly likely that one consequence of this revolt will be not only the resignations or early retirements of a number of leading prelates but also the reconsideration, in due time, of central doctrinal issues and practices, the most obvious of which is the Church's insistence on celibacy and an all-male priesthood. I suspect, though, that it is far easier to contemplate the possibility of "internal" doctrinal changes than, for example, a declaration by the Vatican that the structure of Church governance must be radically transformed in a "democratic" direction. Instead, no doubt, there will be much praise of the pope for recognizing the need for doctrinal changes and emphasis on the adequacy of such centralized control to meet any crises that might arise.

Returning to our consideration of American constitutional practices, perhaps we should distinguish between two different conceptions—one normative and the other descriptive—of protestantism. The normative claim is that the agencies of constitutional interpretation should be significantly pluralized, whether one focuses on the legitimate roles to be played by Congress or the president or, ultimately, on the capacity of ordinary citizens, organized into social movements, to engage in constitutional dialogue. The descriptive claim is that the actual practices of our civil religion are in fact much more decentralized than one would ever gather from reading standard-form civics books or the opinions of the Supreme Court itself, with its own institutional interest in denying the degree of actual pluralization. If that is so, then the normative argument becomes a claim not so much for radical transformation but, rather, for honesty and transparency: We the People should have an accurate understanding of how our institutions actually operate.

Still, this conclusion might be too complacent. To be reminded, as Gerald Rosenberg emphasizes, that the Supreme Court, like the pope, may often be a "hollow hope" with regard to either bringing about or holding back changes in the society at large does not entail that these institutions do not retain some real power whose use can serve (or disserve) the nation. To be told, for example, that the Court will be "ultimately" responsive to new political movements, even if it might take several decades for transformative appointments to have their affect, is certainly cold comfort for the individuals, movements, or institutions that must pay the cost for decisions in the here and now. Some of the Court's most dramatic decisions over the past decade have been more "symbolic" than "real" in their consequences, such as the invalidation of a totally unnecessary federal law prohibiting the possession of a gun near public schools. But some have not, including decisions interpreting, for example, the Americans with Disabilities Act, surely the most important civil rights act passed since the Civil Rights Act of 1964. And of course, no one can deny the material importance of the Court's outrageous decision in *Bush v. Gore* that halted the presidential election process and in effect selected the winner. I assume that similar examples could be offered by Catholics as to decisions by the late John Paul II that "really mattered," in addition to many more that, for better or worse, are principally of symbolic import.

Even if we have a sophisticated understanding of how complex institutions operate, that does not translate into the view that structures of institutional leadership—and the claims made by leaders with regard to their own authority—do not matter at all. There may still be the need for fundamental "reformations" that require not only significant restructurings but also, and just as important, revisions in our very conceptions of the institutions in question. I will be intrigued both to see if any significant political movement makes this a central issue within the United States and, of course, whether the denizens of the U.S. Supreme Court exhibit any more openness to such change than will the Vatican. I will leave it to you to decide whether my skepticism on both points should generate feelings of pleasure or of lamentation.

Notes

1. The canonical citations are *Reynolds v. United States*, 98 U.S. 245 (1878), upholding federal criminalization of Mormon bigamy; *Employment Division, Department of Human Resources of Oregon v. Smith*, 494 U.S. 872 (1990), denying First Amendment protection to the use of peyote as part of the ceremonies of Native American religions.

2. Sanford Levinson, *Constitutional Faith* (Princeton, NJ: Princeton University Press, 1988).

3. See also Sanford Levinson, "'Veneration' and Constitutional Change: James Madison Confronts the Possibility of Constitutional Amendment," *Texas Tech Law Review* 21 (1990), 2443.

4. Quoted in *Constitutional Faith*, 9.

5. See generally William Eskridge and Sanford Levinson, eds., *Constitutional Stupidities, Constitutional Tragedies* (New York: New York University Press, 1998).

6. Geoffrey Wheatcroft, "The Case for Queens and Kings," *New York Times* (June 2, 2002), sect. 4, 19.

In his recent study of the politics of the Civil War era, Mark Neely emphasizes the importance of the fact that Lincoln was entrenched in the White House for four years. "The United States Constitution put the army and navy in the hands of a determined Republican commander-in-chief for four long years. That was the most important fact of political life in the Civil War." Mark E. Neely Jr., *The Union Divided: Political Conflict in the Civil War North* (Cambridge, MA: Harvard University Press, 2002), 195. In that particular case, one might be grateful for America's constitutional rigidity. But to paraphrase Lloyd Bentsen, whether or not we personally knew Lincoln, we know enough to realize that very few of his successors could withstand comparison. Overall, it is not at all clear that the institutional rigidity has served the United States well. Needless to say, there is no systematic study of the issue, and most Americans simply applaud the purported benefits of the fixed-term presidency.

7. I am, of course, emphasizing the more "dissenting" forms of Protestantism, as against, say, the Church of England. Any full analysis of Protestantism would, of course, have to take into account the full variety of approaches toward Scripture, not to mention similar pluralism with regard to questions of institutional authority that will presently be discussed. This being said, I think it is nevertheless accurate to claim that major strains of Protestantism do have the general characteristics that I ascribe to them. Indeed, as occurred during the discussion of the original version of this chapter at Amherst, it may be useful to compare the American constitutional system to a variety of quite nuanced religious possibilities. My use of religious analogies is intended to be heuristic, to spark conversation rather than to end it.

8. See, e.g., *Thomas v. Review Board of the Indiana Employment Security Division*, 450 U.S. 707 (1981).

9. Ibid., 716.

10. *Brown v. Allen*, 344 U.S. 443, 540 (Justice Robert Jackson, concurring).

11. "We are under a Constitution, but the Constitution is what the judges say it is." Charles Evans Hughes, Speech in Elmira, NY, May 3, 1907, in *Addresses and Papers of Charles Evans Hughes* (New York: G. P. Putnam, 1908), 139.

12. 347 U.S. 483 (1954).

13. 358 U.S. 1 (1957).

14. 5 U.S. 137 (1803).

15. 358 U.S. 18.

16. See, e.g., Robert Clinton, *Marbury v. Madison and Judicial Review* (Lawrence: University Press of Kansas, 1989), 5–6; Sylvia Snowiss, *Judicial Review and the Law of the Constitution* (New Haven, CT: Yale University Press, 1990), 65–77, 121–125.

17. 17 U.S. (4 Wheat.) 316 (1819).

18. Robert McCloskey, *The American Supreme Court* (3rd ed., revised by Sanford Levinson) (Chicago: University of Chicago Press, 2000), 241.

19. 395 U.S. 486, 521 (1969), asserting that the Supreme Court is "ultimate interpreter" of the Constitution.

20. 418 U.S. 683, 704 (1974), arguing that "our system of government requires that federal courts . . . interpret the Constitution in a manner at variance with . . . another branch."

21. 410 U.S. 113 (1973).

22. Edwin Meese, "The Law of the Constitution," *Tulane Law Review* 61 (1987), 981.

23. Ibid., 983, quoting Charles Warren, *The Supreme Court in United States History*, vol. 3 (Boston: Little, Brown, 1922), 470–471.

24. All are quoted in *Constitutional Faith*, 40.

25. *Planned Parenthood v. Casey*, 505 U.S. 833 (1992).

26. Jeremy Bentham, *A Comment on the Commentaries [of William Blackstone]*, 196, as quoted in Gerald J. Postema, "Some Roots of Our Notion of Precedent," in Laurence Goldstein, ed., *Precedent in Law* (Oxford: Clarendon Press, 1987), 14. It should be emphasized, incidentally, that Bentham was extremely critical of such authoritarian appeals to precedent.

27. Ibid., 11, quoting Thomas Hobbes in Joseph Cropsey, ed., *A Dialogue Between a Philosopher and a Student of the Common Law* (Chicago: University of Chicago Press, 1971), 55.

28. 505 U.S. at 834.

29. Ronald Dworkin, *Freedom's Law: The Moral Reading of the American Constitution* (Cambridge, MA: Harvard University Press, 1996), 127.

30. See Symposium, "Confounding the Constitution: Treason in the Courts," *The World and I* (March 1990), 357–395. I should note that I have a "liberal" contribution to this symposium, "The Constitution and the Supreme Court," ibid., 380–384, that defends the reaffirmation of *Roe* even as "I largely agree . . . that the [plurality] opinion is extravagant in its claims for judicial authority and that it is foolish, indeed pernicious, to view the Court as anointed with some special powers to resolve fundamental issues like that of abortion." Ibid., 384.

31. Symposium, "The End of Democracy? The Judicial Usurpation of Politics," *First Things* (November 1996), 18–42.

32. *Employment Division, Department of Human Resources of Oregon v. Smith*, 494 U.S. 872 (1990).

33. Ironically enough, had hers been the official "opinion of the Court," RFRA would never have become a political issue, for the whole point of the act was to reestablish the "compelling interest" doctrine that had been repudiated by Justice Scalia's majority opinion. Justice O'Connor did not repudiate it; she simply misapplied it.

34. See *City of Boerne v. Flores*, 521 U.S. 507 (1997).

35. *Board of Trustees of the University of Alabama v. Garrett*, 531 U.S. 356, 365 (2000), referring to "the long-settled principle that it is the responsibility of this Court, not Congress, to define the substance of constitutional guarantees."

36. *United States v. Morrison*, 529 U.S. 598, 616, n. 7 (2000), referring to the "cardinal rule of constitutional law" that "ever since *Marbury* this Court has remained the ultimate expositor of the constitutional text."

37. See Robert C. Post and Reva B. Siegel, "Equal Protection by Law: Federal Anti-discrimination Legislation After *Morrison* and *Kimmel*," *Yale Law Journal* 110 (2000), 441; Post and Siegel, "Protecting the Constitution from the People: Juricentric Restrictions on Section Five Power," *Indiana Law Journal* 78 (2003), 1.

38. See the review of John L. Allen's *Cardinal Ratzinger: The Vatican's Enforcer of the Faith* (New York: Continuum International Publishing Group, 2000) by Adrian Hastings, "The Grand Inquisitor of the Modern Church," *The Tablet*, available at http://www .thetablet.co.uk/cgi-bin/book_review.cgi/past-00007.

39. Alexander M. Bickel, *The Supreme Court and the Idea of Progress* (New York: Harper & Row, 1970), 91. In their 2003 essay, supra note 37, Post and Siegel emphasize the increasingly "juricentric" tone of Supreme Court opinions, by which they mean the Court's claim not only to supremacy in the sense of having the last word but also, and more significantly, to an exclusive authority to interpret the Constitution in a way that leaves other institutions silenced. They make the valuable point that one might continue to support "last-word" notions of judicial supremacy while at the same time expecting the Court to show great respect—and often deference—toward the views of other institutions, particularly if they can make plausible claims to being more democratic. Their use of the term *juricentric* is, of course, quite similar to my use of the term *papalist*, just as their seeming endorsement of a (modest) judicial supremacy suggests that one can articulate notions of "protestantism" that are more institution centered than those found in dissenting sects from which I draw my own use of the term.

40. See Richard H. Pildes, "Democracy and Disorder," in Cass R. Sunstein and Richard A. Epstein, eds., *The Vote: Bush, Gore & the Supreme Court* (Chicago: University of Chicago Press, 2001), 140.

41. It is possible that the majority of the Court has adopted, at least implicitly, a version of "social choice" theory that emphasizes various problems with traditional democratic theory, ranging from empirical theories of "capture" of the legislative process by well-organized special-interest groups that seek to gain access to the coercive powers of the state to gain what economists call illegitimate "rents" from the unorganized majority, to theoretical arguments, associated especially with Kenneth Arrow, as to the "impossibility" of achieving a political process that will in fact reflect something called "majority preferences." There is, to be sure, much to be said on behalf of these criticisms, though a full discussion is well beyond the scope of this chapter. One should recognize, though, that any theory of judicial role almost inevitably contains, whether or not explicitly, conceptions of the political process in terms both of normative ideals and empirical realities. Moreover, the judiciary itself can be subjected to "social choice" analysis. See, e.g., Einer Elhauge, "Does Interest Group Theory Justify More Intrusive Judicial Review?" *Yale Law Journal* 101 (1991), 31.

42. Michael Tackett, "Nation Waits on Supreme Court; Justices Caught at Intersection of Law and Presidential Politics," *Chicago Tribune* (December 12, 2000), 1. Or consider Will Lester, "Americans Split on Recount, Polls Say; Big Majority Trusts Court to Decide Fairly," *New Orleans Times Picayune* (December 12, 2000), 23, emphasizing that public opinion polls were showing that three-quarters of the public believed that the U.S. Supreme Court would decide the case fairly.

43. See Herbert M. Kritzer, "The Impact of *Bush v. Gore* on Public Perceptions and Knowledge of the Supreme Court," *Judicature* 85 (July–August 2001), 32–38 (hereafter "Kritzer"). See also James L. Gibson, Gregory A. Caldeira, and Lester Kenyatta Spence, "The Supreme Court and the U.S. Presidential Election of 2000," *British Journal of Political Science* 33 (2003), 535–536. For older studies of public opinion and the Supreme Court that demonstrate a high level of public support, see, e.g., Roger Handberg and William S. Maddox, "Public Support for the Supreme Court in the 1970s," *American Political Quarterly* 10 (1982), 333, 337, analyzing some explanations of public support for the Court based on national surveys conducted in 1972, 1974, and 1976 by the Center for Political Studies; Richard Lehne and John Reynolds, "The Impact of Judicial Activism on Public Opinion," *American Journal of Political Science* 22 (1978), 896, 897, using the Dolbeare-Hammond study on public support for the Court. I am grateful to Chris Schroeder for bringing these earlier studies to my attention.

44. Kritzer, 38.

45. See Lino Graglia, "The Myth of a Conservative Supreme Court: The October 2000 Term," unpublished manuscript on file with the author (2001). Chris Schroeder aptly comments, however, that

[T]here are actually three conservatisms represented on the Court (sometimes within a single justice): judicial role conservatism (classic judicial restraint); ideological conservatism (aggressive reversal of bad precedents); and Oakeshottian conservatism (continuity with past valued; modest changes better than abrupt). It's the inability of the ideological conservatives to gain a consistent majority that prevents this Court from meeting Graglia's standard [of a truly conservative Supreme Court]. E-mail from Chris Schroeder to Sanford Levinson, September 24, 2001 (on file with the author).

46. See J. M. Balkin and Sanford Levinson, "Understanding the Constitutional Revolution," *Virginia Law Review* 87 (2001), 1045–1109.

47. E-mail from Larry Kramer, Professor of Law, New York University School of Law, to Sanford Levinson, December 13, 2001 (on file with the author).

48. Kritzer, 38, analyzing postelection polls taken between January 10 and 14, 2001.

49. Ibid.

50. Gibson et al., supra note 43, 443. No other racial or ethnic groups appear to have been selected for measurement.

51. Ibid., 555.

52. *Lawrence v. Texas*, 539 U.S. 558 (2003); *Grutter v. Bollinger*, 123 S.Ct. 2325 (2003); *Roper v. Simmons*, 125 S.Ct. 1183 (2005). On the loss of Republican support, Professor Kritzer writes that "[o]ne can speculate on the reason for the drop in confidence among Republicans: Is it due to decisions dealing with issues such as gay rights and affirmative action, or the Court's unwillingness to intervene in the Terri Schiavo case? Is it due to attacks on the courts generally by Republicans and conservative leaders? Unfortunately, it is not possible to pinpoint the reason for this sharp decline." See Herbert Kritzer, "The American Public's Assessment of the Rehnquist Court," *Judicature* 89 (November/December 2005), 168, 171.

53. Joseph Carroll, "Americans' Rating of the U.S. Supreme Court" (September 15, 2005), available at http://poll.gallup.com/content/default.aspx?ci=15331&pg=2.

54. See Herbert Kritzer, supra n. 52. Professor Kritzer examines a full run of public opinion data generated by five different survey sources over the roughly two decades of William Rehnquist's service as Chief Justice. He finds significant variation among the sources, so that "one series might be showing a tendency of increasing support while another is steady or declining." This being said, he notes that the two most recent polls regarding the Supreme Court, conducted in May and June 2005 by the Gallup Organization and the Pew Research Center for the People & the Press, both show "distinctive drops over the last four years." The Pew finding that 57% of its respondents are favorable to the Court "is at the lowest level since it began, falling under 60% for the first time." A late 2004 survey by the National Election Survey, which asks respondents to measure their feelings toward given institutions along a 1–100 range, found that the average among its respondents was 62.5, almost exactly between 67.2 in late 2000 (though most of the poll was conducted before *Bush v. Gore*) and the low of 57.7 in 1980.

55. See Larry Kramer, "Foreword: We the Court," *Harvard Law Review* 115 (2001), 1, 16–74, 90–110, for an important delineation of the difference between "popular constitutionalism," by which the citizenry retains an important role in constitutional interpretation, and "judicial supremacy," which views any interpretive role as delegated entirely to the public's agents in the judiciary. Dean Kramer elaborates his argument in *The People Themselves: Popular Constitutionalism and Judicial Review* (New York: Oxford University Press, 2004).

56. Mark V. Tushnet, *Taking the Constitution Away from the Courts* (Princeton, NJ: Princeton University Press, 2003).

57. See Lewis LaRue, "Neither Force Nor Will," in Eskridge and Levinson, eds., *Constitutional Stupidities, Constitutional Tragedies*, 57–60; L. A. Powe Jr., "Old People and Good Behavior," ibid., 77–80.

58. Though see Sanford Levinson, "Life Tenure and the Supreme Court: What Is to Be Done?" in Roger C. Cramton and Paul D. Carrington, eds., *Reforming the Court: Term Limits for Supreme Court Justices*, 375–383 (Durham, NC: Carolina Academic Press, 2005).

59. Robert Dahl, "Decisionmaking in a Democracy: The Supreme Court as a National Policy-Maker," *Journal of Public Law* 6 (1957), 279.

The Ethos of Sovereignty

WILLIAM E. CONNOLLY

The Gang of Five

I often vote for candidates from the Democratic Party. I note this fact to mark a defining feature of politics in a democratic state. Democratic politics requires partisanship. Does it also depend on judicial access to an impartial standard, procedure, or constitution through which to regulate partisanship? The answer is complex. The public authority of democratic constitutionalism cannot be sufficiently established by fidelity to a written text alone, even if citizens confess loyalty to that constitution. It cannot, (1) because a Constitution consists of words whose meanings are not definitively fixed or settled even when initially composed; (2) because those words must later be applied in new and unforeseen circumstances; and (3) because the spirit through which the text is interpreted will give priority to a democratic ethos if it is to be a regime of constitutional democracy. If judicial authorities in a demo-constitutional state override these three considerations too often or too seriously, trust in the wisdom of judicial decisions becomes corroded.

Knowing this much, you will not be surprised to learn how outraged I was over the handling of the recount issues during the presidential election of 2000 by the Florida secretary of state, the governor, the state legislature, the Bush campaign, the hired Republican guns who intimidated the recount commission in one district, and above all, the Gang of Five Republicans on the Supreme Court who stopped the recount process before Bush's razor-thin lead could be placed in jeopardy by a recount. I did not expect the parties to this contest to rise above partisanship in the sense of applying a neutral or objective standard wholly independent of it. I doubt such a place to rise exists. I expected the majority of the Supreme Court to fold partisanship for the integrity of democratic elections into its interpretation of the porous words of the law and the Constitution, using those considerations to chasten partisanship for the candidate it favored. In this instance, however, the Gang of Five justices first jumped headlong into a situation they could have avoided or entered hesitantly and then halted the vote counting authoritatively. They allowed Republican Party partisanship to override partisanship for democracy in a setting where the applicable principles and laws provided ample room for maneuver. That electoral partisanship reduced public confidence in the Supreme Court and eroded bonds of trust between partisans upon which the legitimacy of demo-constitutionalism depends.

Most of the Gang of Five present themselves as "strict constructionists." This allows them to claim that no partisanship is involved in their decisions. But the doctrine of strict constructionism received a body blow from their action. Citizens who had not paid much attention to esoteric debates over the logic of constitutional interpretation now found the doctrine and this decision placed side by side. Its cover was blown. That was mostly to the good. But because strict constructionism retains a more prominent presence in popular discourse about constitutional interpretation than any contending doctrine, its deflation as *the* measure of judicial responsibility exacerbates public cynicism about the gap between judicial pretense and performance.

In the middle of this quagmire, Justice Souter, who had been appointed by a Republican president, emerges as a hero. Here are a few statements from his dissenting opinion:

> If this court had allowed the state to follow the course indicated by the opinions of its own Supreme Court, it is entirely possible that there would ultimately have been no issue requiring our review.
>
> None of the state court interpretations were unreasonable to the point of displacing the legislative enactment quoted. As I will note below, other interpretations were of course possible and some might have been better than those adopted by the Florida court's majority.
>
> The [state legislature's] statute does not define a "legal vote" . . . The State Supreme Court was therefore required to define it, and in doing that the court looked to another election statute . . . which contains a provision that no vote may be disregarded "if there is a clear indication of the intent of the voter as determined by a canvassing board."
>
> The majority might have concluded that "rejection" should refer to machine malfunction . . . There is, however, nothing nonjudicial in the Florida majority's more hospitable reading . . . Whatever people of good will and good sense may argue about the merits of the Florida Court's reading, there is no warrant for saying that it transcends the limits of reasonable statutory interpretation."[1]

Justice Souter acknowledges that the judges found themselves in uncharted territory or at least in considerable legal uncertainty and indeterminacy. His language of "good will," "good sense," and "reasonable statutory interpretation" conveys the sensibility he brings to such moments of uncertainty and indeterminacy. He also expresses a presumptive partiality for democracy when he seeks to allow "the state the opportunity to count all disputed ballots now." When Souter encounters uncertainty in electoral law, he fills it with partisanship in favor of counting every vote.

What does this event teach about the challenge of sovereignty in a demo-constitutional state? What, more closely, is the relation between sovereignty and law in these moments of legal-constitutional uncertainty? What kind of sensibility on the part of judges and ethos on the part of citizens are pertinent to democracy and rule of law in such recurrent circumstances?

The Paradox of Sovereignty

According to theorists from a variety of intellectual traditions, the Florida election case reflects a fundamental paradox at the center of the rule of law in a democratic society. Jean-Jacques Rousseau, Carl Schmitt, Franz Kafka, Paul Ricoeur, Hannah Arendt, Bonnie Honig, Jacques Derrida, Gilles Deleuze, and Giorgio Agamben, although they disagree on numerous other issues, concur in asserting that a democratic state that seeks to honor the rule of law is also one in which a sovereign power both inside and above the law is also brought into play. Because the paradox of sovereignty expresses the lawlessness upon which the rule of law depends, it is often obscured or hidden from public view. The doctrine of strict constructionism is merely one of the means by which this dicey condition is obscured. Often the paradox of sovereignty is asserted with respect to the founding of a state, but almost always those who acknowledge a paradox of founding discern its echoes and reverberations in law and politics later as well.[2] Rousseau, perhaps the key founder of modern democratic theory, puts the paradox this way:

> In order for an emerging people to appreciate the healthy maxims of politics and follow the fundamental rules of statecraft, the effect would have to become the cause; the social spirit which should be the result of the institution would have to preside over the founding of the institution itself; and men would have to be prior to the laws what they ought to become by means of laws.[3]

For a government of self-rule through law to come into being out of a nondem-ocratic condition, "effect would have to become cause." That is, the social ethos needed to nourish democratic rule requires the right kind of laws already there to nourish it, and good laws cannot come into being unless they are preceded by that ethos. Rousseau resolved the paradox of democratic founding through recourse to the fiction of a wise legislator above the law who imbues people with the ethos of self-rule even before good laws are legislated by them. But he knew this fiction was insufficient to the actuality of people already set in history. Moreover, even before Wittgenstein's account of how every rule and law encounter uncertainty and indeterminacy as they bump into new and unforeseen circumstances, Rous-seau understood that issue too. He knew that the paradox of founding returns as a recurring paradox of democratic governance. His response to its appearance after the founding is to engineer a founding that reduces the future arrival of new and unforeseen things to a minimum. It is to imagine a world where time moves very slowly and a homogeneous culture is already there. Hence his portrayal of the kind of place where self-rule through law is possible: a small, isolated polity; a simple, common public faith; a highly unified educational system; yearly festivals and rituals in which all citizens participate; the regulation of theater; a common mode of dress for adults that discourages amorous relations with people from other countries; tight rules of chastity to regulate the passions; a nuclear family in which the male is supreme; the minimization of commerce; its close regulation with parties outside the polity; a society of self-subsistent farms; severe limits on economic inequality; a citizen militia to which all adults were susceptible; and so on and on. The point of these institutions, disciplines, prohibitions, and injunc-tions is to install the same sentiments, habits, and self-restraints in the citizenry, to create an ethos of commonality. Self-rule, he thought, is circular: Its conditions of possibility require the habitualization of citizens to a set of common sentiments that they then express as their own will.

Rousseau could offer a good account of strict constructionism. He might say that while it is represented by advocates as the correct way to read the constitu-tion impartially, it actually functions to cover up the paradox of sovereignty and to instill within the populace sentiments and dispositions oriented to readings the cultural right already invests in the constitution. Strict constructionism juridical-izes the ruse Rousseau invested in the wise legislator. "It is this sublime reason, which rises above the grasp of common men, whose decisions the legislator places in the mouths of the immortals in order to convince by divine authority those who cannot be moved by human prudence."[4] Replace "the legislator places in the mouths of the immortals" with "the judges infuse into the words of an immortal text," and you dissect the political formula of strict constructionism.

Perhaps no democrat has plumbed the paradox of sovereignty as deeply as Rousseau. He is wise to negotiate its terms rather than to simply transcend them. And his understanding that an ethos must be infused into people if self-rule through law is to flourish has stood the test of numerous attempts to dissolve the paradox of sovereignty into a transcendental equation between law and morality or proceduralism or narrow renderings of a social contract. To negotiate the paradox is to come to terms somehow with the indispensability of a positive ethos to democratic politics, law, and sovereignty. But for all that, the particular ethos Rousseau supports is too out of touch with defining features of the contemporary condition to pass muster today. His response demands a small, isolated polity crawling at a snail's pace through time, while we live in large states, closely woven into a global network of interdependencies, moving at a rapid pace. Rousseau helps us to discern the issue but not to negotiate a response through which democracy, law, and sovereignty speak affirmatively to each other in a fast-paced world. He does, however, help us see why so many erstwhile democrats tilt against the rapid windmill of time today and how nostalgia for a slow world that has been lost can so easily be hitched to a contemporary politics of democratic fundamentalism.

Before pursuing a response to the paradox of sovereignty that speaks to the contemporary condition, let's review, albeit briefly, a perspective that seeks to transcend the paradox itself. Immanuel Kant contends that it is incumbent upon us to act *as if* the law of the state and the universal moral law will progressively move into closer congruence as history proceeds. The integrity of morality itself requires this faith or "hope," even if the empirical course of history suggests otherwise. The hope is that the arrival of an ethical commonwealth will someday allow the coercive state to wither away, and a condition will emerge in which the commands of the moral law, the dictates of legislated law, and the hearts of the citizens will converge. But Kant also contends that while this hope is central to the integrity of morality itself, the actual discrepancy between the dictates of order and the tendencies of people to override them requires a strong operational presumption in favor of obeying the official sovereign. He appeals to the sovereign, in this case the king, not for wide freedom of citizen action but for wide freedom of thought among

highly educated subjects. It is through this latter freedom and publicity that enlightenment might gradually flow from Kantian philosophers into a moral ethos
of public life and the sensibility of the legal sovereign. Reading between the lines,
you could say that, for Kant, sovereignty in the largest sense circulates between
the ruler, the universal dictates of morality, philosophers who ground morality in
reason, and the people (who have the kernel of the moral law inside them), while
positional sovereignty is reserved for the ruler. Kant "hopes" freedom of thought
will gradually make the moral law clearer to the positional sovereign and that,
by this means, it will more fully be expressed in public laws and the will of the
people.[5]

Translated into contemporary terms, the Kantian treatment of morality as a law
you are obligated to obey provides the supplement through which to respond to
uncertainties in the logic of sovereignty. To draw on the moral law in making sovereign decisions of state would be to supplement the incompleteness of common
constitutional understandings with the certainty of universal moral directives.

Kant does not, however, actually resolve the paradox. Rather, he projects a
hope that it might become resolved in the indefinite future. And that hope reflects
a fundamental assumption about morality that Kant took to be undeniable and
universal. If this latter assumption is called into question—that is, if it is shown
to be deeply contestable—the Kantian hope must also be reconsidered. How do
we *know* that morality and law have the same basic *form*? How do we know that
both find expression as laws making a claim to acceptance and obedience upon the
subjects who receive them?

Kant agreed that we indeed do not *know*, by argument alone, that morality necessarily takes the form of a universal law you are obligated to obey. He contended,
rather, that this idea of morality is something every ordinary individual recognizes
apodictically, prior to argument about whether this or that rule is actually moral.
Here is how he articulates the very linchpin of his moral philosophy:

> For whatever needs to draw the evidence of its reality from experience must depend
> for the ground of its possibility on principles of experience; by its very notion, how-
> ever, pure yet practical reason cannot be held to be dependent in this way. Moreover,
> the moral law is given, as an apodictically certain fact, as it were of pure reason. Thus
> the objective reality of the moral law can be proved through no deduction, through no
> exertion of the theoretical, speculative, or empirically supported by reason; and even if
> one were willing to renounce its apodictic certainty, it could not be confirmed by any
> experience a posteriori. Nevertheless, it is firmly established of itself.[6]

Kantian morality is anchored in the last instance in the soft belly of apodictic recognition, not the tight order of knowledge, evidence, or argument. The difficulty is that this very recognition is not, in fact, received everywhere by all reasonable people. The lawlike form receives greatest prominence in predominantly Christian cultures, where people have already been culturally inducted into that experience of morality. It loses its "apodictic" force in settings where such a process of induction has not occurred. And in fact, numerous Epicureans, Confucians, Buddhists, Spinozists, Humeans, Nietzscheans, Jamesians, as well as Jewish and Christian mystics, simply do not bestow this shape upon morality as such. These parties embrace a positive ethic of cultivation not grounded in Kantian recognition.[7] While Kantians are tempted to treat such types as morally defective—witness Kant's reactions to Epicurus and Spinoza—those who have been inducted into a non-Kantian image of ethics treat that charge as the attempt to bully us by unethical means to accept a contestable image of morality.

To articulate the point in spatiotemporal terms, within and across numerous territorial states today, people honor a larger plurality of final moral sources than Kant's image of apodictic recognition can accommodate. It is dogmatic on this critical point. Moreover, if and as such a plurality becomes loudly articulated and politically pertinent, it becomes increasingly apparent that Kant and Kantians lack sufficient resources of argument through which to pull everyone into the moral culture they recognize. Only a political monopoly over the institutional resources of cultural induction—including in this country long-term control over the Supreme Court—could promote such an objective.

Today, the Kantian model of morality either must be enforced rigorously by cultural authorities backed by sovereign coercion or it faces diverse minorities within the United States and everywhere else who do not experience morality as law in the first instance. If the coercive strategy is adopted, the Kantian hope for voluntary congruence between law and morality is abrogated. It comes to be experienced by many as an arbitrary imposition rather than a recognition. The Kantian hope to resolve the paradox of sovereignty, under such circumstances, would devolve into a cultural war to induct citizens into a common set of understandings by disciplinary means. The paradox of sovereignty would be repressed rather than resolved. Indeed, the intensification of cultural war in the United States provides one symptom of the paradox and of the refusal by many to come to terms with it openly.

There are other attempts to resolve the paradox. But I suspect that each succumbs to a comparable result. Either the purported resolution buries the paradox beneath a crude doctrine of constitutional neutrality or it leans upon a concept of morality that cannot become universalized without force in a pluralistic world. The paradox must be negotiated rather than resolved or repressed if the democratic element in democratic constitutionalism is to be honored.

The Sacred and Biopolitics

Giorgio Agamben also finds a paradox within sovereignty. He thinks it has become stark in late modernity as the state inserts itself more deeply into biological life—that is, as issues of biology become prominent in state decisions regarding abortion, artificial insemination, the line between life and death, organ transplants, strategies of citizen induction, and standards of "racial" inclusion and exclusion. He also contends that the practice of sovereignty is tied to the sacred. The aura of sovereign authority is sustained through a link to the mystique of the sacred.

The paradox of sovereignty, for Agamben, resides in the fact that the democratic state requires a final authority to resolve questions of law, but the final authority is often insufficiently informed by a law that precedes it. Modern sovereignty carries forward, if implicitly, the pagan logic of *homo sacer*, or the sacred man. *Homo sacer* is "the life that cannot be sacrificed and yet may be killed."[8] It is connected to sovereignty because the "sovereign sphere is the sphere in which it is permitted to kill without committing homicide and without celebrating a sacrifice."[9] The "logic" that binds sovereignty, the sacred, and biopolitics together, Agamben contends, leads (inexorably?) to a state in which a supreme power can annihilate a whole minority in the name of national unity. It is the nexus between the paradox of sovereignty, the sacred, and biopolitics that makes the concentration camp the paradigm of modern politics, with the German Nazi regime expressing its outer limit. If Agamben is right, the emergence of biopolitics propels the paradox of sovereignty beyond a constitutional dispute over an American election into the very logic of the Holocaust.

It is because he finds this logic so compelling that Agamben insists that it must be overcome entirely. Here are two formulations in which he announces that necessity:

> And only if it is possible to think the relation between potentiality and actuality differently—and even to think beyond this relation—will it be possible to think a constituting power wholly released from the sovereign ban. Until [this happens] a political theory free from the aporias of sovereignty remains unthinkable.

> Only if it is possible to think the Being of abandonment beyond every idea of law
> will we have moved out of the paradox of sovereignty toward a politics of freedom from
> every ban.[10]

Nowhere in Agamben's book, however, is a way out actually disclosed. The response of Hannah Arendt—to pull the state out of biopolitics—is considered and appropriately rejected as unviable. But nothing else is offered to replace it. Agamben thus carries us through the conjunction of sovereignty, the sacred, and biopolitics to a historical impasse. His analysis is almost enough to make you return to Rousseau or Kant. However, the value of his analysis resides in its revelation of powerful cultural pressures to cover up the paradox. Some defenders of monistic strategies of resolution may well think a democratic state would fall apart into warring factions if the terms of the paradox were widely disseminated. But as I have already suggested, under contemporary conditions of expansive cultural plurality, to succumb to this temptation is to wage cultural war to return to a past that cannot be recaptured. Perhaps it is possible both to resist the fantasy to return to a past (that never entirely was) and to slip through Agamben's insistence that the paradox must be *overcome*. I want to suggest that although Agamben's analysis is insightful in identifying three critical elements in the paradox and in pointing to dangers that flow from it, the very formalism of his analysis disables the most promising way to negotiate it. To show this, I examine three key elements in his account: the meaning and role of the sacred, the relation between biopolitics and sovereignty, and the "logic" of sovereignty.

The Sacred

Agamben's account of the sacred, drawing its credibility from one quotation written in the early days of the Roman Empire, needs to be revised. I concur that sovereignty and the sacred touch one another historically partly because sovereignty is historically linked to divinity and partly because the very existence of a political regime can turn on the ability to locate one body to resolve key issues of governance. But the sacred is not well defined as the site of that which is both the highest and the most susceptible to annihilation. The sacred is said to deserve awe because it is closest to the divine or at least touches the highest concerns of human existence. Something might be sacred because it is held to represent divinity or be a book that is divinely inspired or be a ruler divinely authorized or be a set of rituals expressive of the highest human relation to the divine. Those who disturb or snub such things are said to be worthy of punishment, or even death, not simply because they touch the sacred but because they do so in a blasphemous way. They translate a divine being into an idol or mock a sacred text or ridicule a beloved priesthood. When Spinoza challenged the faith of the elders in the beleaguered Hebrew community of Amsterdam in the seventeenth century, the elders accused him of defiling their faith. He was cursed and banned. The action fits Agamben's model of one who is "included while being excluded;" but it does not fit that of one who is to be killed without being sacrificed because he forms part of the sacred. Spinoza is banned (included as a pariah through enforced exclusion) because he defiled the sacred. When Ayatollah Khomeini of Iran offered a reward for the execution of Salman Rushdie, the latter became a target of annihilation, again not because he participated in the sacred but because he defiled it. When I call a faction of the Supreme Court the "Gang of Five," some will take that to show lack of awe for a body that stands at the critical point where sovereignty and the sacred touch. I return to this issue later.

Agamben's attempt to fold a double sense into the logic of the sacred should be rejected in favor of the conventional rendering he seeks to overturn. The sacred is that which is to be approached with awe. There might well be ambivalence in people's orientation to the sacred, one they do not themselves acknowledge because of fear of retribution by God or their compatriots. Those most punitive toward others who "defile" what they take to be sacred sometimes themselves harbor such ambivalence. Their punitiveness displaces ambivalence. That is familiar enough. Spinoza, Nietzsche, and Freud, among others, read the punishment of blasphemy in this way. And each became accused of blasphemy because of that very analysis. None says that *homo sacer* is the one who can be killed without being sacrificed.

The issue is important because in a political culture of deep pluralism—a culture in which people honor different existential faiths and final sources of morality and then bring pieces of those faiths with them into the public realm—different images of the sacred repeatedly bump into each other. To construe the sacred in the more conventional way in a culture with the potential to negotiate an ethos of deep pluralism is to pave the way to relax the authority of those who seek to impose their understandings of the sacred upon others who do not confess it. It sets the stage for a more public and active pluralization of the sacred. And perhaps it encourages renegotiation of the ethos of sovereignty in a pluralistic culture. At this point, I merely suggest that a return to the conventional idea of the sacred loosens the nexus between sovereignty and the sacred without eliminating presumptive respect for sovereign decisions.

Biopolitics and Sovereignty

Agamben contends that biopolitics has become intensified today. That intensi-fication translates the paradox of sovereignty into a potential disaster. His analysis seems not so much wrong to me as overly formal. It may reflect the classical liberal and Arendtian assumption that there was a time when politics was restricted to public life and biocultural life was quarantined from politics. According to this picture, the penetration of biology into culture was more or less reserved to private life. In fact, though, every way of life involves the infusion of norms, judgments, and standards into the affective life of participants at both private and public levels. Every way of life is biocultural and biopolitical. Aristotle, Epicurus, Lucretius, Au-gustine, Spinoza, Rousseau, and Hegel, writing during different periods, all appre-ciate the layering of culture into several registers of biological life and the mixing of biology into culture. They treat the biological not as merely the genetic or the fixed but as labile zones of corporeality infused with cultural habits, dispositions, sentiments, and norms.

Biocultural life has become intensified today with advances in the techniques of infusion. But the shift is not as radical as Agamben makes it out to be. In late-modern life, the technologies deployed by physicians, biologists, geneticists, corporate advertisers, televangelists, media talking-heads, and psychiatrists sink deeply into the grammar of human biology. They help to shape the cultural being of human biology. Agamben's review of new medical technologies to keep people breathing after their brains have stopped functioning captures something of this change, showing how a sovereign authority now has to decide when death has ar-rived rather than letting that decision reflect the slow play of biocultural tradition. Numerous such judgments, previously left to religious tradition in predominantly Christian cultures, now become explicit issues of law and sovereignty in religiously diverse states.

Agamben tends to describe the state as the "nation-state." He does not ask whether disturbing developments in the logic of sovereignty are bound not merely to the conjunction between biopolitics and sovereignty but to a fateful conjunc-tion between them and energetic attempts to consolidate the spirituality of a nation when multiple pressures work against realization of that objective. If and as the reactive drive to restore the fictive unity of a nation is relaxed, it becomes more possible to negotiate a generous ethos of pluralism that better copes with the nexus among biology, politics, and sovereignty. More than anything else, I want to sug-gest the dubious drive to convert plurality into nationhood translates biopolitics into practices of sovereignty that are punitive, corrective, exclusionary, and marginalizing. The shape of the ethos that infuses the practice of sovereignty is therefore critical, not merely the conjugation of sovereignty and biopolitics.

The "Logic" of Sovereignty

Agamben retains one practice of several theorists he criticizes: He acts as if an account of the "logic of sovereignty" reveals ironclad paradoxes that could be resolved only by transcending that logic altogether. His mode of analysis engenders the eschatological gesture through which it closes. I doubt, however, that politics or culture often possesses as tight a logic as Agamben delineates in generating either coherence or paradox. Biocultural life does not display a consummate logic. It is messier, more layered, and more complex than that. The element of illogic in its materiality ensures that it corresponds entirely to no design, pattern of efficient causality, or simple set of paradoxes. Agamben displays the hubris of academic intellectualism when he encloses political culture within such a tight logic.

Some academics express that hubris by presenting a tight model of causal explanation, others by displaying a closed model of historical realization, and others by resolving the first two images into tightly defined paradoxes. All three stances overstate the extent to which the complexity of biopolitical culture is resolvable into a consummate logic of explanation, interpretation, or paradoxicality. The attraction of each perspective is that it allows social and cultural theorists to assume the role that ecclesiastical authorities once sought to play in Christian states: that of authoritative public visionaries who articulate the larger picture of the actual, the possible, and the desirable in which sovereignty, law, and politics are encased. Kant, for example, participated in such a political drive. He sought to replace ecclesiological authority with the public authority of academic (Kantian) philosophers who continued the Christian tradition by other means. The continuing attraction of the Kantian problematic in academic philosophy is bound to the authoritative standing it bestows upon academic philosophers in cultural life. Agamben, of course, translates Kantian antinomies into paradoxes. But just below that facelift beats the heart of a scholar who reduces cultural life to a logic.

If you loosen the logic Agamben articulates, you may both express more appreciation for the materialization of culture than he does and locate more space to maneuver within the paradoxes he delineates. There is a paradox of sovereignty, but it is a social or cultural paradox, one with more room for negotiation, adjustment, and honing than Agamben suggests. The best way to approach this issue, perhaps, is to delineate two ambiguities residing in sovereignty that escape Agamben's attention.

The first ambiguity, almost detected by Agamben, is an equivocation in the idea of sovereignty between acting with final authority and acting with irresistible power. This finds expression in the *OED*, in the definition of sovereignty as "supremacy in respect of power, domination, or rank; supreme dominion, authority or rule." The idea of finality flows through these terms; but in some, it expresses final authority, whereas in others, it expresses irresistible effect. Both find some presence in the terms *rank* and *rule*. Agamben senses this difference in his assertion that the sovereign decides the exception. But within the idea of the exception "decided" by sovereignty, an oscillation lingers between a juridically established authority that decides the exception and a social power that asserts itself in an irresistible way. This ambivalence within sovereign finality finds expression in Christian theology as well as in human law. The point of the nominalist critique of scholastics who had projected an immanent purpose into the world is that such a projection implicitly undermines the very idea of God's omnipotence. A sovereign God, the nominalists contended, is one governed by no prior purpose limiting His power. So they attacked the doctrine of an expressive or enchanted world through which Christian theology before them had bestowed meaning and direction upon human life. They expanded the sense of contingency in the order of nature by subtracting purpose, belonging, and intrinsic meaning from it in the interests of honoring a God of absolute sovereign power over the order of being. They increased God's sovereign power while decreasing the sovereign purpose He expressed. Their opponents, of course, said that they subtracted meaning and purpose from the world over which God presided. Today, they might be called nihilists.

This oscillation and debate subsist within the contemporary idea of political sovereignty, as the finality of sovereignty circulates uncertainly between its authoritativeness and its irresistibility. This is not simply a confusion about the idea, as if it could be eliminated simply by a sharper clarification of the term. *It is the zone of indiscernibility that the practice of sovereignty inhabits.* The practice of sovereignty lives on this zone of indiscernibility.

The significance of the dissonant conjunction between effective and expressive sovereignty becomes apparent when linked to a second oscillation. Alexis de Tocqueville captured much of it in his exploration of nineteenth-century American democracy. "The principle of sovereignty of the people," he says, "which is always

to be found, more or less, at the bottom of almost all human institutions, usually
remains buried there."[11] In European societies, divine right invested sovereign
authority in the king; but below that authority, enabling and confining it, were
the traditions infused into the multitude. This underground interplay among the
multitude, tradition, and official sovereignty enabled some initiatives by the official sovereign, resisted others, and rendered others barely thinkable. Think of a
monarch who sought to convert England from Christianity to Buddhism in one
generation. He might face the fate that met Pharaoh Ikhaneton when he converted
Egyptians to a new, austere faith. They barely conformed to its external dictates for
a generation and then reverted to the old rituals upon his death.

The multitude, infused with manifold particular traditions, comes even more
into the fore in a democratic regime. It helps to set the ethos in which official sovereignty is set. Better put, *in democratic constitutionalism, sovereignty circulates uncertainly among the multitude, the traditions it embodies, and constitutionally sanctioned
authorities*. These elements can be specified more closely, though never completely,
according to need and context. Thus, the police in American cities both express
and help shape the ethos of sovereignty. They can find evidence or plant it, follow
the spirit of Miranda or render it ineffective, intimidate a section of the populace
or act evenhandedly depending on the unstable confluence of legal rulings given to
them, the larger ethos in which they participate, and the professional police ethos
carved out of dangers, loyalties, and hostilities in the city. What would happen to a
Court that "decides" cops must walk without guns or, less dramatically, that they
are free to shoot at any suspicious looking citizen? An unconscious context of the
thinkable and the unthinkable, the habitually expected and the impermissible, the
morally permissible and the morally outrageous enters into sovereign readings of
constitutional texts.

According to Tocqueville, the thing that infused the ethos of sovereignty in the
nineteenth century was above all the Christian tradition. That is the main reason
Amerindians could not be included in the polity. They lacked Christianity. So when
a Supreme Court decision supported the autonomy of the Cherokee people in the
southeastern United States, the sovereign ethos of Christian superiority overturned
that mere legality, even though a minority of Christians protested the hegemony of
that religious ethos. In this case, the irresistible demand that European stock and
Christianity provide the unifying basis of the republic overturned the positional
ruling of the Court. Tocqueville shows how such a slippery circulation of sovereign

power/authority operates. Here is what he says about how the "American government" and "the white population" enter into asymmetrical relations each time a new area was reserved by treaty for the "Indians":

> Who can guarantee that they will be able to remain in peace in their new asylum? The United States pledges itself to maintain them there, but the territory they now occupy was formerly secured to them by the most solemn oaths. Now, the American government does not, it is true, take their land from them, but it allows encroachments on it. No doubt within a few years the same white population which is now pressing around them will again be on their tracks in the solitudes of Arkansas; then they will suffer again from the same ills without the same remedies; and because sooner or later there will be no land left for them, their only refuge will be the grave.[12]

An irresistible faction of the white population defined and decided the exception in this historic instance. Was any court going to order all Christian whites in and around Georgia to march north and west instead of allowing the Cherokee to be sent to Oklahoma in the march of death? Tocqueville himself had regrets about this result. But he did not dissent militantly from it because of his view that in America sovereignty must circulate among the people, the highest court, and a Christendom that forms the first "political institution" of American civilization. Lacking Christianity, Amerindians were set up to be the sovereign exception, the people to be excluded from the territory they occupied first. In every territorial civilization, Tocqueville says, "there are certain great social principles which a people either introduces everywhere or tolerates nowhere."[13] Strict constructionists embrace this equation at a visceral level, concurring with Tocqueville that Christianity, which exercises no explicit constitutional power over the state, functions as the first political institution below it in giving meaning to the porous words of the Constitution.

The sovereign process Tocqueville describes with respect to Amerindians is already in the eighteenth and nineteenth centuries invested in a fateful conjunction between biopolitics and sovereignty. The living space available to Amerindians was squeezed by the effective sovereignty over the land of white Christians. But the circulation Tocqueville charts does not conform to the airtight logic of sovereignty Agamben characterizes. If a political movement successfully changed the cultural ethos in which presidents governed, courts decided, and the white populace responded to decisions, the paradox of sovereignty would still remain, biopolitics would still operate, and the relevant constitutional language would still be insufficient to determine judicial decisions. *But a modified ethos of constitutional action might nonetheless incline the effective range of court decisions and popular action in a different direction.*

The relevance of this point to the contemporary world is underlined by saying that the conjunction of biopolitics and Article 48 of the Weimar Republic did not alone generate the Nazi Holocaust against Jews, the Roma people, and homosexuals. A series of intense relays between those forces and a political culture already infused with anti-Semitism and resentment against defeat in World War I generated the devastating result. Without the last element—the element I call the ethos of sovereignty—the conjunction between biopolitics and Article 48 might have proceeded in a different direction. The point is to see that, given the paradox which helps constitute it, an ethos of sovereignty is both external to sovereignty and internal to it, both part of it and one of its cultural conditions of possibility.

Gilles Deleuze and Felix Guattari concur in the perspective adopted here. Agreeing that there is a paradox at the center of sovereignty, they nonetheless find the most powerful sources of fascism to flow from a series of "resonances" among state sovereignty, fascist gangs, and a larger populace participating in the micropolitics of fascism.

> But fascism is inseparable from the proliferation of molecular focuses in interaction, which skip from point to point to point, *before* beginning to resonate together in the National Socialist State. Rural fascism and city or neighborhood fascism, youth fascism and war veterans' fascism, fascism of the left and fascism of the right, fascism of the couple, family, school, and office: Every fascism is defined by a micro-black hole that stands on its own and communicates with the others before resonating in a great, generalized, central black hole . . . Even after the National Socialist State had been established, microfascisms persisted that gave it unequaled ability to act upon the "masses."[14]

The modern conjunction of biopolitics and the paradox of sovereignty does not, then, suffice to spawn fascism or even fundamentalism. Additional forces are required before either crystallizes. If those same forces are turned in another direction, the paradox of sovereignty becomes consistent with a democratic culture appreciative of existing diversity and presumptively responsive to new patterns of diversification. Put another way, the sovereign is not simply (as Agamben and Schmitt tend to say) *he* (or *she*) who first decides that there is an exception and then decides how to resolve it.[15] Sovereign is *that* which decides an exception exists and how to decide it, with the *that* composed of a plurality of forces circulating through and around the positional sovereignty of the official arbitrating body.

Such a result may be discouraging to those who seek a tight explanation of the economic and political causes of legal action (the realists), a closed model of legal process (the idealists), or a tight model of legal paradox (the authoritative theorists of crisis). But it draws closer to the operative complexity of sovereignty. It has another advantage as well: It points to strategic issues to address by those who give partiality to democracy and plurality in negotiating the paradox of sovereignty.

In American democracy, sovereignty circulates uncertainly among a Supreme Court now sanctioned *positionally* (after an early period of struggle and self-assertion) to decide contested issues authoritatively, a populace marked by an uneven distribution of power, and orientations to the sacred into which the Court and much of the populace are inducted. Today, one important tradition is respect for the integrity of national elections as an expression of the most elemental act of democratic citizenship. If that act is abrogated significantly, much else about democracy is placed in jeopardy. So, when the Gang of Five overturned the Florida Supreme Court, stopping the vote count before it was necessary to do so, it exercised its positional sovereignty in opposition to the democratic element in the civilizational constitution of sovereignty. The Gang gave priority to court hubris and party partisanship over partisanship for democracy in a setting where other alternatives were consistent with the porous words of the law and the Constitution.

What of those, like me, who protest this action? Do we not owe the Court respect and obedience, nonetheless, precisely because it occupies a position critical to constitutional democracy? We owe *positional* respect to the institution called upon to make authoritative decisions when pressing circumstances compel them. That responsibility is met by a presumption to obedience to Court decisions and by the public admission that democratic constitutionalism needs some such body. But to participate in a wider partiality for democracy is to acknowledge other responsibilities as well: to uncover the paradox of sovereignty, to reveal how its negotiation draws on a larger ethos, to pursue a democratic, pluralist ethos of sovereignty, and to expose how the constitutive ambiguity between positional and cultural sovereignty was exploited in this case for narrow partisan purposes. When the implication of sovereignty in a larger ethos that conditions it and infuses it becomes widely appreciated, it also becomes clearer to more people how important it is today to struggle for a generous ethos of pluralist democracy in which the positional sovereignty of the Court operates. We meet our first responsibility by a presumption to obedience that might be overridden on some occasions and our second by contesting actively and vociferously the partisan partiality of the Gang of Five.

There is a related issue here, too. An ethos of sovereignty appropriate to the contemporary condition is not merely one that displays partiality for the integrity of democratic elections. It must also *become* one that points beyond the equation embraced by several members of the Court between a civilization of Christianity, narrowly defined, and strict construction of constitutional provisions. My sense is that strict constructionism could not survive as a doctrine if its tacit link to an exclusionary version of Christianity were publicly exposed. A narrow, exclusionary definition of Christianity sets the ethos in which strict constructionism is practiced. This narrow image of Christianity is the *that* to which conservative judges implicitly appeal when they encounter constitutional provisions compatible with multiple judgments in new, unexpected situations.

In this respect, a justice like Antonio Scalia agrees with Tocqueville, though it is doubtful that a contemporary Tocqueville would continue to agree with him. Tocqueville found Christianity to play a key role in the ethos of sovereignty in early nineteenth-century America. He might well give a different reading today, however, as the diversity of theistic and nontheistic faiths on the same political territory continues to grow.

A lot has happened between 1830 and 2006. Stirred by the compression of distance through the acceleration of pace, biopolitical culture has bumped through several transformations. A significant pluralization of operational faiths on the same territory is one of those shifts. A new plurality of religious and nonreligious orientations forms a constitutive part of biopolitical culture today. In these circumstances, to draw a sharp line between a Christian civilization and those who inhabit the territory but are either un-Christian or not Christian enough would be to add new constituencies to the demonization of Amerindians that marked the ethos of sovereignty in nineteenth-century America.

To renegotiate the ethos of sovereignty in the contemporary context requires an audacious pluralization of the sacred and a corollary relaxation of what it takes to defile the sense of the sacred embraced by you or others. Such a project is demanding, of course, but no more so than the relatively successful attempt earlier to infuse a new plurality within Christianity or, after that, to fashion a more secular public culture or, after that, to accept a broadened range of ethnic diversity. When partisans of this or that confessional faith actively draw a specific confession of the sacred into public life, as most regularly do today, it becomes legitimate for others to contest some of its key assumptions actively and publicly and to explore critically pertinent aspects of its texts and rituals, particularly when the confessors seek to apply those dictates to everyone.

The demanding tasks are (1) to maintain presumptive respect for the practice of positional sovereignty, (2) to pluralize the number and type of legitimate existential faiths (including secular and nontheistic faiths) that enter into the ethos of sovereignty, and (3) to relax further than many have heretofore accepted what counts as an assault upon the sacred confessed by yourself or others.

The project is to generalize partiality for democracy and to infuse agonistic respect for diverse existential faiths into the ethos of sovereignty. The launching pad for that project is the understanding that positional sovereignty is both indispensable to the rule of law in a democracy and constitutively insufficient to itself. It is conditioned by, and expressive of, a larger ethos. The struggle to negotiate a generous ethos forms part of the respect democrats bestow upon the indispensability and uncertainty of sovereignty.

Notes

1. Justice Souter's opinion as quoted in its entirety in *The New York Times* (December 14, 2000), 28–29. The quotation from Souter in the next paragraph is also from page 29.

2. For two essays that are particularly pertinent on this point, see Bonnie Honig, "Declarations of Independence: Arendt and Derrida on the Problem of Founding a Republic," *American Political Science Review* (Winter 1991), 97–113; and Alan Keenan, "Promises, Promises: The Work of Arendt," *Political Theory* (May 1994), 297–322.

3. Jean-Jacques Rousseau, *On the Social Contract: With Geneva Manuscript and Political Economy*, trans. Judith Masters (New York: St. Martin's Press, 1978), bk. 1, 46. I discuss this paradox with respect to the relation among territory, global politics, and democracy in chap. 5 of *The Ethos of Pluralization* (Minneapolis: University of Minnesota Press, 1995). A thoughtful and detailed engagement with its effect on Rousseau's theory is developed by Steven Johnston in *Encountering Tragedy: Rousseau and the Project of Democratic Order* (Ithaca, NY: Cornell University Press, 1999).

4. Rousseau, *On the Social Contract*, 69–70.

5. Here is one expression of the hope: "If an ethical commonwealth is to come into being, all single individuals must be subject to a public legislation, and all the laws which bind them must be capable of being regarded as commands of a common law giver . . . But if the commonwealth is to be ethical, the people, as a people, cannot itself be regarded as the law giver. For in such a commonwealth all the laws are expressly designed to promote the morality of actions (which is something inner, and hence cannot be subject to public

laws) whereas in contrast these public laws . . . are directed only toward the legality of actions." The statement goes on to project the hope of a future harmony between inner and
outer. Immanuel Kant, *Religion Within the Limits of Reason Alone*, trans. Theodore Greene
and Hoyt Hudson (New York: Harper Torchbooks, 1960), 90. For a study that supports the
reading of Kant advanced here, see Ian Hunter, *Rival Enlightenments: Civil and Metaphysical Philosophy in Early Modern Germany* (Cambridge: Cambridge University Press, 2001).

6. Immanuel Kant, *Critique of Practical Reason*, trans. Lewis Beck (New York: Macmil-
lan, 1993), 48–49.

7. For a fine essay that compares Confucianism to Thoreau and Foucault as an ethic
of cultivation, see Brian Walker, "Thoreau on Democratic Cultivation," *Political Theory*
(April 2001), 155–189. Walker's essay should be read in conjunction with Jane Bennett, *Thoreau's Nature*, 2nd ed. (New York: Rowman and Littlefield, 2001), to which it is indebted.

8. Giorgio Agamben, *Homo Sacer: Sovereign Power and Bare Life*, trans. Daniel Heller-
Roazen (Stanford, CA: Stanford University Press, 1995), 82.

9. Ibid., 83.

10. Ibid., 44, 59.

11. Alexis de Tocqueville, *Democracy in America*, 2 vols., trans. George Lawrence (New
York: Harper & Row, 1969), 58.

12. Ibid., 336. I explore Tocqueville's rendering of the relation between the Christian
civilization of America and Amerindians who were excluded by it in *The Ethos of Pluralization*, chap. 6.

13. Tocqueville, *Democracy in America*, 294.

14. Gilles Deleuze and Felix Guattari, *A Thousand Plateaus*, trans. Brian Massumi (Minneapolis: University of Minnesota Press, 1987), 214.

15. Chantal Mouffe examines ambiguities in Schmitt's conception of the exception and
the sovereign decision in *The Democratic Paradox* (New York: Verso Press, 2000), chap. 2.
She also thinks that Schmitt's focus on the exception and the decision becomes problematic
when you come to terms with his prior commitment to decisions that enforce, as he calls it,
"homogeneity" among those included and, hence, excluded. To relax that latter demand is
to set the stage for strategies to renegotiate the ethos of sovereignty.

The Triumph of a Departed World:
Law, Modernity, and the Sacred

PETER FITZPATRICK

Let us return to the past, that will be progress.

— Giuseppe Verdi

Departure I

Exordial agony is relieved for now by the specificity of my inviting brief.[1] With its sanction, I may explore whether the world of the sacred still persists, and that will indeed be my impelling concern. For this purpose, the brief goes on, I can attempt to "theorize the sacred," consider "law's relation to the sacred," and more pointedly, address "the continuing relevance of ideas of the sacred to law." The renderings of modern law or its rituals in religious terms abundantly illustrate such continuing relevance.[2] Yet in occidental modernisms, the departure of the sacred is usually conceived as complete or almost so. What supervenes is a now rational or secular world, and one often exemplified in law. As my fecund brief has it, and in marked contrast now to the continuing relevance of the sacred to law, ". . . law stands in stark opposition to the sacred, a crass, worldly substitute for mystery, miracle, faith, or fatalism. Law is both a primary instantiation, and defender of, the secular." "Primary" indeed in that the sacred involves a determinant reference beyond the existent world, yet modern "secular" law and "legal science" distinctively deny the effect on themselves of any such reference.

There would seem at first to be a similar divide in modern existence between a continuity with the sacred and a break from it. The newly created secular or rational world is one freed infinitely from any determining reference to a sacred realm set beyond our profane reality. Yet there is a view, clean contrary if less remarked, that sees modernism as an ironic apotheosis of the sacred rather than its utter denial, and this perception is something more thoroughgoing than those partial or exceptional or "residual" resemblances some find between what were once manifestations of the sacred and their modern secular counterparts. Notably, and taking these authors as indicative but also exemplary, Adorno and Horkheimer in their critique of Enlightenment would render modernism itself as perfected myth, myth here being a form of the sacred, and they would find the sacred pervading the very modernity that would deny it:

> In the enlightened world, mythology has entered into the profane. In its blank purity, the reality which has been cleansed of demons and their conceptual descendants assumes the numinous character which the ancient world attributed to demons.[3]

With this "disenchantment of the world," with "this dissolution of myth and the substitution of knowledge for fancy," and with the world straitened to "the known, one and identical," the now somehow numinous reality takes what was beyond, what was transcendent, into itself.[4] Yet in so doing, it would still claim intrinsically to oppose, surpass, and displace the world of the sacred—something which Adorno and Horkheimer also observe, inevitably.[5]

The sacred then, and given the story so far, can be taken as perfected *and* negated in modernity, and overlaying this divide with the similar one in my brief, law could perhaps be taken as a pointed concentration of that opposition. My whole argument will ultimately be focussed on modern law as the realization yet denial of the sacred and on what that hiatus tells us about the quality of law in modernity. That focus will reveal law as "taking the place" of the sacred in modernity yet doing so in a "secular" way that obviates any determinate and determinant reference beyond the existent world. What was once determination beyond is taken with-in law—with-in but nonetheless now illimitably because the surpassing constraints provided by the gods or nature are no more. Even though modern law assumed the demonic ability to come from beyond an existent world and to possess and determine what is brought within, it can do this only from within that world. This determining by law from within entails the constituent denial by law of a determinate realm beyond. Since law is nonetheless of a realm beyond, for law itself both that realm and law's being of it cannot be determinate. Law assumes the sacral efficacy of bringing this not-determinate, this pure indeterminate, into determination. To produce and maintain such determination, law cannot be simply of the indeterminate. It must itself have determinate and determinant existence within. Law thence brings the indeterminate and the determinate together in various sacral modes.

What I hope to show with this more sinuous irony, then, is not just the triumph of a departed world of the sacred through its covert continuation in or as law but also its triumph *as* departed—to show how, in its very departure and with the block on recognizing that departure, the sacred shapes and constrains, even constitutes, the ways in which we perceive and experience, or fail to perceive and experience, modern law. What this triumph does not import, then, is some simple if unacknowledged equivalent of the sacred "in" modernity. Nor does it import some emendation through which the sacred may still play some residual part "in" modernity. Rather, the combined presence and denial of the sacred go to form modern law operatively. At least, that is what the argument will be.

That the hypersacral law just outlined transcends secular solidity is readily intimated by apostles of Enlightenment secularism. For one, the imperative that law have transcendent purchase was almost obsessively emphasized by Rousseau for whom it remained the case that "[g]ods would be needed to give men laws" and for whom the primal lawgiver needed a transcendent "great soul" so as to generate acceptance of his laws.[6] Yet, if the transcendent domain of such gods and demigods is now quite vacant and nondetermining, how can the claim to such a domain be made out in a determinate and determinant rule? Kant would spectacularly seek to avoid the question by enjoining the people not to enquire into such matters—something that would mean abjuring the Enlightenment demand that one dare to know.[7] In terms of my argument so far, the law would combine the indeterminate beyond with determinate rule, but still for Kant, this would have to be, and operatively so, a "law so holy (inviolable) that it is already a crime even to call it in doubt *in a practical way*, and so to suspend its effect for a moment;" and indeed, the authority for such a law must "as a practical principle of reason" be thought of as coming from God.[8] Whatever the effecting necessity this points to, it is not just consequentially a practical principle of reason. Rather, what is intimated by pronouncing it *"already* a crime to call" the law in doubt *"and so to suspend its effect *for a moment"* is an imperative sustaining of being.[9] In this chapter, that sustaining is constituently tied to the sacral quality of modern law. And what the sustaining of modern law requires, in turn, is sacrifice.[10] That is the sacral mode which preoccupies the present chapter. In its giving empathic effect to the sacred and to law in modernity, sacrifice can no longer be a sacrifice to the covetous gods beyond. It becomes an "introverted" sacrifice, a sacrifice to the perfected immanence of a now disenchanted world—and, more pointedly, a sacrifice to that world's reifications as they pervade and empower "its" law.[11]

The Sacred as Such

Exordial agony resurfaces with having now to encompass the immeasurable sacred in some summary way. And it is hardly relieved by the looming demand for attention that comes with Agamben's currently famed account of law and the

sacred, notably in his *Homo Sacer: Sovereign Power and Bare Life*.[12] As that account could fairly be taken to provide the impetus, even if somewhat of a negative impetus, of much that is to follow here, it may be as well to deal with it at
the outset. As is excessively well known, Agamben resurrects "an obscure figure
of archaic Roman law," the figure of "*homo sacer* (sacred man)," a figure that for
Agamben embodies "bare life."[13] What is "bare" about the life of *homo sacer* is that
it can be taken by anyone and that this has to be done without sacrificing such a
life.[14] Thence, Agamben would place bare life as definitively apart from the law.
It is "included in the juridical order *solely* in the form of its exclusion (that is, of
its capacity to be killed)"; "as such," it is "outside both human and divine law"
and demarcating of them.[15] No matter how "obscure" or even dubious its origin,
Agamben trajects the unsacrificeable *homo sacer* into the core of modernity as no
less than constituent of its "political realm."[16] In this way, the sacred, carried by
homo sacer, is of modernity even as excluded by its law—a proposition that could
resonate supportively with my thesis of the modern sacred triumphing in its very
departure were it not that I am about to disagree with it.

In a work earlier than the one being engaged with here, Agamben once depicted
the sacredness of *homo sacer* in rather different terms. As he then helpfully pointed
out, "the sacred is necessarily an ambiguous and circular concept. (In Latin, *sacer*
means vile, ignominious, and also august, reserved for the gods; both the law and
he who violates it are sacred)."[17] This *homo sacer*, then, would seem to be very
much of the law, designated sacred by the law, one of "those men whom," as Mac-
robius observes, "the laws order to be 'sacred' to certain deities," and who are considered as "of the gods," as already sacrificed; hence, in giving effect to the laws, no
further sacrifice is possible and such men can "be stripped of their bodies and sent
thither."[18] It is through being adjudged guilty of a crime, through transgressively
going beyond the existent law, that *homo sacer* is deemed sacred.[19] Obligingly, the
gods themselves were prone to transgress.

That classic conception of the sacred as "necessarily . . . ambiguous" is now departed from by Agamben as being a modernist deviation; rather, he now affirms an
"autonomous" *homo sacer* as the carrier of bare life and with it the "most ancient
meaning" of the sacred, a sacred having an "originary" quality and a singularity
that cannot be dissolved "into an assumed originary ambiguity of the sacred," a
quality placing it distinctly and distinctively outside the law.[20] I will later engage
more sympathetically with several of these aspects of Agamben's work, but for
now, there will be a perverse insistence on, and expansion of, the "originary ambiguity" of the sacred.

Let me start my argument proper, however, with another reduced or constrained meaning of the sacred—with what that captures and fails to capture of the sacred. In that reduction, typical of modernity, the sacred is made fixed or inviolate, a matter of unshakable belief or of what enduringly is, yet something also to be protected, "held" against challenges to it. Sacredness is thence attributed to property and the nation, law and the Constitution, life and stem cells. Doubtless this represents a much-remarked dimension of the sacred generally.[21] Intimating the contrary case bluntly for now, this very stasis or closure can, however, be sustained only in self-contradiction. To remain ostensibly whole, the demarcated entity must accommodate and adjust to all that would ever confront it. There is a dual yet mingled etiology here. One is the inexorability of illimitable change. The other is an imperative constant. Each can only "be" in relation to the other. That point can now be amplified as taking us beyond unidimensional or monadic conceptions of the sacred, whether Agamben's or the modern, and initially by way of the expansive and ambivalent manifestation of the sacred in premodernity.

The questioning of confined conceptions of the sacred fuses now with the ineluctable question of how we, in the fastness of our present, can perceive the sacred in premodernity. Allow me to plunge immediately into "the answer," deriving it initially from a meditation on Spanish imperialism and Inca civilization in which Wilson Harris seeks liberating resources seemingly lost to conquistadorial ages, ages which would see the world they despoil as finished and "so finished it could be sold again, without insight, or understanding of the unfinished past, the unfinished present."[22] Of course, resorting to a current verity, we cannot encompassingly know alterity or "the other," or more specifically, we cannot know the alterity that is the past. And of course, resorting to another such verity, our apperceptive ability is tied to our own times.[23] Yet our present, our evanescent now, cannot be contained either in itself or in its relation to the past or to anything else. Eschewing then, with Foucault, "any monotonous finality" here, we are left with dispersion and "disparity."[24] But in the unfinished quality of both the present and the past, each will continually change in the intimacy of a relation that is their indistinction. So, and for the very same reasons, if we cannot know the past distinctly, neither can we not not know it. Admittedly, we cannot lay claim to a pristine retrieval of the sacred, or of anything else, but we are existentially impelled to seek constituent connections that may be no more modest. The immodest effort now will be to identify dimensions of being exemplified by an alembic sacred and then to connect these dimensions as so exemplified to modernity and to "its" law.

Going straight to the top, as it were, those dimensions of the premodern sacred appear at what is perhaps their most distinct in the god of monotheism. This will be taken as my prime instance of the sacred because monotheism will inform the pending account of the modern sacred. A singular perfection obliged this monotheistic god to take on chasmically dual characters, characters that will reappear in various guises throughout my argument. One character was the omnipresent and fully determinate god, the god of perfect order, the god of constancy, caught by "his" own laws, by "nature," and forbidden by Malebranche to "disturb the simplicity of his ways"[25]—a god, in short, unable to be other than what he is. "Is not freedom," opines Bataille, "the power God lacks . . . since he cannot disobey the command that *he is*, the command of which he is the guarantor?"[26] The alternative god, in stark contrast, is entirely transgressive of any determinate order, a god of infinite and pure possibility. He can, says Cassirer, only ever be other than what he "is"—"absolutely unconditional and subject to no limiting rules and norms,"[27] pure transgression. This is the god of miracle, of nature confounded, of mystery and revelation, boundless, an ineffable god, a god in whose presence there can only be dissolution.

These deific characters may also be somehow combined. For Abu Ali ibn Sina (Avicenna), God was both rationally and "simply" contained yet uncontainedly different from everything else and apprehended most completely in the "realm of the imagination—not through discursive reason."[28] Or for Plotinus, the One "is Everything and Nothing; it can be none of the existing things, and yet it is all."[29] More pointedly for present purposes, and for Nicholas de Cusa, despite being made up of such opposing dimensions and despite being beyond comprehension, God could still be affirmed as "Oneness, for Oneness is Being," or more congenially, "God is *unitas complicans* or Enfolding Oneness."[30] In all, the monotheistic sacred provided an ultimate unifying reference that was transcendently self-founding and comprehensively constituted the world.[31]

These dimensions of being inhabit other configurations of the sacred, and I will shortly come to sacrifice as the most significant configuring in this setting. For now, I will briefly take the myth of origin as a supporting instance, one that will soon prove pivotal in instancing and developing my overall argument by way of Freud's use of that genre. It is common in myths of origin to pit variations of order and incipient manifestation against chaos, possibility, and the disparate. With the myth of origin, however, as with other types of the sacred, the divide between these dimensions is a prelude to their creative combining. And in that combining, both a foundation and a continuate constitution is provided for the community adhering to the myth, for a being-with in community.

In what terms could this transcendent sacred transpose to the profane world, a world of finitude? The domain of the premodern sacred was perceived, in contrast to the modern, as one of "energy" and "forces," and the profane was the place of a set "substance" and of "things." [32] For Eliade, "the outstanding reality is the sacred; for only the sacred *is* in an absolute fashion, acts effectively, creates things and makes them endure." [33] Neither effective action nor the creation of things nor their enduring can *be* in stasis any more than they can *be* in nothing but change. Operatively, the sacred becomes the combining of its antithetical dimensions into force and form—the putative point at which "newness enters the world" and continues to endow it with substance. [34] Thence, and for Bataille, "the sacred is essentially that which, although impossible, is nonetheless there." [35] Here we may discern just why the "obscure figure" of *homo sacer* resonates so with a uniform modern reality since, having been consigned to the gods, he is already and fully of the sacred, yet he is palpably and "nonetheless there" in an all-too-determinate world where he is wholly, irredeemably transgressive. Yet even as "there," as a resolution in between its antithetical dimensions, the sacred as phenomenal force can only ever be an expedient, a resolution "for the time being." More bluntly, resolution as the outcome of the sacred mode is a deception. [36] The resolved reality which the ritual or office or system or symbolism would enclose—and would shore up with iterations, incantations, and solemnities—that reality subsists in its unsettling appetence for what is illimitably beyond it. And what is beyond "remains 'here below,' remains in rapport" with the enclosed reality. [37] The enclosing, the protecting of the reality, the bringing to form and identity is always a denial of what could otherwise be or have been, and when explicit, that denial is a sacrifice—coming now to sacrifice as (etymologically) "a rendering sacred," what Bataille calls "the most intense aspect of the sacred." [38]

Sacrifice as Such

Sacrifice, conclude Hubert and Mauss, "consists in establishing a means of communication between the sacred and the profane worlds," a means through which these worlds "can interpenetrate and yet remain distinct." [39] There is also for Hubert and Mauss a fusion of the sacred and the social through sacrifice:

> The sacred things in relation to which sacrifice functions, are social things. And this is enough to explain sacrifice. For sacrifice to be truly justified, two conditions are neces-

sary. First of all, there must exist outside the sacrificer things which cause him to go outside himself, and to which he owes what he sacrifices. Next, these things must be close to him so that he can enter into relationship with them, find in them the strength and assurance he needs, and obtain from contact with them the benefits that he expects from his rites. Now this character of intimate penetration and separation, of immanence and transcendence, is distinctive of social matters to the highest degree.[40]

Indeed, sacrifice is usually associated with assurance, with the seeking and sustaining of bounds to, and between, social and personal existence. To repeat somewhat, this sacrificial bound also relates to what is beyond. It does not mark off what is utterly or completely beyond. Sacrifice straddles and connects the domain of the bounded within and the domain of that beyond onto which the boundary ever opens. Neither domain definitively contains sacrifice. Sacrifice enacts and subsists in the sacred. Yet it is also of the profane, trajecting the bounded within, joining it to the incipience or realization of the possibility beyond. The sacrificial motion, then, must come from the beyond as well as from within. In this, it would give some effect "for the time being" to that alterity which inexorably "approaches from within and without at the same time."[41] It creates a commonality between what is within and what is without.

The coeval positioning of this alterity can be discerned in Bataille's alternation in the matter of sacrifice. For him, the sacred and the sacrificial would stand "against the world of practice" and inhabit "the domain of death" to the point where a sacrifice becomes a completeness of relation to the alterity without.[42] The impossibility of "being" in such a sole relation, as well as the insistent connection to a finite within, are intimated in the deracinated "human sacrifice" Bataille arranged in Paris as a way of "loosing the sacred" and paving the way for a complete revolution, a revolution that would "flood the streets of the city with blood"; exquisitely, the victim "was to sign a presacrificial agreement absolving his murderers of legal responsibility. The legal considerations finally thwarted the plan. . . ."[43] In sum, the sacrificial boundary is ever ambivalent. Sacrifice inseparably identifies what is and opens it to the possibility of its being otherwise, to the potentiality of its elimination. Rigidity in the ritual and other forms of the sacrifice is a testament and a response to that danger. And *homo sacer* embodies something of its realization. Having been already consigned to the beyond, already sacrificed, *homo sacer* is on the verge of elimination and only awaits the quietus that will complete it.

The carrier of this ambivalence in sacrifice is its victim. "Everything converges on the victim . . . , all the participants which come together in sacrifice are united in it; all the forces which meet in it are blended together."[44] Aptly for the force of relation to the beyond, this victim will be a differentiated marginal figure, a "differential mark."[45] Yet that same relation to the beyond attests to the illimitably potent incipience carried by the victim. So, victimhood, even within the profane world, does not always import weakness or insignificance. Girard's list of candidates, for example, "includes prisoners of war, slaves, small children, unmarried adolescents, and the handicapped," but the list extends also to "the king" whose very centrality and anticipatory rule set him apart, make him also marginal to the settled social norm.[46] Even more exalted a victim can be found in what Hubert and Mauss aptly take to be the "highest expression" of sacrifice, an expression that will soon be this chapter's increasing concern, the sacrifice of the god.[47]

The poignant contrast that the victim makes present is identified by Bataille as one in which the victim's being different fuses unsurpassably with sameness: being chosen for sacrifice gives the victim "a recognizable figure, which now radiates intimacy, anguish, the profundity of living beings."[48] The victim's position becomes ours. A more manifest figure of sameness would be the victim's becoming a concentration of and "substitution" for "the community," the Hebrew scapegoat providing a vivid instance with its carrying, into the wilderness beyond, the sins of the community symbolically heaped upon it.[49] An even more thorough realization of sameness, of identification with the victim, can be found in those sacrificial rituals where members of a community temporarily abandon the restraints of their normal roles and feast on their victim, thereby assimilating "the characteristics of the whole"—of the victim as a putative whole.[50] In all, with its enclosing affirmation, "sacrifice . . . is a moment which is not what it is—destruction, abandon—and this is its irony."[51] Yet for the sacrificer, identification with the victim cannot of course be complete; it cannot go to the point of self-destruction. The uncomfortable "fact" of sacrifice is that it entails the death or denial of the victim but does so to institute life—"in it the principle of all life resides."[52] We sacrifice others, says Derrida, "to avoid being sacrificed oneself."[53]

To draw together the argument so far and to orient it toward my culminating concerns with the sacred in modernity and in modern law, let me offer an interpretation of a fabled sacrifice that straddles the premodern and the modern. This is Freud's tale of totemic sacrifice in his *Totem and Taboo*.[54] The choice may at first seem strange. To describe Freud's anthropology of the premodern and his ethology as dubious would be a flattery. And his fanciful tale itself is advanced by Freud as a myth of origin[55]—although, as we shall see, he wavered at times as to its epistemological status. In all, it may be wondered how the myth, cast as it is in an irretrievable prehistory, could possibly connect to the modern condition. Notwithstanding, Freud's tentacular genius insinuates his myth into the question of sacrifice in a way that plants it generatively within modernity. Sacrifice was, in a sense, preadapted to the transition. If one follows the Brahmins far enough, we find that the gods depend on sacrifice not only for their sustenance and efficacy but also for their existence and, cruelly, for their very immortality.[56] With sacrifice, the gods are dispensable, and Freud's contribution, in effect, is to realize that this is the case for modernity, to reveal that what is being sacrificed to, and rendered sacred, is the monadic social bond itself, a bond made effective in law.

Freud's is a myth of the origin of law, of society, of individual being, and of much else. It comes in two stages and these correspond to and would "socialize" those two dimensions of the monotheistic god and of myths of origin touched on earlier. The dimension of fully determinate order is reflected in Freud's first stage and opening scene, a scene of stilled and utter completeness, a "primal horde" comprehensively subordinated to the power of the primeval father, a neosacral power of ultimate determining force. This was a world where nothing could be other than what it is. Nonetheless, somehow the subordinated sons "came together," in their own right as it were, by drawing on "the social fraternal feelings, which were the basis of the whole transformation" that was now to come; thence, the now rebellious sons perform "the first great act of sacrifice" by killing and consuming the father—something akin to the victimvorous sacrifice just described.[57]

After this first stage, the elimination of the father's pervasive power means that the world is now one of pure possibility, a world commensurate with the second dimension of the monotheistic god and of the myth of origin outlined earlier—a dimension and a world now where everything can only be other to what it is. This is the second originating of Freud's myth. It leads to the sons realizing that they cannot subsist in dissolute individuality, that no one of them could take the place of the father's pervasive domination, and that they had internalized the power of the ingested father by bringing it to bear now on themselves; hence, "the dead father became stronger than the living one had been."[58] It would seem that the power of the dead father is greater because the object of the living father's power was only that which invariantly is, whereas the dead father becomes an authority ruling incipiently over all that could be: "the revenge taken by the deposed and restored father was a harsh one: the dominance of authority was at its climax."[59]

What becomes central to my argument now is not only the impetus for this transition but also its epistemological elusiveness. All that is consistent in its various manifestations is its tautology.[60] At its most bland, the transition is simply a matter of the brothers entering into "a sort of social contract."[61] Not only does this abrupt formulation ignore the standard criticism of the idea of the social contract that it presupposes the capacity it produces, but there is also the more significant point that Freud was concerned in his myth to identify the social origin of psychoanalysis. The tautology now diverges into two branches. With one, the social ensues from a scene where it already existed as those "social fraternal feelings" of the sons that "were the basis of the whole transformation."[62] With the other branch, Freud repeatedly makes up for the poverty or uncertainty of social explanation by resorting to the very domain of the psychoanalytical that was supposed to be accounted for by the social. So, the social cement, the authority of the dead father, is produced by the Oedipal guilt or remorse at having killed him. Yet, as Freud recognizes, the same "contradictory feelings" producing Oedipal guilt or remorse had to be in existence before the murder so as to be made operative by it.[63] The ultimate refuge for Freud, but a refuge always uncertainly inhabited, was to shift the epistemological basis of his story from myth to science and to do so the more vehemently as the very science he espoused came to contradict what he claimed to be so. Or being even more brutal about it, his patchy and impatient drawing on science as he first formulated the myth was even then inconsistent in crucial ways with what the science was actually saying. In sum, the modernist Freud sought scientific grounding, but Freud was also and explicitly presenting a myth of origin for modernity, and his science could not accommodate the futural force of such myth. The myth of origin has to projectively account for what we are in any future now. Freud sought to satisfy this imperative in psychoanalytic and in social terms, and the social terms, at least, were realized in law.

One of the more engagingly egregious of Freud's inconsistencies comes with his claim that "the totemic clan" was "the next form of human society" after the primal horde.[64] Not only that, the sacrifice of the totemic animal as the "surrogate father" was for Freud both the first form and the prototype of society, of law, and of religion; thus, the "totemic culture everywhere paved the way for a more advanced civilization."[65] It would have ruined the story as universal history, as implanted in the nature of things, but Freud's passing references to Hubert and Mauss on sacrifice could have been extended to their considered rejection of his authorities for "the universality of totemism," a totemism that, so they find, "appears only in a few isolated tribes of Australia and America."[66] Yet Hubert and Mauss can also alert us to something of Freud's argument that, tendentiously now, will soon advance my own. Freud's reasons for why an animal is sacrificed as the emblematic totem are explicitly speculative except for one that would correspond with Hubert and Mauss in their chapter on "the sacrifice of the god."[67] They see the sacrificial unity of god and victim as the paradigm of sacrifice, and I will return to that combination, but that leaves the obvious difficulty of how the impalpable god can be operatively sacrificed. It was frequently the case, Hubert and Mauss deduced from numerous instances, that an animal took the place of the god and was often consumed by the sacrificers.[68] In Freud's terms now, they "acquire sanctity" in the consumption of "a sacrosanct victim": "the participation in the same substance establishes a sacred bond between those who consume it."[69]

It is in this sacrifice that the lineaments of law are concentrated and come to bear. The totem represents and gives effect to the social bond, carrying with it the "original" terms of settlement, the group's primal laws, "sacred" taboos "which could not be broken," starting with the prohibition on killing the father and on killing the totem animal.[70] Yet determinate prohibitions do not contain the totemic victim. It remains beyond and always incipiently transgressive. Like the ever-resurgent gods when they and their substitutes are sacrificed, the totemic victim is repeatedly killed.[71] It is then consumed in a festival or feast in which the whole group must participate. What is prohibited is the killing of the totem animal apart from this ritual, and that is the most heinous of crimes—a direct and destructive affront to the social bond. Freud's nicely dissonant idea of the festival encapsulates what is involved here. The killing and consumption of the totem animal are seen by Freud as a festival and, for him, a festival generically "is a permitted, or rather an obligatory, excess, a solemn breach of prohibition" in which "every instinct is unfettered and there is licence for every kind of gratification."[72] In the excess of the feast, in its breaking of the ur-prohibition on the killing of the totem animal, existing determination is suspended, the beginning of things is revived, and fresh determination can ensue.[73] This killing, Freud is concerned to emphasize, is "justifiable only through the participation of the whole clan," through a reassertion of the commonality, and it is in this relation to a continuing commonality that Freud equates the totem with the law.[74]

In reflecting and effecting this commonality, law has both to endow it determinately yet be ever capable of accommodating its infinite possibility. Both these dimensions of law are made operative in the totem, as we have just seen. What now becomes crucial are the constituent terms in which these two dimensions combine in and as law, and as modern law. Freud is unequivocal on this score: For the sons, it "became a duty to repeat the crime of parricide again and again in the sacrifice of the totem animal, whenever, as a result of the changing conditions of life, the cherished fruit of the crime—appropriation [by the sons] of the paternal attributes—threatened to disappear."[75] So, the whole responsive regard of the law to infinite possibility, its "doing justice" to the "changing conditions of life," all of this is enfolded in the preservation of patriarchal rule and instrumentally subordinated to it. That containing nexus was derived, as we also saw, from tautology and from scientism and surmise. Nor is all of this a matter of a hugely uncertain "back then" that would now be configured differently. Like all effective myths of origin, Freud's would account for our current condition. That origin persists in both its stages. As for the first, any "group formation" retains in it "the survival of the primal horde" with its ordered completeness.[76] Patriarchal power itself, however, and this is the second stage, becomes and remains mediated by the self-subjection of the sons. They do this "by themselves."[77] This involves a shift in "that every internal compulsion which makes itself felt in the development of human beings was originally—that is, in the *history of mankind*—only an external one."[78] To effect this internal compulsion, the sons bind their very subjectivity in "a covenant with the father."[79] This covenanting is impelled in a variety of related ways. For one, "the unlimited power" of the father is internalized by the sons through their remorse for the parricide, a remorse that "set up the super-ego by identification with the father; it gave that agency the father's power."[80] Even more pointedly, at least for my purposes, this remorse produced a constant "attempt at atonement,"[81] literally at-one-ment, a turning again to the one that is the father. As with the formative force of the primal horde, this remorse or guilt "persists among us," seemingly undiminished, becoming sedimented in both "a collective mind" and "modern subjectivity."[82]

With the sons' "sense of guilt," there also persists their "rebelliousness."[83] This is something that cannot be determinately contained since the ultimate power of paternal determination is no more and the sons have absorbed the unlimited power of the primal parent. This power, inevitably, has to be reigned in. With the creation by the sons of "the first form of social organization," along with its "moral restriction," there has to be a "renunciation of instinctual gratification."[84] Such gratification was given periodic play in the totem feast, but it now has to be more uniformly contained in a variety of continuous self-sacrifice. In the result, the "great event" of the primal parricide ever "since it occurred, has not allowed mankind a moment's rest."[85] Or in terms of one of Freud's more famous titles, there is an inbuilt "discontent" or, more exactly, "dis-ease" afflicting civilization.[86] Yet there always remains, and this is the obsessive impulsion of *Totem and Taboo*, the prospect and possibility of "regression" to the primitive, to the savage absence of a superego.[87]

Modernity as Such

Freud, rather too expansively, sees his own savage myth generating a theogony "of every form of religion."[88] The monotheistic god is found to be a substitute for the father, and the ready comparison is drawn with the consumption of the god in the Eucharist.[89] Feuerbach and Nietzsche had already inverted the Christological demand for our guilt-ridden and complete commitment to a god sacrificed for both our "original" and existent sins.[90] Yet in this scheme, sin or transgression remained simply that, something to be rejected entirely in reaccepting a monistic invariance. Quite to the contrary, Freud found that with the sacrifice of the primal father "the unity of the world was broken,"[91] and the world, the modern world, is ever unsettled. No matter what the pervasive force of the primal father, and no matter how effectively it continues, "the conscious individual personality" inheriting the "rebelliousness" of the sons cannot be eliminated.[92] Like "us" and our slaying of God as recounted by Nietzsche's supremely sane madman, the sons killed the god/father "by themselves."[93] With the persistence of that ability to dispose of even the most exalted determination, there can no longer be any enduringly ultimate efficacy. Change and circumstance can now continuously and constituently come into the world. This being so, the terrain marked out by totemic sacrifice must be remade iteratively. All of this may seem to run counter to a Freud for whom, supposedly, deviation calls for adjustment to the normality manifesting the social bond—sacrifice reconstituted as therapy. The Freud being trumpeted here, however, is one wedded to the creative recognition of irresolvable conflict.[94]

Yet if the sons reveal that individuated existence requires rebellion, that existence cannot subsist simply in itself. Freud's generosity, coming now to *Group Psychology and the Analysis of the Ego*, provides us with the kernel of necessity in the arrogations of patriarchal power. In writing that work, mostly in 1921, Freud saw "human groups" coming to "exhibit once again" the condition of the primal horde.[95] He associates this with the emergence of leadership somewhat equivalent to the primal father in *Totem and Taboo*, but in a "correction" administered to that account, he now says that "individual psychology must . . . be just as old as group psychology" and that in the primal horde "there were [these] two kinds of psychologies."[96] The sons of the primal horde were individuals who were not, after all, existently encompassed by the all-powerful father. Instead, as Freud had already revealed in *Totem and Taboo*, they "lived together in a community," they had "social fraternal feelings," enabling them to "come together" and kill the father.[97] The only need, then, for the second origin, for the social contract following the killing of the father, was to stage the self-submission of the individual sons to patriarchal authority. In short, the individual sons had already formed a commonality apart from the father. But whether before the killing or in the superfluous social contract following it, the sons could not form an effective commonality simply as distinct individuals because the only commonality this would afford would require them to be the same as each other, and distinct individuality would thence be lost. It was, then, a condition of their very individuality that there be some commonality determinately and determinably limiting individuality. That commonality cannot continue in being, cannot continue as being, unless it is ever responsive to the changing relations between the sons. In all, the elements of Freud's totemic social bond had to be already in the relations between the sons of the primal horde. As the embodiment of merely existing order, of a monotonous stasis, the father had to be (repeatedly) dispensed with in the parricidal sacrifice and its totemic reiterations.

On reiterations and formations of being: In commenting on Nietzsche's parable of deicide, with its "tiresome celebrity," Blanchot observes that "God means God, but also everything that, in rapid succession, has sought to take his place."[98] There are two facets to this persistence. One involves the large and acknowledged host, a heavenly host, of similarities drawn of late between the god of monotheism and putatively secular institutions and concepts, especially political and legal institutions and concepts.[99] As we saw close to the outset, both Rousseau and Kant found that, even in the enlightened world, law had to assume a sacral or deific character. To take another instance, the revived concern with that avatar of the patriarchal god, sovereignty, involves a constant tussle over how any conceptual containment can match sovereignty's deific combining of determinate existence with unconstrained efficacy. This takes us to the second facet of godlike persistence, to Nietzsche's having his madman recognize that, although we have killed God ourselves, "you and I," the deed remains beyond us, "more remote to . . . [us]

than the remotest stars." [100] We are left waiting, striving, in the "festivals of atonement" and "sacred games . . . we have to invent," [101] festivals and games striving to
restore the broken unity of the world, striving to attain the one of atonement—to
attain the origin or to attain an encompassing of the sovereign. These latter are but
instances, and it is time to turn to modernity in its generic relation to the sacred.

The initiating marker of that relation to the sacred for this chapter was Adorno
and Horkheimer's announcing that in the enlightened world a once transcendent
and resolving reference now immanently inhabited that very world. Instead of separating out a realm apart, the sacred now suffuses a world that has itself become
"one and identical." [102] To be effective in the world, this now numinous reality cannot simply be an intangible pervasion. It must, as it were, take place within finite
differentiations. That is where transcendence inexorably re-enters for, as Deleuze
and Guattari have it, "whenever immanence is interpreted as immanent *to* Something, we can be sure that this Something reintroduces the transcendent." [103] So,
sovereignties, origins, the nation of modern nationalism, numberless imperial ex-
emplarities claimed by "the West," all these integrally assert a transcendence, even
if a transcendence that can only be implicit because the world's resolving reference
is now, supposedly, purely immanent to itself.

The emplaced yet transcendent arrogation of a singular world, of "universal"
reality, entails an unacknowledged sacrifice. This is not just a matter of the standard perception that any social formation in its specificity involves the denial or
exclusion of what is "other" to it. Nor is it just a matter of the inevitable failure to
emplace the universal positively with the result that "we" are constituted in a negative opposition to "them," to such as the excluded savages—including, at Freud's
prompting, the savage instincts which we are to contain in self-sacrifice.[104] Nor,
further, is it just a matter of appropriating Agamben's tenuous introduction of
homo sacer to the modern world and relying only on his elegant formulation of the
"inclusive exclusion" of a life, its inclusion "in the juridical order solely in the form
of its exclusion." [105] This emphasis on inclusion does point us, however, toward
an apt sacrificial dimension because the victim, as we saw, must be ambivalently
excluded and included. The inclusive force of modern sacrifice is, however, more
encompassingly resolute than Agamben would allow. Admittedly, those who are
excluded from a reality that is universal or complete can only be utterly apart from
that reality. As such, they could only be included in that reality as excluded. Yet,
since the reality is universal, it must also include everything and extend to what
is quite excluded in its affirmation. On one side, then, are the carriers of the uni-

versal, those whose action is possessed of a sealed immanence, of an enwrapped plenitude. On the other side are those acted upon, the excluded who are called to be the same yet repelled as different, bidden perpetually to attain what is intrinsically denied them.

There are, however, differences to be observed. The sacred and the sacrificial can provide no resolving reference in modernity. The modern universal cannot be endowed with enduring content in some quondam reference beyond. Nor can such content perceptibly form within this universal, for to come to the universal from within is never to encompass or to be able to hypostatize it. The bringing of the universal into a determinate, and determinant, particularity can thence never be something irenically set. The particularity of its instantiation will be continually subject to dissipation. Or from the perspective of the universal itself, from the perspective of what is being continually "turned into one," [106] there can be no enduring differentiation within. Borrowing the term, and something of the thought, from Agamben, there is now an "indistinction" between inclusion within and exclusion from the modern universal, and all our lives are at least incipiently "bare," suspensively sacrificed, lacking as they do the protection of explicit sacral demarcations. [107]

Law as Such

In this scene of ultimate insecurity, we are now, with modernity, consoled by law. This is a law "put in place" of a sacred realm beyond, a law that Vitoria, in the advent of modernity, had prised away from its dependence on that realm. [108] Much of that law's significance came from its trenchant opposition to that very sacred with which it had once been characteristically identified. A now secular law intrinsically countered and historically displaced the sacred. [109] Yet the mantric elevation of law as the carrier of certainty and predictability in the modern age is nowadays matched just as often by its observed changefulness, so much so that the epoch-making quality of modern law and its attendant assurance can be forgotten.

Early manifestations of this assurance were revealingly extreme and could be matched in this by explicitly sacred archaic codifications. I will take just a few instances. One was the *référé législatif* of the revolutionary regime in France which, in 1790 at least, was so assured of law as an almost self-sufficient repository of enduringly set order that it forbade the interpretation of the law by judges who had to refer to the legislature matters where it could not be simply applied. [110] This elevation of the lapidary code reached its apotheosis with the Napoleonic variants introduced with the expectation of fixing forever "the empire of liberty" in what Kelley describes as "an almost totalitarian effort of social control."[111] However, the universal nation itself, to take one further instance for now, was quite outdone in that very quality by Bentham's insatiable and, as it transpired, influential striving after universality through law. Seeing himself as both the scourge of any transcendent reference and the "Newton of the moral sciences," Bentham envisaged the eventual attainment through law of total and "certain order," and there was for him a mutual dependence between order and truth.[112]

All of which is a none-too-pale reflection of that first deity of monotheism encountered earlier, the god whom, returning to my indulgent brief, "we know . . . through His laws," through his being confined within these laws. This, to borrow from another revolutionary scene, became "the laws of nature and of nature's God." Such a divinity was one bound in the perfected order of his laws, one already forbidden by Malebranche to "will against the eternal and immutable perfections of his essence."[113] We can "know" this god, to repeat, in the undisturbed "simplicity of his ways."[114]

That these legal artifacts can hardly be consigned to a spent history appears readily enough from the belief in, yet impossibility of, the constituent claims of the rule of law. For its calculable order to prevail, for law "not men" to rule, this law has to be closed yet also complete. If it were open rather than closed, something could enter and rule with or even instead of law. The same consequences could follow if this law were incomplete, if it were not a whole *corpus juris.*

There is, however, a contrary condition that has to be met if law is to rule, a condition to do with the ascription of changefulness. Law cannot simply secure certainty and predictability. It has to change in response to the illimitable unpredictability and uncertainty that ever confront it. Should it fail to do so, it will cease to rule situations changing around it or be unable to extend to them. If the rule of law is to be necessarily responsive, then it cannot be closed or complete. It must assume, as Carty puts it, a quality of "everywhereness," although liberal versions of the rule of law are content for it to extend to anything rather than everything.[115] There is an accommodating deity matching these requirements also. "In other traditions," my companiable brief goes on, law "is a bridge to mystery, to the miraculous," and the second god of monotheism encountered earlier was a god of mystery and the miraculous, a god infinitely protean and self-transgressive—not only, then, perfectly determinate but also perfectly indeterminate. What kind of law could issue from the perfectly indeterminate? An instance is revealed in Agamben's account of one such "other tradition" as a law of "absolute mutability."[116] In the debate within that tradition questioning "the state of the Torah as it existed in the sight of God," one answer deduced that the Torah must have been "a medley of letters without any order—that is, *without meaning*."[117] This is "the god of the unreadable book."[118] If, then, "one way in which we know God is through his laws," again invoking my brief, a law of this inscrutable kind would reveal not a god encompassed and bound by law as the simplicity of his ways, but an unknowable god, a god who "moves in a mysterious way / His wonders to perform," an avatar being Rousseau's deifically creative yet immeasurably distant lawgiver.[119]

There were nonetheless sacred modes, mysterious as they may well have been to behold, which sought to combine this deific movement with a perfected, a complete fixity. The resourceful God of Abu Ali ibn Sina, the One of Plotinus, and the Oneness of Nicholas de Cusa were instanced earlier. Freud's totem was likewise obliging. And the totem was the law. Something of an equivalent legal artifact, and itself epochal, was propounded by Hobbes as the philosopher of the first English revolution, as the "demon-king of modernity" in Tuck's marvellously compacted description.[120] In advancing a new basis for earthly rule, one severed from an erstwhile connection to a realm beyond, Hobbes advanced his Leviathan as a "mortal god;" and "Leviathan" for his contemporary audience would have had a resonant reference to that Leviathan of awe-inducing power in the Book of Job.[121] The terms in which Hobbes's Leviathan have become predominantly perceived would endow it with a surpassing totality of ruling power. This was not for Hobbes a matter of static completeness, however. It meant that the power could not be hindered and could extend to anything—a "giving life and motion to the whole body" politic.[122] There was, crucially for present purposes, a comparatively unremarked side to Leviathan, a Leviathan bound in a responsive regard to his subjects, and what Hobbes does is to combine these dimensions of Leviathan in law as the expression of Leviathan's power.[123]

The operative claims for enlightened law were, as we have seen in various French and Benthamite instances, hardly less extensive or more unassuming. Law was now destined to be either that domain of complete order vacated by the godhead or the illimitable deific ability to bring the nonexistent into effect. Lacking an empyrean to connect them, these claims would, without more, remain fastened to their respective impossibilities—to an immutable stasis or to a boundless vacuity.

Law thence becomes the neosacral combining of these claims in enforceable social relations. In this combining, a combining which cannot be effected in finitude, law itself takes on an operative transcendence. Now, says Blanchot, law "affirms itself as law and without reference to anything higher: to it alone, pure transcendence."[124] With that pure transcendence, law assumes a position set apart, immune in itself to what it effects. Summarily, then, modern law, Freud's totemic law, takes on dimensions and functions of the sacred but retains "in itself" the antinomy between those dimensions—an antinomy that, with the departure of the sacred, can no longer be overcome by a resolving reference beyond a world now irredeemably profaned. Hence, the incessant failure of efforts to render the godless law singularly and comprehensively in terms of the uniform world, in terms of a reality immanent to itself. More specifically, these are terms that would, in numberless attempts, render law as fact, as mental state, as instrument of sovereign or society, and so on. Aided as ever by Kafka, this could be seen as "the problem of our laws":" The laws are ours, they effect our being-with each other, but we cannot know "the law"; and "it is an extremely painful thing to be ruled by laws that one does not know."[125]

It could be, then, that the intensity of the opposition between modern law and the sacred is not because they are different but, rather, the same yet having to appear different and opposed. Yet again, there is a difference to be observed, however. As pure transcendence, modern law has no transcendent content of its own. Put another way, its dimension of illimitable responsiveness is not tied to its dimension of determinate existence. It is ever capable of becoming other to what it determinately is. With its incohesive responsiveness, law becomes ineluctably contingent on what is apart from it for its operative cohesion and content. So, there is a point to the attempts at rendering modern law in terms of its dependence on society or sovereign, but only up to a point. No matter what the source of law's dependence for its content, in its pure transcendence, in its outstripping any mundane content whatsoever, law can never be definitively bound to any such content. As Montesquieu would have it, the power of the judiciary is "in a certain way nil," but it is a power nonetheless.[126]

There can, then, be no abiding or palpable purchase on this law, and we are always excluded by it. Yet this same law, the law through which we each become in "our" commonality, also extends inclusively to us. In our being excluded yet included by it, we are, to repeat, ever suspensive victims "before" the sacrificial law. With the departure, or concealment, of the immortal gods, this sacrifice is now one to the content enshrined in the law itself, combined with whatever law employs or "finds," what it creates and reifies, as its own attributes—a sacrifice, for example, to responsibility in law, to law's rationality and utility, to the very pervasion of its rule, and to the imperative quality of the norm it includes.[127]

Departure II

To return now to the beginning, to the triumph of a departed world, "depart" once meant to part or to divide, and an intimation of that meaning persists in the two orientations of depart: departing to or toward and departing from. My argument has been that the explicit sacred has departed from modernity but that, in so doing, it has departed toward and become an implicit condition within the modern, and that it has triumphed as departed. In modernity, dimensions of being, the existent and the possible, could no longer join together through a transcendent yet delimited reference into a creative, determinant force. Although these dimensions endure inexorably, they cannot within modernity be joined in terms of the sacred. For now, they can neither subsist apart nor be resolvably joined. The formation of being that joins these dimensions in creating enforceable relations between us is law.

Yet if law would effect this joining, it must assume a position of transcendence. The formative and neosacral combining of these seeming contraries in law, the finite realization in this way of each in the other, and hence the assuming by law of the violent, creative force of the sacred, all these import a transcendence by law, but now a "pure transcendence," as Blanchot has it.[128] In its purity, the law, the neosacral law of modernity, can have no content of its own. Entrenched constitutions and the manifest hold of the rule of law notwithstanding, law's secular solidity is imaginary. That, however, is not to confine law in its dependence on others for its content. As we saw in glossing Freud's "at once intimidating and derisory myth,"[129] our being distinct, yet in-common evoked an appositive, force-filled space ultimately, if not exclusively, occupied by law. This law could neither be constrained by nor definitively turned toward any determination apart from itself. As the commensurate carrier of the sacred in modernity, law effects its pervasive triumph.

As with the premodern sacred, sacrifice still seems to be, borrowing Bataille's view again, "the most intense aspect of the sacred,"[130] even if in modernity it has to be an unavowed sacrifice. And with sacrifice in and as law, there is a further bar to its recognition since, in its pure transcendence, its vacuity of content, there is now a lack in law of anything to be sacrificed to. The conveniently voracious gods are more than matched, however, by the "new idols" that seek domination of our being-in-common and that endow law with content, the nation-state being the most explicitly prominent in modernity.[131] Is sacrifice itself, the sacrifice that "maintains the sanctity of the law,"[132] but an endowment from without and not intrinsic to law? Might law then extend beyond and even displace sacrifice?[133] Could the sacred, dependent as it would seem to be on some manifest presence, have effect without that presence being formed in sacrifice? These are questions tangential to my brief and will be saved for another day. We could, however, perhaps intimate a response by dissipating the surrounding silence, by recognizing the expressly "inclusive exclusion" of premodern sacrifice revealed in its premodern form—recognize, returning to Hubert and Mauss, what is owed and remains close in sacrifice.[134]

What then is needful in seeing modern law revert to the terms of premodern sacrifice? It is that law is oriented toward not only a disregard for the other but also an utter regard. It is that the contained truth of the law is only and ever "held" to its substance and certitude against, yet also with, an other. It is that the ineffable law always escapes confining calculation and cannot be enduringly rendered in terms of the known or knowable. It is that law's rendering in the legal decision, in the sacrificial cutting off, is inevitably partial and arbitrary, and the recognition of responsibility for the excluding violence done thereby. And it is the plangent provocation always to seek, as Derrida would enjoin, the "lesser violence."[135]

Notes

This chapter owed much initially to Stewart Motha, to his abundant generosity and intellectual enterprise. Paul Passavant commented to telling effect on the first draft. It was then sustained in leavening conversations with Johan van der Walt. Finally, it is pervaded by a happy indebtedness to Martha Umphrey, Austin Sarat, Lawrence Douglas, and the questioners after it was delivered as a Keck Lecture at Amherst College, all of whom provided much provocation to further thought. I am indeed fortunate in the particular "little platoon we belong to in society" (Burke).

1. This and the ensuing references to my brief come from a letter of February 2, 2001, from Martha Umphrey, Austin Sarat, and Lawrence Douglas.

2. Preeminent elaborations of such continuing relevance can be found in Pierre Legendre, *L'amour du censeur: essai sur l'ordre dogmatique* (Paris: Seuil, 1974); and Peter

Goodrich, *Languages of Law: From Logics of Memory to Nomadic Masks* (London: Weidenfeld and Nicolson, 1990), chap. 3.

3. Theodor W. Adorno and Max Horkheimer, *Dialectic of Enlightenment*, trans. John Cumming (London: Verso, 1979), 28.

4. Ibid., 3, 39. For an exploration of this shift in relation to law as sacrifice, see Johan van der Walt, "Law as Sacrifice," *Journal of South African Law* 2002 (2002), 710; and to law as myth, see Peter Fitzpatrick, *The Mythology of Modern Law* (London: Routledge, 1992), 27–43 *et passim*.

5. Adorno and Horkheimer, *Dialectic*, 46.

6. Jean-Jacques Rousseau, *The Social Contract*, trans. Maurice Cranston (London: Penguin, 1968), 84, 87.

7. Immanuel Kant, *The Metaphysics of Morals*, trans. Mary Gregor (Cambridge: Cambridge University Press, 1996), 95.

8. Ibid. (emphasis in the original).

9. Ibid. (emphasis added).

10. Jean-François Lyotard, *Toward the Postmodern*, trans. Christopher Fynsk (Atlantic Highlands, NJ: Humanities Press, 1993), 181–182, 186.

11. Adorno and Horkheimer, *Dialectic*, 3, 55.

12. Giorgio Agamben, *Homo Sacer: Sovereign Power and Bare Life*, trans. Daniel Heller-Roazen (Stanford, CA: Stanford University Press, 1998). For a more extensive engagement with the points that follow, see Peter Fitzpatrick, "Bare Sovereignty: *Homo Sacer* and the Insistence of Law," in *Politics, Metaphysics, and Death: Essays on Giorgio Agamben's Homo Sacer*, ed. Andrew Norris (Durham, NC: Duke University Press, 2005). In that same collection, Agamben nuances his engagement with law considerably—"The State of Exception," trans. Giorgio Agamben and Kevin Attell. See also on this score, Giorgio Agamben, *State of Exception*, trans. Kevin Attell (Chicago: University of Chicago Press, 2004).

13. Agamben, *Homo Sacer*, 8.

14. Ibid., 71.

15. Ibid., 8, 73 (emphasis added).

16. Ibid., 9.

17. Giorgio Agamben, *Language and Death: The Place of Negativity*, trans. K. E. Pinkus and Michael Hardt (Minneapolis: University of Minnesota Press, 1991), 105. Thanks to Nasser Hussain for this key reference.

18. See W. Ward Fowler, *Roman Essays and Interpretations* (Oxford: Clarendon, 1920), 16; and Harold Bennett, "Sacer Esto," *Transactions of the American Philological Association*, lxi (1930), 7–8.

19. Fowler, *Roman Essays*, 23. For transgression in its relation to the idea of the modern sacred being offered in this present chapter, see Michel Foucault, "Preface to Transgression," in *Language, Counter-memory, Practice, Selected Essays and Interviews*, trans. Donald F. Bouchard and Sherry Simon (Ithaca, NY: Cornell University Press, 1997).

20. Agamben, *Homo Sacer*, 74, 80.

21. And this dimension is usually seen as typical of the sacred generally. See, e.g., René Girard, *Violence and the Sacred*, trans. Patrick Gregory (Baltimore: Johns Hopkins University Press, 1977), 39.

22. Wilson Harris, *The Dark Jester* (London: Faber & Faber, 2001), 100. My thanks to Martha Umphrey for an informed prompting to pursue the analysis that now follows. The formulation provided by Wilson Harris will also resonate with, in Nancy's term, the "finished" quality of sovereignty and of other neosacral entities touched on later in this chapter. Jean-Luc Nancy, "War, Right, Sovereignty—Technē," in *Being Singular Plural*, trans. Robert D. Richardson and Anne E. O'Byrne (Stanford, CA: Stanford University Press, 2000).

23. Cf. in this setting, Jean-Luc Nancy, "The Unsacrificeable," trans. Richard Stamp and Simon Sparks, in *A Finite Thinking* (Stanford, CA: Stanford University Press, 2003).

24. Michel Foucault, "Nietzsche, Genealogy, History," in *Language, Counter-memory, Practice*, 138, 142.

25. See P. Riley, *The General Will Before Rousseau: The Transformation of the Divine into the Civic* (Princeton, NJ: Princeton University Press, 1986), 40.

26. As quoted in Jean-Luc Nancy, *The Experience of Freedom*, trans. Bridget McDonald (Stanford, CA: Stanford University Press, 1993), 12 (emphasis in the original). Thanks to Pablo Ghetti for this reference, and apologies to him for its underdevelopment here.

27. Ernst Cassirer, *The Philosophy of the Enlightenment*, trans. F. C. A. Coelln and J. P. Pettegrove (Boston: Beacon Press, 1955), 238.

28. Karen Armstrong, *A History of God: The 4,000-Year Quest of Judaism, Christianity and Islam* (New York: Ballantine Books, 1993), 184, and generally 181–184.

29. Ibid., 102.

30. See Henry Bett, *Nicholas of Cusa* (London: Methuen, 1932), 122; and Jasper Hopkins, *A Concise Introduction to the Philosophy of Nicholas of Cusa*, 3rd ed. (Minneapolis: Arthur J. Banning Press, 1986), 4.

31. Jean-Luc Nancy, *La création du monde ou la mondialistion* (Paris: Galilée, 2002), 31. I am, yet again, grateful to Pablo Ghetti for this reference.

32. Roger Caillois, *Man and the Sacred*, trans. Meyer Barash (Glencoe, IL: The Free Press of Glencoe, 1959), 34.

33. Mircea Eliade, *The Myth of the Eternal Return or, Cosmos and History*, trans. Willard R. Trask (Princeton, NJ: Princeton University Press, 1965), 11 (emphasis in the original).

34. The phrase comes from Salman Rushdie, *Imaginary Homelands: Essays and Criticism 1981–1991* (London: Granta Books/Penguin, 1991), 394.

35. Georges Bataille, *The Accursed Share: An Essay on General Economy: Volume II The History of Eroticism: Volume III Sovereignty*, trans. Robert Hurley (New York: Zone Books, 1991), 214.

36. Girard, *Violence*, 5–7; Adorno and Horkheimer, *Dialectic*, 50–51.

37. Joseph Libertson, *Proximity, Levinas, Blanchot, Bataille, and Communication* (The Hague: Martinus Nijhoff, 1982), 7.

38. Respectively, Walter W. Skeat, *A Concise Etymological Dictionary of the English Language* (New York: Capricorn, 1963), 459; and Bataille, *Accursed Share*, 230. And given the function just outlined in the text, cf. Lyotard's description of sacrifice as "the first representational economy": Jean François Lyotard, *Heidegger and "The Jews,"* trans. Andreas Michael and David Carroll (Minneapolis: University of Minnesota Press, 1990), 21.

39. Henri Hubert and Marcel Mauss, *Sacrifice: Its Nature and Function*, trans. W. D. Halls (London: Cohen & West, 1964), 97, 99.

40. Ibid., 101–102.

41. Libertson, *Proximity*, 78.

42. Bataille, *Accursed Share*, 222.

43. Marianna Torgovnick, *Gone Primitive: Savage Intellects, Modern Lives* (Chicago: University of Chicago Press, 1990), 108.

44. Hubert and Mauss, *Sacrifice*, 29, 44.

45. Cf. Jacques Derrida, "Signature Event Context," trans. Samuel Weber and Jeffrey Mehlman, in *Limited Inc* (Evanston, IL: Northwestern University Press, 1988), 10.

46. Girard, *Violence*, 12.

47. Hubert and Mauss, *Sacrifice*, 77.

48. Bataille, *Accursed Share*, 59.

49. E.g. Girard, *Violence*, 7, 96–97. Although the scapegoat is commonly adduced as an example of substitutive sacrifice, and it certainly has similarities to other victims of such sacrifice, it can be doubted whether it is actually a sacrifice—doubted at least if one espouses consistency in biblical exegesis. See under "Azazel," in *Illustrated Dictionary & Concordance of the Bible*, ed. Geoffrey Wigoder et al. (Jerusalem: Jerusalem Publishing House, 1986), 140. On substitution, cf. Jacques Derrida, *The Gift of Death*, trans. David Wills (Chicago: University of Chicago Press, 1995), 86.

50. Hubert and Mauss, *Sacrifice*, 40. For a resonant comparison with dining at the Inns of Court, "eating terms," see Peter Goodrich, *Oedipus Lex: Psychoanalysis, History, Law* (Berkeley: University of California Press, 1995), 94–95.

51. Libertson, *Proximity*, 63.

52. Hubert and Mauss, *Sacrifice*, 92.

53. Derrida, *Gift of Death*, 61.

54. Sigmund Freud, *Totem and Taboo*, trans. James Strachey (London: Routledge & Kegan Paul, 1960).

55. Sigmund Freud, *Group Psychology and the Analysis of the Ego*, trans. James Strachey, in *Civilization, Society and Religion* (Pelican Freud Library Vol. 12, London: Penguin, 1985), e.g., 175.

56. Hubert and Mauss, *Sacrifice*, 91–92.

57. Freud, *Totem and Taboo*, 141, 146, 151.

58. Ibid., 143.

59. Ibid., 150.

60. What follows on tautology and on the alternating epistemological bases of Freud's account is explored in more detail and referenced in Peter Fitzpatrick, *Modernism and the Grounds of Law* (Cambridge: Cambridge University Press, 2001), chap. 1.

61. Sigmund Freud, *Moses and Monotheism*, trans. Katherine Jones (New York: Random House, Vintage Books, n.d.), 104.

62. Freud, *Totem and Taboo*, 146.

63. Ibid., 143, 159–160; Sigmund Freud, *Civilization and Its Discontents*, trans. James Strachey, in *Civilization, Society and Religion*, 325; cf. Jacques Derrida, "Before the Law," in *Acts of Literature*, trans. Avital Ronell (New York: Routledge, 1992), 198.

64. Freud, *Group Psychology*, 157.

65. Freud, *Totem and Taboo*, 101, 142, 144, 147–148.

66. Hubert and Mauss, *Sacrifice*, 5. Freud refers to them in *Totem and Taboo*, 78 and 140n.1.

67. Hubert and Mauss, *Sacrifice*, chap. 5; and for Freud's reasons, see *Totem and Taboo*, 126–134, 161, and *Moses and Monotheism*, 104. For his connecting deific and animal sacrifice, see *Totem and Taboo*, 148–149, 151.

68. Hubert and Mauss, *Sacrifice*, e.g., 81, 89, 91.

69. Freud, *Totem and Taboo*, 137, 140.

70. Freud, *Moses and Monotheism*, 104.

71. Hubert and Mauss, *Sacrifice*, 83, 89, 92.

72. Freud, *Totem and Taboo*, 140, for the quotation, and see generally 140–142.

73. Ibid., 145–146.

74. Ibid., 140; Freud, *Civilization*, 284; Sigmund Freud, "Why War?" trans. James Strachey, in *Civilization, Society and Religion*, 351.

75. Freud, *Totem and Taboo*, 145.

76. Freud, *Group Psychology*, 155.

77. Freud, *Totem and Taboo*, 143.

78. Sigmund Freud, "Thoughts for the Times on War and Death," trans. James Strachey, in *Civilization, Society and Religion*, 69 (emphasis in the original).

79. Freud, *Totem and Taboo*, 144.

80. Freud, *Civilization*, 325.

81. Freud, *Totem and Taboo*, 149.

82. Ibid., 157–158. For the point about "modern subjectivity," see Celia Brickman, *Aboriginal Populations in the Mind: Race and Primitivity in Psychoanalysis* (New York: Columbia University Press, 2003), 90. Chapters 2 and 3 of this book offer an enthralling development of this continuate strand in Freud's scheme.

83. Freud, *Totem and Taboo*, 152.

84. Ibid., 142; Freud, *Moses and Monotheism*, 103–104.

85. Freud, *Totem and Taboo*, 145.

86. Freud, *Civilization*, 329.

87. Freud, *Group Psychology*, 151; Brickman, *Aboriginal Populations*, 86, 96.

88. Freud, *Totem and Taboo*, 148.

89. Ibid., 154.

90. Ludwig Feuerbach, *The Essence of Christianity*, trans. George Eliot (New York: Prometheus Books, 1989), especially chap. 5; Friedrich Nietzsche, *On the Genealogy of Morals*, trans. Douglas Smith (Oxford: Oxford University Press, 1996), second essay.

91. Freud, *Totem and Taboo*, 153.

92. Ibid.; Freud, *Group Psychology*, 154–155.

93. Freud, *Totem and Taboo*, 143. Nietzsche's madman observes that "they have done it themselves:" Friedrich Nietzsche, *The Gay Science*, trans. Josefine Nauckhoff (Cambridge: Cambridge University Press, 2001), 120 (para. 125).

94. See Cornelius Castoriadis, "Psychoanalysis and Politics," in *Speculations After Freud: Psychoanalysis, Philosophy and Culture*, eds. Sonu Shamdasani and Michael Münchow (London: Routledge, 1994), 3; and generally Adam Phillips, *Equals* (London: Faber & Faber, 2002).

95. Freud, *Group Psychology*, 154.

96. Ibid., 155.

97. See Freud, *Moses and Monotheism*, 103; Freud, *Totem and Taboo*, 141, 146.

98. Maurice Blanchot, *The Infinite Conversation*, trans. Susan Hanson (Minneapolis: University of Minnesota Press, 1993), 144.

99. Perhaps the most widely noted equation is that between modern political concepts and "political theology" advanced by Carl Schmitt in *Political Theology: Four Chapters on the Concept of Sovereignty*, trans. George Schwab (Cambridge, MA: MIT Press, 1985), 49. Derrida and Nancy have provided many recent and telling formulations. See, e.g., John D. Caputo, "Without Sovereignty, Without Being: Unconditionality, the Coming God and Derrida's Democracy to Come," *Journal for Cultural and Religious Theory* 4: 3 (2003), 9; Jean-Luc Nancy, "The Confronted Community" and "Deconstruction of Monotheism," trans. Amanda Macdonald, *Postcolonial Studies* 6: 1 (2003), 23, 37.

100. Nietzsche, *Gay Science*, 120 (para. 125).

101. Ibid. I have substituted "sacred" for Nauckhoff's translation of "holy" for *helig*. Admittedly, both would be strictly appropriate but "sacred" would seem to match more adequately something that is taking the place of God.

102. Adorno and Horkheimer, *Dialectic*, 39.

103. Gilles Deleuze and Félix Guattari, *What Is Philosophy?* trans. Graham Burchell and Hugh Tomlinson (London: Verso, 1994), 45 (emphasis in the original).

104. "The history of civilization is the history of the introversion of sacrifice": add Adorno and Horkheimer, *Dialectic*, 55.

105. Agamben, *Homo Sacer*, 7, 8.

106. Skeat, *Etymological Dictionary*, 584.

107. Agamben, *Homo Sacer*, 170.

108. Francisco de Vitoria, "On Law," in *Francisco de Vitoria: Political Writings*, eds. Anthony Pagden and Jeremy Lawrance, trans. Jeremy Lawrance (Cambridge: Cambridge University Press, 1991), 155, 164; Anthony Pagden, *The Fall of Natural Man* (Cambridge: Cambridge University Press, 1982), 62–65.

109. For an account of displacement more nuanced than the norm, see Girard, *Violence*, 18–27.

110. Julius Stone, *Legal System and Lawyers' Reasonings* (London: Stevens, 1964), 213.

111. Donald R. Kelley, *History, Law and the Human Sciences: Medieval and Renaissance Perspectives* (Princeton, NJ: Princeton University Press, 1984), 42–43.

112. David Lieberman, *The Province of Legislation Determined: Legal Theory in Eighteenth-Century Britain* (Cambridge: Cambridge University Press, 1989), 281; Jeremy Bentham, *An Introduction to the Principles of Morals and Legislation* (London: Athlone Press, 1970), 273.

113. See C. Walton, *De la Recherche du Bien: A Study of Malebranche's Science of Ethics* (The Hague: Martinus Nijhoff, 1972), 38.

114. See Riley, *General Will*, 40.

115. Anthony Carty, "English Constitutional Law from a Postmodernist Perspective," in *Dangerous Supplements: Resistance and Renewal in Jurisprudence*, ed. Peter Fitzpatrick (London: Pluto Press; Durham, NC: Duke University Press, 1991), 196.

116. Giorgio Agamben, *Potentialities: Collected Essays in Philosophy*, trans. Daniel Heller-Roazen (Stanford, CA: Stanford University Press, 1999), 165.

117. Ibid. (emphasis in the original).

118. Lyotard, *Heidegger*, 22.

119. William Cowper, *The Poems of William Cowper, Vol. 1* (Hymn 35, "Light Shining Out of Darkness") (Oxford: Clarendon Press, 1980), 174; Rousseau, *Social Contract*, 84, 87.

120. Richard Tuck, *Hobbes* (Oxford: Oxford University Press, 1989), 102.

121. Thomas Hobbes, *Leviathan* (Chicago: Encyclopedia Britannica, 1952), 100. As for Job, see chap. 41.

122. Hobbes, *Leviathan*, 47.

123. These dimensions, and especially the revisionist one, are explored in Fitzpatrick, *Modernism*, 93–95, 106–107.

124. Maurice Blanchot, *The Step Not Beyond*, trans. L. Davis (Albany: SUNY Press, 1992), 25.

125. Franz Kafka, "The Problem of Our Laws," trans. Willa and Edwin Muir, in *The Collected Short Stories of Franz Kafka* (London: Penguin, 1988), 437–438.

126. Montesquieu, *Esprit des Lois*, Book 11, chap. 6.

127. All of which can be to cast the law's creativity in an overmomentous mode. At

times, a lighter touch would be apt. The rootless rituals of the law provide an abundance of instances, as where an august Chief Justice of the Supreme Court of the United States derives the design of his robe from a production of Gilbert and Sullivan's *Iolanthe*. See Bernard Schwartz. "Term Limits, Commerce, and the Rehnquist Court," *Tulsa Law Journal* 31 (1996), 521, 530–531. I am grateful to Adam Thurschwell for much refining my vague memory of this.

128. Blanchot, *Step Not Beyond*, 25.

129. Mikkel Borch-Jacobsen, *The Freudian Subject*, trans. Catherine Porter (Stanford, CA: Stanford University Press, 1988), 237.

130. Bataille, *Accursed Share*, 230.

131. Friedrich Nietzsche, *Thus Spoke Zarathustra*, trans. Walter Kaufmann, in *The Portable Nietzsche* (New York: Viking Press, 1954), 160–163.

132. Lyotard, *Toward the Postmodern*, 181.

133. Cf. Nancy, "Unsacrificeable," read in the light of the note in Johan van der Walt, "Psyche and Sacrifice: An Essay on the Time and Timing of Reconciliation," *Journal of South African Law* 2003 (2003), 635, 645, n. 36; complementing that, in turn, by the relation between community and law set by Nancy in Jean-Luc Nancy, *The Inoperative Community*, trans. Peter Connor (Minneapolis: University of Minnesota Press, 1991), 28.

134. Hubert and Mauss, *Sacrifice*, 101.

135. See Richard Beardsworth, *Derrida & the Political* (London and New York: Routledge, 1996), 20.

INDEX

Abbasid caliphate, 92
abortion, 115; politics of, 116; Supreme
    Court and, 126
Abou El Fadl, Khaled, 69
absolute, problem of the, 11
absolute monarchy, 22n6
absolute mutability, law of, 173
absurd, law as, 3–4
accusatorial procedure, 43
ACLU (American Civil Liberties Union),
    116, 120
administrative law, 48
Adorno, Theodor W., 155–156, 170
affirmative action, 134n52
Agamben, Giorgio, 7–8, 9, 19–20, 137,
    142–147, 150, 157–158, 159, 170, 173
Alito, Samuel, 125
ambivalence: and Constitution, 12; pure
    and impure and, 23n11; secular law and,
    63–64; taboos and, 4–5
American Revolution, 11–12
Americans with Disabilities Act, 121, 129
Amerindians. See Native Americans
amidah, 75n1
anti-antirationalism, 72, 89n148
antirationalism, 71–72, 88n144
antirationalist theology, 66–67
Aq-qoyunlu, 94
Aquinas, St. Thomas, 42, 80n40
Arendt, Hannah, 9, 11, 137, 143
Aristotelian moment, 41
Aristotle, 39–41, 145. See also rhetoric
Article 48, Weimar Republic, 150
atonement, attempt at, 167
Augustine, St., 42, 44, 81n40, 145
Avicenna, 160, 173

Balasuriya, Tissa, 122
Balkin, Jack, 127
bare life, 158
Bataille, Georges, 5, 160, 161, 162, 163,
    175
Becket, Thomas, 83n72
"Before the Law" parable, 5–7, 8
Bellah, Robert, 13
Benedict XVI, Pope, 127
Bentham, Jeremy, 99–100, 117
Benthamite system, 20
The Bible, 12, 64; secular law and, 42
Bickel, Alexander, 122
bigamy issue, 129n1
Bill of Rights, 126–127
biopolitics, 142–153; intensification of,
    145–146
Black, Hugo, 12
Blackmun, Harry A., 119
Blanchot, Maurice, 169, 174, 175
blasphemy, 144
Boerne decision, 121
Boff, Leonardo, 122
Bork, Robert, 12
Brennan, William J., 116
Brown v. Board of Education, 18, 114
Buddhism: morality, shape of, 141; plural-
    ism and, 68. See also Tibet
burden of proof, 43
Burger, Warren, 112
Bush, George H. W., 116
Bush, George W., 123
Bush v. Gore, 18, 19, 122–124, 129

cafeteria Catholics, 127–128
Caillois, Roger, 4

canon law, 41–42; explanation of, 79n38; origins of, 47–48; overlaps with secular law, 50–51; probabilism and, 67; Roman culture and, 52; subject matters covered by, 47–48
capital punishment, 58
Carty, Anthony, 172
Cassirer, Ernst, 160
Catholic Church, 18; cafeteria Catholics, 127–128; excommunication by, 122; papal infallibility doctrine, 69, 112; pluralism in, 68, 70; secular law and, 83n69; sexual abuse issue, 128. See also canon law
cave parable (Plato), 65
"The Center Holds" (Dworkin), 119
Cherokee people, 148–149
chess, 101–102
Christ. See Jesus
Christianity: dual jurisdictions in, 42; illusion, notion of, 66; Jewish law and, 52, 57, 63–71; kingships and, 49–50; liberalism and, 76n7; morality and, 141; secularist theology and, 41–51; sovereignty and, 148–149. See also canon law; Catholic Church
Church Councils, 41–42
civil law, 50–51; probabilism and, 67
civil religion, 13–15
Civil Rights Act of 1964, 129
Civil War politics, 130n6
Clinton, William Jefferson, 120
College de Sociologe, 21n4
common law, 49, 50–51; probabilism and, 67
compelling interest test, 120
Confucius, 141
Congress: interpretative role of, 121–122; Supreme Court and, 122
Connolly, William E., 14, 18–19, 135–154
Constitution: cult of the, 12; destabilizing potential of, 12–13; as holy text, 109–110; majestic generalities of, 126–127; and presidency, 110; as sacred text, 26n63
A Constitutional Faith (Black), 12
Constitutional Faith (Levinson), 18, 109, 111

constitutionalism, 148
Cooper v. Aaron, 114–115
Crapanzano, Vincent, 12
crime: Christian law and, 44–45; Jewish law and, 58–60, 61–62. See also new criminal law
Crone, Patricia, 93
Curran, Charles, 122
Cusa, Nicholas de, 160, 173

Dahl, Robert, 127
death: biopolitics and, 145; of homo sacer, 25n45; sacrifice and, 163
death penalty, 58
deicide, 169–170
DeLay, Tom, 125, 126
Deleuze, Gilles, 137, 150, 170
democracy and sovereignty, 139
democratic pluralism, 18
depart, defined, 175
Derrida, Jacques, 10–11, 137, 163, 176
dhikr objective, 101
dina de-malkhuta dina, 53, 54–55, 57, 65, 86n94; and state law, 90n154
dinin, 54
discriminatory practices, 121–122
disenchantment of the world, 156
diversity and sovereignty, 150–151
divine lawgiver, 3
Donahue, Charles, 48, 52
Douglas, Lawrence, 1–27
dual jurisdictions, 42
due process, 43
Durkheim, Émile, 4, 21n4
Dworkin, Ronald, 119

effective sovereignty, 147–148
elections, 151
Eliade, Mircea, 161
enforceability of law, 21n5
Engels, Friedrich, 29
Enker, Arnold N., 59, 61–62
Enlightenment, 16, 156, 157; liberal values and, 73; and polytheism, 76n11
Epicurus, 141, 145
ethos of sovereignty, 18–19
Eucharist, 168

everywhereness, 172
expressive sovereignty, 147–148

farce, law as, 3
fascism, 150
fatwas, 92, 101
Faubus, Orville, 115
fetishism, 26*n*60
Feuerbach, Ludwig, 168
fiqh, 92, 95
First Amendment, 1; neutrality among religions, 14. *See also* Free Exercise Clause
Fish, Stanley, 39
Fitzpatrick, Peter, 2, 19–20, 155–183
Florida election results, 2000, 135–154
Foucault, Michel, 159
founding fathers, 10–12, 25*n*56
Fourteenth Amendment, 120, 126–127; on discriminatory practices, 122
Fourth Lateran Council, 82*n*56
Fox, Matthew, 122
Fraher, Richard, 43, 45–46, 48–49, 64
freedom of belief, 36
Freedom's Law: The Moral Reading of the American Constitution (Dworkin), 119
Free Exercise Clause, 109, 120; Native American religions and, 120
French, Rebecca, 64, 66
French *référé legislatif*, 171–172
Freud, Sigmund, 4, 20, 144, 163–169, 173, 174, 175
fundamentalism, 31–32; judgments in, 73–74; and profanity, 37–38; sovereignty and, 150. *See also* secularist theology

Gang of Five, 135–137, 144, 151
gay rights issue, 134*n*52
Genghis Khan, 94
Ghazali, Abu Hamid al-, 92, 95–98
Girard, René, 163
global war against terrorism, 125, 126
Gnostic tradition, 66
God: absolute monarchy and, 22*n*6; characters of, 160; deicide, 169–170; founders and, 11–12; monotheism, 160, 172; sovereignty of, 147

Graglia, Lino, 123
Gregory, Pope, 44
Grey, Thomas, 26*n*63
Group Psychology and the Analysis of Ego (Freud), 168–169
Grutter decision, 124
Guattari, Felix, 150, 170
guilt, 2, 3; Arendt, Hannah, on, 21*n*3; atonement and, 167; Oedipal guilt, 165

halakha, 52, 54–55; and human judgment, 87*n*119; pluralism and, 68; types of law in, 56–57
Hallaq, Wael, 95, 99, 102
Harris, Wilson, 159
Hasan, Uzun, 94
Hasidism, 32
hazz concept, 97
Hegel, G. W. F., 145
Helmholz, Richard, 49, 50
Henry II, England, 83*n*72
Hinduism, 52; law of, 85*n*91; sacrifice and, 164
Hobbes, Thomas, 117, 173
Holocaust, 150
holy, unclean and, 23*n*12
holy vision, 39
homogeneity, 154*n*15
homo sacer, 7–8, 20, 158, 170; death, responsibility for, 25*n*45; resonance of, 161; sacrifice and, 162; sovereignty and, 142–143
Homo Sacer: Sovereign Power and Bare Life (Agamben), 158
Honig, Bonnie, 137
Horkheimer, Max, 155–156, 170
Hubert, Henri, 161–162, 163, 165–166, 176
hudud, 93
Hughes, Charles Evans, 113
human sacrifice, 162
Hume, David, 141

Ibn Khaldun, 93
ibn Sina, Abu Ali, 160, 173
Ibn Taymiyya, 94, 101, 103
ideological conservatism, 133*n*45
ifta', 92

Ihya' ulum al-din (al-Ghazali), 95
Ikhaneton, Pharaoh, 148
illusion: Tibetan Buddhism and, 65–66; of
   truth, 39
imperfections, human, 38, 40
Inca civilization, 159
incest taboo, 4
Innocent III, Pope, 45
inquisition, 49
invocation of divinity, 11
irreligion, 31
Islam, 16–17, 34, 91–108; Christian theology
   and, 52; history of legal thought, 94–
   95; kingship in, 92–93; pluralism in,
   67–68, 70; probabilism in, 67; rationalist theology in, 66. *See also* shari'a;
   Sufism
isolation, 9–10
ius commune, 49

Jackson, Andrew, 113
Jackson, Robert, 112–113
James, William, 141
Jefferson, Thomas, 110, 113
Jesus: and legalism, 44; Sermon on the
   Mount, 52
Jewish law, 51–63; Christian law and, 52,
   57, 63–71; emergency powers in, 62,
   87n104; enforcement of, 58–60; exceptional leniency in, 58–59, 60; leniency
   in, 63–64; new spiritual law, 55–56;
   pluralism in, 67–68, 70; probabilism in,
   67; secular realm in, 61–62; and state
   law, 86n100. *See also halakha*; Mosaic
   law; Noahide law
Job, Book of, 173
John Paul II, Pope, 129
Judaism: cafeteria metaphor, 128; Christian
   theology and, 52; Hasidism, 32; Holocaust, 150; messianism, 32; in Middle
   Ages, 84n84; and morality, 141; prayer,
   29, 75n1; rationalist theology in, 66;
   scapegoats in, 163. *See also* Jewish law
judicial murder, 63; pluralism and, 69;
   probabilism and, 67
judicial role conservatism, 133n45
judicial supremacy, 113–115; defenses of,
   115–116; Meese, Edwin, and, 115–116

Kafka, Franz, 2–8, 137, 174
Kant, Immanuel, 139–141, 146, 157, 169
Katz, Marion Holmes, 16–17, 91–108
Kelley, Donald R., 172
Kennedy, Anthony, 116, 119, 127
Kentucky and Virginia Resolutions of 1798,
   113
Khomeini, Ayatollah, 144
kingship, 49–50; in Islam, 92–93; and Jew-
   ish law, 59; social order and, 61
Koran, 91
Kramer, Larry, 123
Kritzer, Herbert, 123–124
Kung, Hans, 122

lapidary code, 171–172
Lawrence v. Texas, 124
leadership, 169
Lectures on the Religion of the Semites
   (Smith), 4
legal cosmology, 34
legalism, 52; Jesus and, 44; of Mosaic law,
   34
legitimacy of power, 11
Lemon test, 14–15
Leviathan, 173
Levinson, Sanford, 12, 18, 109–134
Lewis, Anthony, 116
liberalism, 32; Christian origins of, 76n7;
   Enlightenment and, 73; secularist liber-
   alism, 73–74
Lincoln, Abraham, 113, 130n6
logic of sovereignty, 146–153
Löwith, Karl, 29
Lucretius, 145

Madison, James, 109–110, 113
Malebranche, Nicolas, 160, 172
Mamluk period, 94
Man and the Sacred (Caillois), 4
Maqrizi, 94
Marbury v. Madison, 114, 121
Marshall, John, 114
Marshall, Thurgood, 116
Marx, Karl, 29, 31
maslaha concept, 102–103
materialization of culture, 146–147
Mauss, Marcel, 161–162, 163, 165–166, 176

McCulloch v. Maryland, 114
Meese, Edwin, 115–116, 118
messianism, 32
Middle Ages, 16; Jews in, 84n84. *See also* new criminal law
millenarianism, 32
minimal rationality tests, 121–122
minority legal systems, 68–69
modernism, 155–156
modernity, 19–20
monotheism, 160, 172
Montesquieu, Baron de, 174
morality: hope for harmony in, 153n5; and law, 139–41; and pluralism, 144
Mormon bigamy issue, 129n1
Mosaic law, 34, 52; covenant with, 54
mufti, 92
murder: in sovereign sphere, 24n38. *See also* judicial murder
murder taboo, 4
Muwafaqat (al-Shatibi), 103
mysticism, 32–33; morality, shape of, 141; Sulami, Abd al-Salam al-, 101; traditions of, 66
myth: dissolution of, 156; origin myths, 164

nation-state, 145–146
Native Americans: religions, 120; sovereignty and, 148–149
natural law, 53
Nazi Holocaust, 150
neo-Platonist tradition, 66
new criminal law, 43, 45; brutality of, 45; justifications for, 46
Nietzsche, Friedrich, 141, 144, 168, 169–170
nihilism, 147
Nixon, Richard, 115
Noahide law, 53, 54–55, 56–57; capital punishment and, 58; kingship and, 59; social order and, 61
nonestablishment, 14

Oakeshottian conservatism, 133n45
O'Connor, Sandra Day, 116, 119, 120, 125, 127
Oedipal guilt, 165
oneness of God, 160

On Revolution (Arendt), 11
ordeal, trial by, 82n56
Oregon v. Smith, 120
originalism, 12
origin myths, 164–166
Ottoman Empire, 69; *qanun* in, 94
overlapping jurisdictions, 50–51

paganism, 73; in antiquity, 36; tolerance and, 76n11
papal infallibility doctrine, 69, 112
paradox of the sacred, 20
patriarchal power, 167
Perot, Ross, 110
Perry, Michael, 12–13
pietism, 32–33
Pildes, Richard, 122
Planned Parenthood v. Casey, 116, 117–118, 120, 127
Plato, 38–41; Tibetan Buddhism and, 65; tradition of, 66
Plotinus, 160, 173
pluralism, 32, 34, 67–68; in Catholic Church, 68, 70; fundamentalism and, 73–74; imperial legal systems and, 68–69; in Islam, 67–68, 70; in Jewish law, 67–68, 70; morality and, 144; in religion, 152; role of, 70
plurality concept, 118–119
polarization of religious/secular, 31–32
political theology, 181n99
polytheism, 76n11
positional respect, 151
Post, Robert, 121
Postema, Gerald, 117
postmodernism, 12
Povarsky, Chaim, 55
Powell, Adam Clayton, 115
Powell, Lewis, 116
Powell v. McCormack, 115
power: legitimacy of, 11; patriarchal power, 167; social power, 147
Powers, David, 95
pragmatism, 32, 34, 67–68, 69–71; fundamentalism and, 73–74; new criminal law and, 46
precedent concept, 117–119
presidency, 110

primal horde, 164, 165, 167; leadership and, 169

prison chaplain's parable, 5–7, 8

probabilism, 34, 67; fundamentalism and, 73–74

problem of the absolute, 11

profane/profanity, 4; in Jewish law, 53; Latin root of, 16, 36; law and, 30; sacrifice and, 162; usages of, 36–37

"The Profanity of Law" (Stolzenberg), 29–90

Protestantism, 130n7

Proudhon, Pierre-Joseph, 29, 31

public utility, 46, 62–63; pragmatism and, 70

punishment in Hindu law, 85n91

qadis, 92

qanun, 93–94

Qawaʿid al-ahkam fi masalih al-anam (al-Sulami), 99–100

Qurʾan, 91

Qutb, Sayyid, 91

rabbis. See Jewish law

Rashba, 62

rationalism, 32–33, 66–67, 88n144; secularist theology and, 67

Ratzinger, Cardinal, 122

Reagan, Ronald, 116

rebellion, 167, 168–169

référé legislatif, 171–172

Rehnquist, William, 119, 125

religion: civil religion, 13–15; plurality of, 152; and rhetoric, 40–41, 78n35. See also God; specific religions

Religious Freedom Restoration Act (RFRA), 120–121

religious skepticism, 31

renunciants, 97

renunciation, demands for, 99

respect, positional, 151

Reynolds v. United States, 129n1

rhetoric, 39–40; pragmatism and, 69–70; probabilism and, 67; religion and, 40–41, 78n35

Ricoeur, Paul, 137

rituals: of law, 183n127; and sacrifice, 24n34, 166

Roberts, John, 125

Robertson Smith, William, 4, 7

Roe v. Wade, 18, 115, 123, 127; as precedent, 117, 118

Roman law, 43–44; Christianity and, 52

Roosevelt, Franklin D., 113

Roper v. Simmons, 124

Rosenberg, Gerald, 128

Rousseau, Jean-Jacques, 13, 19, 137–139, 145, 157, 169, 173

rule of law, 137–142

Rushdie, Salman, 144

sacred: Agamben, Giorgio, and, 143–144; attribution of, 159; and biopolitics, 142–153; departed world of, 155–157; Latin root of, 2; modernism and, 155–156; perceptions of, 161; transcendence of, 170

sacred man, 7–8, 20. See also homo sacer

sacred texts, 12–13, 26n63

sacrifice, 20, 161–168; law and, 157; rituals and, 24n34, 166; totemic sacrifice, 163–168; transcendence of, 175–176

sanctum/sanctuarium, 36

Sarat, Austin, 1–27

Scalia, Antonin, 116, 120, 152

scapegoats, 163, 179n49

Schiavo, Terri, 134n52

Schmitt, Carl, 22n6, 137, 150

secular democracy, 14

secularism: concept of, 30–31; of Enlightenment, 157; secularist theology and, 71–75

secularist theology, 15–16, 32, 71–75; Christianity and, 41–51; defined, 35; error, mindfulness of, 73; Jewish law and, 51–63; liberalism and, 73; mutations of, 71–75; origins of, 36–41; pragmatism, 69–71; and profanity, 38; rationalist tendencies and, 67; subjectivity and, 72

secular law, 32; ambivalence and, 63–64; Aquinas, St. Thomas, on, 80n40; Augustine, St., on, 81n40; Catholic Church

and, 83*n*69; hostility to, 74; religious necessity for, 46–47; in Tibet, 64–65
self-rule through law, 137–138
separation of Church and State, 14–15
Sermon on the Mount, 52
Shafiʿi, al-, 98
shariʿa, 17; fundamental duties under, 105;
history of, 94–95; Ibn Taymiyya and,
101–102; as law, 91–95; lower self and,
97; objectives of, 105–106; pluralism
and, 68; as sacred, 95–106; secondary
duties, 105–106; Shatibi, Abu Isaq al-,
on, 102–106; *siyasa* distinguished, 94;
and spirit life, 98; Sufism and, 98–99;
Sulami, Abd al-Salam al-, on, 99–101
Shatibi, Abu Isaq al-, 102–106
shurta, 93
Siegel, Reva, 121
sin, 168
Sinaitic law. *See* Jewish law
siyasa, 93; shariʿa distinguished, 94
skepticism, religious, 31
social choice theory, 132*n*41
The Social Contract (Rousseau), 13
social contracts, 165
sociality, 9–10
social power, 147
social utility. *See* public utility
Souter, David, 116, 119, 127, 136–137
sovereign ban, 8
sovereign sphere, 24*n*38
sovereignty: and biopolitics, 142–153; defined, 147; ethos of, 18–19; fascism and,
150; *homo sacer* and, 142–143; logic of,
146–153; morality and, 139–141; paradox
of, 137–142; practice of, 147
Spanish imperialism, 159
Spinoza, Baruch, 141, 144, 145
standards of proof: in canon law, 48–49;
Christian law and, 46
Stevens, John Paul, 119
Stolzenberg, Nomi, 15–16, 21, 29–90, 93
Stone, Suzanne, 54, 59, 60
strict constructionism, 136, 137–138
subjectivity of legal decisions, 72
Sufism, 17, 95; Ibn Taymiyya and, 101–102;
renunciation, demands for, 99; and

shariʿa, 98–99; Shatibi, Abu Isaq al-,
on, 102–103
Sulami, Abd al-Salam al-, 99–101
Sunni law, 98
Supreme Court, 109–134; approval ratings,
123–125, 134*n*54; conservatisms, types of,
133*n*45; constitutional meaning and, 18;
expansion of authority, 119–125; Gang
of Five, 135–137, 144, 151–152; infallibility of, 112–113; interpretative role of,
112–113, 121; juricentric tone of, 132*n*39;
Lemon test, 14–15; lifetime tenure issue,
126; national majority and, 127; plurality
concept, 118–119; positional sovereignty
of, 19; precedent, concept of, 117–119;
redistribution in, 125; reformation of,
125–129; and religious community,
111–112; sovereignty and, 151–152; symbolic decisions, 129. *See also* judicial
supremacy

taboos, 4–5; as contagious, 5; profanity
and, 77*n*19
*Taking the Constitution Away from the
Courts* (Tushnet), 126
Talmud, 52, 53. *See also* Jewish law
terrorism, 125, 126
texts, sacred, 12–13
theological secularism. *See* secularist
theology
Third Great Awakening, 111
Thomas, Clarence, 116
thresholds, 7
Tibet, 64–65; illusion, notion of, 65–66;
legal cosmology of, 34; pluralism in, 70
Tocqueville, Alexis de, 13–14, 147–150, 152
tolerance, 32, 36; fundamentalism and, 74
Torah, 52, 173. *See also* Jewish law
torture, 82*n*57
Totem and Taboo (Freud), 4, 163–168, 169
totems, 26*n*60
traditions, 30–33
transcendence: of law, 25*n*56, 174, 175; of
sacred, 170; of sacrifice, 175–176
transgression, 168
The Trial (Kafka), 2–8
Tribe, Laurence, 116

Trinitarianism, 32
truth: illusion of, 39; probabilism and, 67
Tuck, Richard, 173
Tushnet, Mark V., 126

Umayyad caliphate, 92
Umphrey, Martha Merrill, 1–27
unclean, holy and, 23n12
United States Reports, 127
universality, 170–171
U.S. v. Nixon, 115
utilitarianism, 99–100

Vatican bureaucracy, 48
Verdi, Giuseppe, 155
victim: of sacrifice, 162–163; sanctity of, 166

Vinaya, 64–65
violence, 10
Violence Against Women Act, 121
Vitoria, Francisco de, 171

wara typology, 97, 99
Weimar Republic, 150
Wheatcroft, Geoffrey, 110
Why I Am Not a Secularist (Connolly), 14
withering away of state, 31, 76n6
Wittgenstein, Ludwig, 138

Yasa code, 94

zhud concept, 99

The Amherst Series in Law, Jurisprudence, and Social Thought

EDITED BY

Austin Sarat, Lawrence Douglas, and Martha Merrill Umphrey

Law and the Sacred (2007)
How Law Knows (2007)
The Limits of Law (2005)
Law on the Screen (2005)